ESSAYS ON TEACHING EDUCATION AND THE INNER DRAMA OF TEACHING

ADVANCES IN RESEARCH ON TEACHING

Series Editors: Volumes 1–11: Jere Brophy
Volumes 12–29: Stefinee Pinnegar

Recent Volumes:

ESSAYS ON TEACHING EDUCATION AND THE INNER DRAMA OF TEACHING: WHERE TROUBLES MEET ISSUES

BY

ROBERT V. BULLOUGH Jr.
*Center for the Improvement of Teacher Education
and Schooling (CITES), McKay School of Education, Brigham
Young University USA*

United Kingdom – North America – Japan
India – Malaysia – China

Emerald Publishing Limited
Howard House, Wagon Lane, Bingley BD16 1WA, UK

First edition 2019

Copyright © 2019 Emerald Publishing Limited

Reprints and permissions service
Contact: permissions@emeraldinsight.com

No part of this book may be reproduced, stored in a retrieval system, transmitted in any form or by any means electronic, mechanical, photocopying, recording, or otherwise without either the prior written permission of the publisher or a license permitting restricted copying issued in the UK by The Copyright Licensing Agency and in the USA by The Copyright Clearance Center. Any opinions expressed in the chapters are those of the authors. While Emerald makes every effort to ensure the quality and accuracy of its content, Emerald makes no representation implied or otherwise, as to the chapters' suitability and application and disclaims any warranties, express or implied, to their use.

British Library Cataloguing in Publication Data
A catalogue record for this book is available from the British Library

ISBN: 978-1-78769-732-4 (Print)
ISBN: 978-1-78769-731-7 (Online)
ISBN: 978-1-78769-733-1 (Epub)

ISSN: 1479-3687

CONTENTS

ABOUT THE AUTHOR

Robert V. Bullough, Jr is a Professor of Teacher Education at Brigham Young University and Emeritus Professor of Educational Studies at the University of Utah. Currently, he serves as associate director of the Center for the Improvement of Teacher Education and Schooling (CITES). Widely published, his most recent books include *Preschool Teachers' Lives and Work: Stories and Studies from the Field* with Kendra Hall-Kenyon (Routledge, 2018) and *Schooling, Democracy, and the Quest for Wisdom: Partnerships and the Moral Dimensions of Teaching* with John Rosenberg (Rutgers University Press, 2018).

ACKNOWLEDGMENTS

I wish to thank Professor Stefinee Pinnegar, editor, colleague, and dear friend for her enthusiastic support of this project at every stage of its development and for many years of remarkable conversation. As always and thankfully, Dr Sharon Black provided skilled and very smart editing. Sharon not only smoothed out the text but also sharpened my meaning when I stumbled. I also wish to thank Craig Kridel who, over many years, has been a wise and wonderful friend and a source of constant inspiration. Excepting Chapter 9, each chapter draws on previously published although mostly extensively rewritten and reworked articles. I am grateful for permission from various publishers for use of the following pieces: Caddo Gap Press gave permission to reprint material from Bullough, R. V., Jr, (2014/2015). Higher education and the neoliberal threat: Place, fast time, and identity. *Journal of Thought*, 48(4/5), 13−32 and Bullough, R. V., Jr (2005). Teacher vulnerability and teachability: A case study of a mentor and two interns. *Teacher Education Quarterly*, 32(2), 23−39. Taylor & Francis granted permission to use materials from the following articles: Bullough, R. V., Jr (2014). Recalling 40 years of teacher education in the US: A personal essay. *Journal of Education for Teaching*, 40(5), 474−491. Bullough, R. V., Jr (2012). Against best practice − Outliers, local studies, and education research. *Journal of Education for Teaching*, 38(3), 343−357. Bullough, R. V., Jr & Hall-Kenyon, K. M. (2011). The call to teach and teacher hopefulness. *Teacher Development*, 15(2), 127−140. Bullough, R. V., Jr (2015). Theorizing teacher identity: Self-narratives and finding place in an audit society. *Teacher Development*, 19(1), 79−96. Bullough, R. V., Jr (2012). Cultures of (un)happiness: Teaching, schooling, and light and dark humor. *Teachers and Teacher: Theory and Practice*, 18(3), 281−295. Sage granted permission to use materials from the following articles: Bullough, R. V., Jr (2014). Toward reconstructing the narrative of teacher education: A rhetorical analysis of *Preparing Teachers*. *The Journal of Teacher Education*, 65(3), 185−194. Bullough, R. V., Jr (2010). Parables, storytelling, and teacher education. *The Journal of Teacher Education*, 61(1−2), 153−160. Springer gave permission to draw on material from: Bullough, R. V., Jr (2011). Hope, happiness, teaching, and learning. In C. Day & J. Lee (Eds.), *New understandings of teacher's work: Emotions and educational change*, pp. 17−32. New York, NY: Springer.

INTRODUCTION

At the conclusion of *The Sociological Imagination,* C. Wright Mills (1959) wrote:

> Know that the problems of social science, when adequately formulated, must include both troubles and issues, both biography and history, and the range of their intricate relations. Within that range of life of the individual and the making of societies occur; and with that range the sociological imagination has its chance to make a difference in the quality of human life in our time. (p. 226)

It is from this quote of Mills that the subtitle of the present volume originated, "*Where Troubles Meet Issues.*" Although it has been many years since I first read Mills' work, this quote stuck and gradually sunk into a secure place in my thinking.

Among my earliest writings are biographical pieces, sometimes more scraps than finished works, within which I tried to make sense of the lives of various educators in relationship to their times, hoping to see where, as Mills wrote, troubles and issues and biography and history meet. Over the decades of my work in education and teacher education, I have often puzzled over what has seemed to be a necessity to choose sides: practice or theory; people or institutions; generalization (quantitative research) or particularization (qualitative research); humanities or social science. Since such choices have social, political, and personal implications, setting conditions of affiliation and membership, and therefore identity, no surprise, a good deal of scholarly activity signals the choice that has been made. As a student in the 1970s, my graduate chair, Paul Klohr, revealing his roots in the pragmatism of Dewey and Boyd Bode, sought a middle position, which he often described as "middle range theorizing," a place where educators – being neither fish nor fowl – lived and worked. Dewey (1929) explored this terrain in his *Sources of a Science of Education.* Currently, the oft-used concepts of micro-, meso-, and macro-focused analyses, each representing in ascending order a different level and type of social analysis, seem to suggest the desirability of locating meeting places somewhere at the points inbetween.

In the 1970s, I sought what I then called a "persons-centered history" of education. I argued, quoting Maxine Greene (1967, p. 186), "What often is missing in educational histories is a focus upon 'the continuing, sometimes desperate efforts of men to choose, shape, and maintain what they consider to be a proper human way of life'" (Bullough, 1979/1989, p. 33). Reading Erik Erikson's (1958) study of Martin Luther helped deepen a sense that turned into a foundational insight, "that individuals are victims, vehicles and, in a sense, ultimately resolutions to the cultural dilemmas they experience – dilemmas which run through and around them" (Bullough, 1979/1989, p. 33). As Erikson (1958) wrote: "Man never lives entirely in his time, even though he can never live outside it; sometimes his identity gets along with his time's ideology, and sometimes it has to fight for its life" (p. 221). Socialization is never one way; we live in tension and that tension shapes identity and the social surround – which is often simply assumed, like water to fish, as given.

The givenness of life, described by Paul Feyerabend (1994) as involving "natural interpretations" that need shaking, elevates *issues* and *history* over *troubles* and *biography*. The sociologist Zygmunt Bauman and his colleague Leonidas Donskis (2013) wrote of this one-sidedness as manifesting what they called TINA (There Is No Alternative), a malady that infects social policy and slips unannounced into political speech, characterizing it as perhaps the greatest evil of our time. "Nowadays, you say, 'we find ourselves in the world of TINA disguised as a world of the rational choice, profit-enhancing and pleasure-maximizing forces of the free market.' [...] A condition of the 'is' and the 'ought' merging and no longer [being] distinguishable – let alone in conflict" (pp. 150–151). They continued, "The world has probably never been so inundated with fatalistic and deterministic beliefs as it is today" (p. 162). Their concern was the dominance of neoliberalism (see Chapter 1) with the result, as Bauman (with Mazzeo 2012) wrote:

> The link between the public agenda and private worries, the very hub of the democratic process, has been broken – each of the two spheres now rotating in mutually isolated spaces and set in motion by mutually unconnected and non-communicating (though certainly not independent!) factors and mechanisms. (p. 97)

Essays on Teaching Education and the Inner Drama of Teaching: Where Troubles and Issues Meet is composed of 11 essays separated as Part I, "On Teaching Education," and Part II, "The Inner Drama of Teaching." While each essay seeks to illuminate the place where troubles and issues and biography and history meet, those contained in Part I are most directly concerned with the institutional, ideational, and social context within which educators live, work, and strive to make sense of their experience. The essays in Part II primarily address specific aspects of the experience of teaching, emphasizing troubles. Hence, the intent of the chapters in the second part of the book is to explore troubles while seeking to elevate them as issues. Taken as a whole, the essays seek to expose assumptions and ideas that enjoy taken-for-granted status in educational thought and practice. By seeking to locate tensions between troubles and issues and biography and history, the intent is to honor the life experience of educators (and of students) by recognizing that within that experience reside seeds of a potentially powerful and compelling, because life-affirming, criticism. Such criticism is life-affirming when it opens imagination to alternative possibilities for living. Where there is tension, there resides hope. The hope is that TINA will be recognized for what it is, privileged and harmful ideology.

ESSAYS IN PART I

Chapter 1, "Place, Fast Time, and Identity: University Teaching and the Neoliberal Threat," explores neoliberalism in relationship to troubles and issues, thereby serving as a contextual backdrop for the essays that follow. The chapter includes a detailed description of what neoliberalism is and how it broadly and variously affects education, including its effects on the lives of those who live and work within higher education, including teacher education.

Chapter 2, "Looking Back on 40 Years of Teaching Education: A Personal Essay," describes the evolution of the purposes and practices of teacher education under neoliberal policy priorities and includes discussion of shifting federal policies in teacher education.

Chapter 3, "Toward Reconstructing the Narrative of Teacher Education: A Rhetorical Analysis of *Preparing Teachers*," offers a Burkian rhetorical analysis of the National Academy of Sciences publication *Preparing Teachers*. The chapter reveals the ideology, biases, and intentions embedded in this influential publication of the best thinking of significant scholars on the practice and reform of teacher education.

Chapter 4, "Against Best Practice: Uncertainty, Outliers and Local Studies in Educational Research," critically analyzes best practice, a celebrated and rarely criticized aim of teacher education. Representing a phrase that easily slips off the tongue of teacher educators interested in diffusing criticism while making a case for possessing distinctive knowledge, "best practice" proves to be a mischievous aim.

ESSAYS IN PART II

Chapter 5, "Getting Motivation Right: The Call to Teach and Teacher Hopefulness," refutes the punishing psychology that has characterized the past few decades of educational reform. Drawing on data from a study of teacher beliefs and commitments related to feelings of being called and remaining hopeful about teaching, this chapter argues for the importance of getting motivation right with all efforts at educational improvement. The chapter provides background for the chapters that follow by reminding readers of the values, beliefs, and commitments that motivate teachers to teach, especially the depth of their service ethic and their concern for the well-being of young people.

Chapter 6, "Theorizing Teacher Identity: Exploring Self-narratives and Finding Place in an Audit Society," picks up and extends the argument in Chapter 5 with an approach to the study of identity formation that draws on life course research and psycho-social constructivist methods and concepts to analyze the work of a head teacher, Mr Kent. The analysis reveals the relationship between issues of teaching within a neoliberal audit culture and the difficulties experienced by Mr Kent – his troubles – that affect his identity as a teacher and administrator.

Chapter 7, "Teaching and Learning with Parables: Reimagining the Self and the World," begins with a discussion of the centrality of storytelling in teacher education and teaching. In teacher education, stories are typically used to describe instructors' views of best practice. Parables are an alternative form of narrative, one that provides means for revealing and perhaps reconsidering embedded meaning, working assumptions about teaching and about themselves as teachers — foundational experiences for exploring identity.

Chapter 8, "Teachability and Vulnerability," explores the vulnerability always present in teaching. Vulnerability is commonly considered a weakness to be overcome or avoided. This chapter draws on a case study of two interns and their mentor to illustrate the role of vulnerability in learning and teacher development.

Chapter 9, "An Inquiry into Empathy and Teaching: Is Empathy All it Is Cracked Up to Be?" provides an extensive review of the extant research on empathy, including a brief study of a preschool teacher's struggles to connect with her students. Empathy is widely taken as an inherent good, a source of hope for teaching across differences, among other expectations. This chapter problematizes the concept to argue that efforts to elevate empathy to a teaching disposition are misguided, perhaps potentially harmful. The concept is in need of reconsideration, including its relationship to the realization of the social justice aspirations that hold such a prominent place in teacher education.

Chapter 10, "Light and Dark Humor and the Inner Drama of Teaching," describes dangers as well as benefits of this widely touted component of teaching: considered by some as an essential quality of good teaching and an unquestioned good. Humor may be harmful, even as some researchers are arguing that it should become an important focus for professional development. This chapter explores light and dark humor, suggesting that the kind and quality of educator humor provide an important gauge of institutional health and well-being.

Chapter 11, "Hope, Happiness and Seeking Eudaimonia," explores the well-being of teachers, an important yet seldom considered condition essential to sustaining quality education for the young. Within policy circles, the strong link between student and teacher well-being is seldom considered. This chapter reviews studies of teacher happiness and hope, with an eye toward establishing Eudaimonia — flourishing — as perhaps the most compelling and consequential cultural aim for educational improvement.

A postscript composed of eight propositions concludes the collection.

PART I
NEOLIBERALISM AND TEACHING EDUCATION

CHAPTER 1

PLACE, FAST TIME, AND IDENTITY: UNIVERSITY TEACHING AND THE NEOLIBERAL THREAT

INTRODUCTION

Reviewing the history of teacher education, Fraser (2007) argued that among the reasons for university involvement was that administrators and some faculty acknowledged,

> Public schools, especially high schools, were growth industries and that the university ought to seize the leadership of the movement, especially in preparation of those slated for "higher positions in the public school system," which could include future high school teachers, superintendents, and normal school professors. (p. 140)

But, not everyone involved in teacher education was pleased by this development, especially normal school educators dedicated to the idea that preparation to teach was best done in separate institutions dedicated to the study and practice of teaching.

> [They] were reluctant to adopt the "standards" of the academic world or, from a somewhat different point of view, to renounce their provincialism and freedom to adjust curricular offerings and other practices to the exigencies of their clientele and local situations. (Monroe, 1952, p. 296)

For some early teacher educators, concern about the possibility of universities moving into teacher education was more principled than self-serving. As Fraser (2007) observed, there was tension "between university desires for academic respectability, which often meant greater focus on theoretical research than on practical applications, and the need felt by leaders of schools and states for well-prepared educators" (p. 139). Some teacher educators were double-minded: wanting to elevate the status and respectability of the study of teaching by affiliating with colleges and universities, but fearing that the practice of teaching would be short-changed by the move, both as an arena of inquiry and as a craft or art form (see Clifford & Guthrie, 1988). University faculty and normal school faculty both understood that dramatic changes would follow when teacher education entered the academy.

Normal schools evolved into teachers' colleges and teachers' colleges into universities, and in the process, the future and fate of teacher education and its faculty became inextricably joined to higher education. This chapter explores the neoliberal university, including what life is like within it as troubles and issues, biography and history, meet.

THE SOCIAL LOCATION OF TEACHER EDUCATION

Like all university faculty, teacher educators' lives are shaped by how work is defined, organized, and rewarded. The social location of teacher educators, however, is somewhat unique. Education schools, like other professional schools including social work and nursing, engineering, architecture, law, theology, and medicine, have established vocational expectations and responsibilities associated with licensure. Teaching, school psychology, and educational administration, like social work, occupational therapy, and nursing, are on the lower occupational rungs. Similarly, within higher education institutions, those who educate educators are widely viewed as lower status than those who teach in business, law, and medical schools. Moreover, within schools of education, teachers of teachers work in the shadow of those who educate administrators and school psychologists. Thus, teacher educators are constantly challenged to prove their worth within the academy; they have to defend the value of the questions and forms of inquiry that characterize their field and work; and they live in a state of persistent "status deprivation" (Goodlad, 1999, p. 29). After all, is it not true, as is commonly believed, that "anyone can teach?" Seeking higher status, many university-based teacher educators have distanced themselves from the practice of teaching, just as early normal school faculty feared, while delegating responsibility for fieldwork of various kinds to lower-paid and sometimes part-time clinical and teaching faculty (Bullough, Hobbs, Kauchak, Crow, & Stokes, 1997).

Despite the uncomfortable fit of teacher education within higher education, teacher educators are typically held to expectations and standards similar to other higher education faculty: service, teaching, and scholarship. As program quality within most professional schools depends on labor-intensive clinical work, teacher educators, like many others, must endure a double life: one foot planted within the schools and the other planted in the academy. Under such conditions, scholarship, the academy's chosen evidence for the value of one's work and worth, is inconsistent with what counts as valuable knowledge in the schools.

NEOLIBERALISM AND THE TRANSFORMATION OF EDUCATION

Universities are changing, with resulting changes in the lives of those who work and live within them. No historical change has been more consequential than higher education's embrace of neoliberalism as a dominating attitude and policy framework. Assumed to be an inevitable consequence of globalism, with its proliferation of markets worldwide, neoliberalism is rooted in neoclassical economics and brings with it a "thorough-going" and profoundly self-serving and competitive individualism (Fredman & Doughney, 2012, p. 44). While neoliberalism means many things, it means in particular a minimal and weakened welfare state and elevation of "the values of the marketplace [...] above all others" (Weinberg, 2018, p. 8). As a form of "economic rationalism," neoliberalism "reduces all human dimensions, social relations, and activities into consumer exchange" (Mullan, Samier, Brindley, English, & Carr, 2013, p. 188), and in this exchange, the highest value is customer satisfaction, especially satisfaction of those who enjoy resources and power.

At every level, the educational manifestations of neoliberalism are evident and far-reaching. The shift of education from the cultural to the economic realm has brought with it "managerialism, audit cultures, values of commodification, efficiency, and effectiveness from a wholly alien sector – the industrial economy" (Mullan et al., 2013, p. 222). Assuming the presumed efficiency of markets in support of a mythologized meritocracy, neoliberalism celebrates radical individualism (Brooks, 2018a) and profit motives, justifying a sweeping deregulation and privatization of many traditional government functions. Among these is public schooling, though evidence supporting the superiority of vouchers and charters to local board-run, community-based public schools is lacking (see Ravitch, 2013; Schneider, 2016). As an article of faith, teachers, like other public sector workers, are presumed to be self-interested, inefficient, and overpaid despite evidence to the contrary. Assuming everything of value can be measured, neoliberalism justifies ranking, rating, and grading everyone and just about everything from departments and schools and school systems to entire universities and even individual teachers. Artificial scarcity is thereby created and controlled with social "goods" purposefully and unequally distributed.

As ideology, the influence of neoliberalism seems boundless; having crept into virtually every level of government policy and aspect of political and social life, it also slips into consciousness (see Kuttner, 2018). Once residing in subjectivity and taken as true, neoliberalism morphs into common sense and lies hidden among other "natural interpretations" (see Feyerabend, 1994).

Whatever the expression, neoliberal outcomes are understood to be inevitable, as flowing law-like from the movement of the invisible hand of the marketplace and of persons exercising that now fundamental human right – the right to choose that is presumed to be universally shared, when clearly it is not. Ironically, when Adam Smith wrote of the wonders of markets, he assumed a marketplace situated within a moral order composed of people who knew something about and were sensitive to the importance of being a brother's keeper. Believing that markets would produce a "liberal reward of labour" (1759/1937, p. 80), Smith was convinced they would support the well-being of families and the children of the working poor, whose hard lives he found so deeply troubling (McCraw, 1992). Unable to imagine how the fickleness, cruelty, and susceptibility to manipulation of markets can destroy virtue, Smith envisioned a future of material abundance shared by all – hollow but still a neoliberal promise. The irony is that while presumptively free markets have, to a degree, enriched many nations, they have simultaneously impoverished large portions of those very nation's populations, widening the gaps separating the wealthy 10% from everyone else (see Stewart, 2018). As Harari (2017) concluded, "It is dangerous to trust our future to market forces, because these forces do what's good for the market rather than what's good for humankind or for the world" (p. 382). There are additional ironies: as the Great Recession revealed, not all markets, indeed if any, are free. In contrast to small businesses, a handful of select and very large businesses are believed to be too large to be allowed to fail. As a result, costs are socialized while benefits are privatized. Markets create needs no one needs fulfilled and fail to satisfy the genuine needs everyone has. If this is not strange enough, market growth depends on fulfilling needs that must remain unfulfilled, for complete satisfaction destroys markets. Ultimately, as the pursuit of profit plays out in higher education a formidable amount of talent is wasted (Brown & Tanneck, 2009).

EXPENSES AND EXPENDITURES

Over the past few decades, state support for higher education in the US dramatically declined. Within higher education institutions, competition for scarce resources soared; year after year, tuitions increased and institutional marketization expanded (Judson & Taylor, 2014). Middle-class parents and college students found themselves mired in deepening piles of debt. By 2017, students (and former students) owed US$1.3 trillion in student loans, 93% loaned directly by the federal government. By 2014, seven million students had defaulted on their loans, while 44 million owed in excess of US$37,000. Much of the increase in tuition offset non-instructional university costs: supporting intercollegiate athletics, funding growing institutional and faculty ambitions, and promoting institutional brands to be (or become) competitive for more able students and to increase external funding, each a central element to achieving coveted rankings that raise the market value.

To ameliorate tuition increases, universities lacking large tax-exempt endowments raised average class size and hired large numbers of comparatively cheap itinerant faculty, by 2014 numbering 70% of all faculty (Swarns, 2014, p. A11), many of them former students whose degrees were not from preferred graduate schools and who failed to obtain regular (and scarce) academic appointments. As a strategy for increasing efficiency and saving money, this practice has its limits. At some point, changing who teaches within the university alters the nature of the students' educational experience, which may undermine the quality (i.e., market value) of that experience, which is essential to sustaining product competitiveness and therefore institutional viability.

Representing diverse origins, costs include coping with excessive administrative expenses associated with perpetual fund-raising; managing and responding to increasingly aggressive and expensive systems of accreditation and accountability; and paying bills accrued from an unexpected source − the generous subsidies for the grants deemed essential to institutional status and survival. Seldom considered, research grants are only rarely self-supporting, so humanities and education students, among others, find themselves subsidizing research and researchers (Newfield, 2008, Chapter 13) as institutions compete for market share and prestige, positioning themselves to achieve ever higher brand recognition and ranking. Ironically, subsidizing grants with tuition money enables professors to buy out of their teaching responsibilities.

Rising costs have led to increased personal and family debt at the same time as the economic rewards for college graduation from non-elite schools have attenuated and become disproportionate (Shell, 2018), reflecting an increasingly stratified status system of higher education. Concerning return on investment, gaps continue to broaden between elite, well-funded private along with a very few select public, research universities and all the other institutions, including those that graduate comparatively large numbers of teachers. Nevertheless, as consumers, parents and students expect returns on their investments, not only in greater maturity and learning but also in future security and employment certainty. But at the same time, employment security is undermined by federal policy and Supreme Court rulings made in support of globalism's demand for maximal labor market flexibility by weakening unions to reduce labor costs to maximize profit.

Despite high start-up and production costs, the university is going and has gone "online" in the hopes of containing costs (see Christensen & Eyring, 2011, p. 385), tightening work-education alignment (Gallagher & LaBrie, 2012, p. 71) and looking ahead toward making a profit (Chistensensen & Eyring, 2013, p. 339). Online, for-profit, teacher education programs are increasing, some of which, like the US Department of Education funded American Board for Certification of Teacher Excellence (ABCTE), are test driven and do not require student teaching. Universities are increasing their online teacher certification business as well. Speaking more broadly, Massive Open Online Courses (MOOCs) have captured the imagination of many educators, although enthusiasm appears to be tempering as the difficulties of the task, likelihood of the rewards accruing to a few select universities, and potential negative consequences for student growth and development (Rice, 2013) are increasingly recognized.

A trend far advanced in the UK follows a path opened by for-profit institutions by packaging education into self-contained, sharply focused, discrete, and marketable modules that promise high portability, ease of consumption, and simple and efficient assessment (see Christensen & Eyring, 2011). Modules profoundly alter the nature of the schooling and teaching experience as they minimize instructional demands. There are several trade-offs. Modules typically remove instructor control over the curriculum, which assures a degree of similarity in outcomes but undermines many of the sources of the joy found in teaching. Though no longer responsible for setting course aims or even determining content, instructors are still expected to support student motivation for learning (Guerlac, 2001, p. 7).

A less obvious result is that the module structure and form as independent slices of content are more conducive to training than to education. The distinguishing characteristic of training — itself representing a service or product — is a high degree of predictability that certain actions will lead to pre-specified outcomes in others and that proof of value is direct, involving a specific demonstration such as passing a test. Training, then, is all about binomials: right and wrong, not better and worse. In contrast, education is inevitably messy, with permeable boundaries and uncertain outcomes dependent on both person and context; proof of educational accomplishment is always indirect and usually long delayed. For this reason, Oxenham concluded, "Competencies simply do not have the necessary robustness to uphold the deeper functions of higher education" (2013, p. 149). Being measurable, skills and competences are given precedence over understandings, and replicative and applicative uses of knowledge are preferred to associative and interpretative uses (see Broudy, 1988). The former represents the sort of knowledge that dominates MOOCs, a "notion of knowledge [...] quite close to the notion of information [...] sets of facts, pieces of data, or concrete bits of a larger process" (Rhoads, Berdan, & Toven-Lindsey, 2013, p. 92).

Reading trends and thinking through a neoliberal lens reveal that the past few decades have effected a new iteration of the research university: the Emerging Global Model (EGM). Understood as a predominant economic driver,

> [These institutions] represent the leading edge of higher education's embrace of the forces of globalism. [They] are characterized by an intensity of research that far exceeds past experience. They are engaged in worldwide competition for students, faculty, staff, and funding; they operate in an environment in which traditional political, linguistic, and access boundaries are increasingly porous. These top universities look beyond the boundaries of the countries in which they are located to define their scope as trans-national in nature. Their peers span the globe. (Mohrman, Wanhua, & Baker, 2008, p. 6)

Credited with defining educational "excellence," these few institutions "head virtually every list of leading universities worldwide" (p. 6), and against them all other institutions are measured (see Majcher, 2008). Market-driven, and profoundly entrepreneurial, EGM universities prize scientific and technological knowledge within the social sciences as well as more technical disciplines. The EGM university functions as a "knowledge conglomerate [...] that puts primacy on the production of new knowledge and the training of expert personnel to carry on this production into the future" (Mohrman et al., 2008, p. 8). Other traditional aims, teaching and service, find a place "to a large extent in the new [university] via their role in making the university into a knowledge conglomerate" (p. 9).

While these developments are widely celebrated, concern has been expressed that with its priorities the financially driven free-market EGM has altered the "fundamental conception of the purpose of the university [...] transforming a college degree into career investment or individual indulgence rather than a public good" (p. 17). The quest for market survival, except for within the very richest of institutions, mostly private, "can pit international research prestige against mass education demands" (p. 19). "Impossible situations [arise] as nations and universities want it all—to play in the international knowledge game while at the same time providing tertiary education for as many people as want and can benefit from a college degree" (p. 19). Despite these concerns, worldwide the EGM has come to be understood as the model of quality higher education in whose hands the future of higher education seems to rest. As Mohrman and her colleagues argued, the "EGM fosters winners and losers"

(p. 25). Losers pick up the leftovers, and among these is the unglamorous work of teacher education.

EFFECTS: PLACE, CYBER-SPACE, AND IDENTITY

Economic globalism accompanied by technological advance not only expanded markets worldwide but weakened the power of place, undermining the stability and forms of relationship that build and sustain identity. For the educational work of universities, no issues are more significant than those associated with loss of stable grounding (see Kuntz, Petrovic, & Ginocchio, 2012).

While the world has become smaller, it has also become more diverse. Globalism "homogenizes human lives by imposing a set of common denominators (state organization, labour markets, consumption and so forth), but it also leads to heterogenization through new forms of diversity emerging from the intensified contact" (Eriksen, 2007, p. 142). But there is no guarantee that contact with strangers will be intense, engaging, or mind-expanding. Indeed, perhaps the most powerful response to these developments by those unable to book a tour is a growing sense of alienation and loneliness (see Brooks, 2018b); feeling threatened and lost, identities are shored up in walled communities and by identity politics and fundamentalism (see Hochschild, 2016). As the social anthropologist Thomas Eriksen (2007) argued,

> Disembedding is always countered by re-embedding. The more abstract the power, the sources of personal identity, the media flows and the commodities available in the market become, the greater will the perceived need be to strengthen and sometimes recreate (or even invent) local foundations for political action and personal identity. (p. 143)

Markets, of course, put some consumers in charge. Thought of and treated as consumers, not scholars or critical thinkers, students, as Judson and Taylor (2014) suggested, are apt to choose products unwisely. Education requires engagement with otherness, the stretching of self and confrontation with limitation. The technologies of the marketplace provide opportunities to engage difference as well as to maintain and sustain sameness, but offering self-confirmation sameness sells. Sameness feels good. It is no surprise, as Eriksen observed, that "globalization does not create global people" (p. 143). As the Boston Marathon bombers illustrate, webs can support insular networks experienced as communities across thousands of miles (Seelye, Schmidt, & Rashbaum, 2013).

Identity politics and threat of difference sharpened by rapidly growing insecurity and economic uncertainty are among the materials used to construct the conservative elite response to the rise and defeat of the middle class detailed by Newfield (2008). The elements of identity politics are well known and easily manipulated even as they are potentially dangerous, as the events surrounding the 2016 American presidential election suggest. These elements always entail "competition over scarce resources," dominance of ascribed within-group similarities over across-group equality, invocation of historical injustices and past suffering, use of cultural myths and images to recall and strengthen shared group experiences, employment of simple contrasts to distinguish in- and out-group membership, and the unflattering comparisons of "invaders" with "first-comers," the last element calling for a defense of place, even if a ghetto (see Eriksen, 2007, pp. 144–146). "Identity politics," Eriksen concluded, "is a trueborn child of globalization" (p. 146). Indeed, globalization triggers group conflict and actualizes differences while providing the opportunity to avoid serious engagement with those differences (p. 145). And this is precisely the sort of engagement that education requires.

TIME: HURRIED AND HARRIED

"Time is an enacted, material, social practice that organizes the functions of temporality" (Moran, 2015, p. 289). Time is varied (see Mayes, 2005a). In neoliberal, advanced market, and managed economies, the "scarcest resource for people on the supply side is [...] the attention of others" (Eriksen, 2001, p. 21). Incessant and intrusive electronic ads followed by aggressive requests for feedback on product satisfaction once a purchase has been made, as well as communication technologies from Instagram and Snapchat to Facebook, all push ever-increasing volumes of information that demand attention like a hungry child. For those pressed for quick responses, time speeds up. Gaps are filled so there is less and less "down time," and time becomes more "dense" (Eriksen, 2001, p. 21), more hurried but less durable. Losing duration and linearity weakens belief in progress (p. 47), leaving behind a nagging feeling of always being behind, of reacting but of never quite being in control of one's life. Academics resent this feeling, even as they conclude there is nothing to be done about it, and so work intensifies (Fredman & Doughney, 2012; Menzies, &, Newson, 2007). Nothing is better than having a scheduled meeting unexpectedly canceled which may open a small space for solitude. At home, the slow time involved in feeding or helping a child get dressed and engaging in other family activities leads to impatience. It is impossible to speed up a child. Those sitting in church, in class, or at a ballgame, let text messages fly and, being addicted to speed and holding an expectation that everyone is always available, senders get frustrated when a return response is delayed. While half listening to a minister or graduation speaker, the individual checks email or plays a video game.

Wired and plugged-in students cannot maintain attention, having adapted to what Eriksen (2001) describes as the "tyranny of the moment" (p. 33). Students expect to be entertained by their teachers, who sense they are losing a battle. Student minds flit about and defy faculty members' best attempts at netting. Outside of class, young people would simply click and change the channel or, as in olden times, fast forward.

For university faculty, information overload narrows knowledge, as no one seems able to read broadly or deeply, and those who try spend a large portion of their time filtering the flow of materials, attempting to sort out the junk; 93% of all humanities articles and 48% of all social science articles are never cited (Filion & Pless, 2008). Efficiency encourages reliance on review articles, and citing an article one has not actually read produces all sorts of mischief. As publication pressures intensify, a range of clever strategies for increasing productivity have emerged – not limited to teacher education. Bauerlein, Gad-el-Hak, Grody, McKelvey, and Trimble (2010) described one such strategy:

> The pace of publication accelerates, encouraging projects that don't require extensive, time-consuming inquiry and evidence gathering. For example, instead of efficiently combining multiple results into one paper, professors often put all their students' names on multiple papers, each of which contains part of the findings of just one of the students. One famous physicist has some 450 articles using such a strategy. (A80)

No wonder the number of publications now roughly doubles every 20 years, and journals pile up – or rather DOIs (digital object identifiers) pile up. Real journals are expensive, but Bauerlein et al. (2010) offer a straightforward solution: fewer journals, less publishing.

Accelerated time affects university faculty work in additional ways. In short time, quick and increasingly trivial studies are favored over long-term projects. In reviews, recent publications are privileged over earlier publications, encouraging production of ungrounded and often repetitious works, a problem that few reviewers can recognize.

Lack of memory undermines transmission of culture and weakens the ability to generate explanatory narratives. "Fast-thinking," as Eriksen (2001, p. 113) suggested, is preferred to slow, reflective thought – the sort of thinking involved when pondering ideas and wrestling with vexing problems, and the sort of problems that resist technical solutions. Reflection, as Dewey (1933) argued, necessitates learning how to "pause" (p. 14). Dangers of a rush to judgment and of confirmation bias arise, suggesting strong connections between slowness and integrity (Cilliers, 2006, p. 109). Oddly, the faster we go, the busier we get, and the less likely it is that our actions will result in desired changes in institutional life. Systems change more slowly than their environment, and lasting changes require slow time (Cilliers, 2010). The result is that the fast thinking valued in game shows actually undermines individual and institutional efficiency; by becoming an "end in itself [simply going faster] is not a means to a better future" (Sutherland, 2014, p. 59).

Finally, fast time and fast thinking are embedded in tenure systems. Tenure may seem to involve a marathon, but given how quickly time passes, how time-intensive consequential research is, and how long it takes to get a piece into print, a sprint is a more apt analogy – often a sprint with misplaced, missing, or misaligned starting blocks. To support scholarship, young faculty are given reduced teaching loads and excused from most forms of service, decisions that distance them from students and from getting to know other faculty members and their work. Generally, in the area of scholarship, the tenure process privileges quick accumulation of capital and professional chatter over the pleasures of engaged conversation. The press young faculty feel is to speak before they have anything worth saying, but speak they must and they do. After all, there are thousands and thousands of journals in print and online hungering for content.

These effects of speeding up time forced Eriksen (2001) to conclude that "Slowness needs protection" (p. 156). Traditional forms of academic work are still most valued by faculty: "The image of an individual scholar pursuing his or her interests according to his or her own rhythm still remains an ideal, especially in the humanities and social sciences" (Ylijoki, 2013, p. 247). Echoing Dewey, Stein (2012) also argued for the value of pausing, but offered a different reason: "Pauses are valuable in that their inherent discontinuity adds multidimensionality to experience" (p. 336). Pauses refresh as university faculty struggle to live a "temporally balanced academic life" (Ylijoki & Mantyla, 2003, p. 75), a possibility increasingly difficult to realize. Inside and outside of the university, friendship, collegiality, loyalty, and trust in and depth of relationship, including love, all depend on the slowness of time.

CAPITAL ACCUMULATION AND COMPROMISED VIRTUE

Lacking strong embeddedness in place and in persons and speeding through life and work can profoundly shape identity, including the identities formed by university faculty. Shoppers are fickle and consumers are not easily satisfied. Oxenham (2013) described the challenge of identity formation this way: "The cost of using unstable things as our building material is that our identities are just as unstable as the materials we have chosen and not everyone is fit enough to adjust to such a quick ride" (p. 22). Stable identities enabling consistent behavior are a condition for moral courage: clearly, the young desperately need adults they can count on.

When almost everyone we know is a competitor for genuinely scarce or presumably scarce goods, few can be trusted, for trust often proves to be an unwise survival strategy. As substitute means for achieving confidence, codes, rules, and systems are formed to make interaction predictable, but systems are very poor substitutes for trust (Seligman, 1997, pp. 173–174). Role prescription is role-play, and within neoliberalism when goods are scarce and consumer is role played, revealing one's market strategy opens the strong possibility of diminishing oneself and losing one's standing. In situations of genuine or imagined scarcity, if someone wins someone else loses. Hence, your loss, for instance in academic standing, is likely experienced by someone else on faculty as his or her gain, not just in merit pay. This certainly is not the way to run a university, department, or program that is serious about learning; helping students discover and then transcend their limitations necessitates their revelation, and this requires trust.

In economics, money is the means of reducing differences to a common standard of worth. Outside the arts, the currencies of higher education are publication and citation counts. Publication quality is often an afterthought. Determining publication quality, including for tenure reviews, requires slow time to read and to ponder, and it requires insider knowledge that itself is often rare. Counting substitutes for careful consideration. Counted articles are dropped into catchments, journal tiers, proxies for quality even though the link between journal impact factors and citations is generally weak and weakening (see Lozano, Laiviere, & Gingras, 2012). The Australian Research Council tried to rank 30,000 journals on international prestige, which unleashed a storm of protest, arising in part from how such rankings drive researchers away from topics and issues of national and local concern. The council found the exercise mostly a matter of smoke and mirrors, politics and marketing. Besides, junk shows up everywhere, and, it seems, so do quality publications.

Online "hits," which are counted and reported by journals for marketing purposes, are easily doped. Since citations seem scarce, surely they must have real value, and more is certainly better than less. The moral problems associated with citation counting are subtle and complex, going well beyond the obvious issue that beginning scholars face delayed citation but immanent tenure evaluation. Some articles are cited for terrible reasons, and works that enjoy massive citation often have rather more to do with scholarly production than scholarship itself: The multiple editions of Robert Yin's book on case study methodology, for example, have been cited well over 150,000 times (methods sell). As currency, citations, and citation indexes are the subjects of market manipulation and, reflecting the Matthew effect, the rich get richer.

In her discussion of complexity theory, Mitchell (2009) offered the following example of how, in the quest to increase market value, academic riches accumulate:

> Suppose you and Joe Scientist have independently written excellent articles about the same topic. If I happen to cite your article but not Joe's in my latest opus, then others who read only my paper will be more likely to cite yours (usually without reading it). Other people will read their papers, and also be more likely to cite you than to cite Joe. The situation of Joe gets worse and worse as your situation gets better and better, even though your paper and Joe's were both of the same quality. Preferential attachment is one mechanism for getting to what [...] Gladwell called tipping points—points at which some process, such as citation, spread of fads, and so on, starts increasing dramatically in a positive-feedback cycle. (p. 253)

Friends cite friends, graduate students cite mentors, and universities with lots of friends and big grant-supported graduate programs and successful branding strategies enjoy prominent place within citation indexes. Poor Joe. He's a loser. What is he to do, especially if he is part-time faculty, an untenured "freeway professor"?

First Joe ought to get better at self-marketing, which ought to be distasteful, but is not necessarily immoral. Yet, self-marketing certainly can lead to serious ethical issues. Like the exemplary famous physicist and his students noted above, Joe might cut a deal with other young faculty, perhaps former classmates, to collaborate – meaning, "I'll put your name on my work if you'll put my name on your work." This strategy has caught on since the average number of authors per paper is dramatically increasing (Grimes, Bauch, & Ioannidis, 2018, p. 11). Joe borrows capital and cooks the books. Certain not to be caught, within his hundreds-of-pages-thick tenure file, Joe portrays his involvement with these articles as greater than it was. Who would know? He might even believe what he writes. Joe might publish what one colleague some years ago described as LPUs – least publishable units, an inflationary strategy. By splitting large studies into several very small publishable bits, Joe appears wealthier than he is. A good person facing a difficult situation, Joe might also tweak what essentially is one study, change the title, and, since so few articles are read, publish it twice.

As Niebuhr (1945) asserted, in desperate situations, good people often engage in morally marginal behavior.

Like many beginners, Joe undoubtedly will be encouraged to mine his dissertation for publications. Should he, or how should he, involve his chair in publication? In the academic marketplace, senior faculty, like junior faculty, are concerned about capital accumulation and academic standing. Capital indicates worth; the press to accumulation has encouraged some chairs to take credit for student work. I recall, for example, a young teacher educator worrying over her chair's insistence on being first author on a major piece even though the chair merely supported the work and did some editing. Revealing strong beliefs in trickle down academic economics, the chair urged that being listed first was not an act of arrogation but of generosity, a matter of increasing market value, an expression of largesse from one who has to one who has not. More citations would follow, the chair argued, and these would benefit her former student. Graduation often changes mentor and protégé roles and relationships, heightening and exposing latent feelings of competition and perhaps revealing feelings of mentor envy of the young. In any case, mentoring of junior faculty requires largeness of spirit that is difficult to sustain since, like one's protégés, mentors live in fast time and everyone is in competition with everyone else.

As noted, fast time leads to shortcuts, including abrogation of essential ethical roles and professional responsibilities. Traditionally, teacher education faculties have made decisions about which students should be recommended for licensure to teach. These decisions have been based on faculty members' professional knowledge, experience with students over an extended period of time and in multiple settings, and understanding of program aims. Seeking what some believe to be better warrants of teacher education student quality, 23 states joined with Stanford University to develop a common portfolio-based assessment system, the edTPA, for beginning teachers. Once the system was developed, Stanford sold the rights to the edTPA to Pearson Education, a massive corporation located in London that employs over 40,000 people worldwide. Offering a range of supporting services and products for sale, including its own ePortfolio System, Pearson charges teacher candidates for assessment of their portfolios, assessments conducted by unknown somebodies. In addition, Pearson administers the National Board for Professional Teaching Standards (NBPTS) assessment despite its having been developed with public funding from the US Department of Education. NBPT candidates pay an assessment fee recently reduced to US$1900. Owning these licenses, good academic capitalist that it is, Stanford is positioned to receive a huge payout. More to the point, faculty across the United States will no longer make determinative assessments of their students' ability to teach. Pearson employees will make the decision. Obviously, the effects of these actions, presumably undertaken to guarantee quality and raise program efficiency, are far-reaching and ethically troubling (Cochran-Smith, Piazza, & Power, 2013).

Markets and consumer values also affect teaching when scores on student satisfaction surveys substitute for slow time faculty observations and discussions about teaching and teaching quality with peers. Students are decent judges of teacher fairness, but often they struggle to reasonably assess content quality or even of the preparation of their teachers. Ethical issues may arise from pressures for time to engage in other valued activities, not the least being scholarship. Time is saved when teachers avoid giving student assignments that require significant discussion and feedback, even though most university faculties place high value on teaching. In fact, the value of teaching to faculty has grown dramatically on US campuses over the past two decades (Cummings & Shin, 2013), perhaps underscoring the centrality of quality teaching to student recruitment, but most certainly to work satisfaction.

UNSEEN FACTORS AND THE CRITIQUE OF NEOLIBERALISM

Much is right about higher education generally and with college and university-housed teacher education specifically, but also much is worrisome, as this chapter has suggested. For the most part, a wide-ranging peace seems to exist with neoliberalism and its influences in higher education. Generally, it is accepted there ought to one education for the elite (or soon to be elite) and another for everyone else (Christensen & Eyring, 2011). In fact, higher education is much involved in the production of a new aristocracy (Stewart, 2018). Even when troubling effects are recognized, the assumptions and values of neoliberalism are generally taken-for-granted, easily spoken, and too seldom interrogated even as contradictions and tensions abound (see Hochschild, 2016). As Baxter (2011) has argued, while identifying "manifest discourses is a relatively straightforward undertaking, it is more complicated to identify discourses from unsaid, taken-for-granted presuppositions" (p. 159).

Universities operate within a national and international marketplace and political context that press the values of neoliberalism. The siren song of EGMs plays loudly in the background of board of trustee meetings almost everywhere, with a predominant refrain of not measuring up. Nevertheless, *U.S. News & World Report* and various other businesses and organizations that have found ranking and rating profitable inflict comparison. Outliers and distinctive institutions that march to a different yet spirited and skilled drummer may find themselves pushed into a significant market disadvantage. As with any other product, including faculty "productivity," value is comparative, even if the distinctions made are microscopic, parsing marginally consequential or even illusionary differences, perhaps based more on institutional reputation than reality (Glenn, 2010). Rather than self-satisfaction, at such moments, embarrassment is probably the more appropriate emotion. Greatness never follows emulation, which promises only mission creep and loss of distinctiveness. A comment and a warning offered by the late John Goodlad (1994) comes to mind: "In the early stages of redesigning settings or creating new ones, it is not wise to go forth seeking models elsewhere" (p. 100). When seeking improvement, generally it is best to turn inward and to an institution's "unique strengths" (Christensen & Eyring, 2011, p. 401).

Vigorous criticism of neoliberalism, what Ball (2016) described as "fearless speech" (p. 1138), in its many faces and forms is essential to the health of higher education, including teacher education. Through immanent critique, the seductive, demeaning, humanly contorting, and community crushing manifestations of neoliberalism need to be identified, especially as they play out in consciousness, in the wider society and within the university (see Agger in Nichel, 2012, p. 142). Immanent critique is a means for restoring "actuality to false appearance" by "first expressing what a social totality holds itself to be, and then confronting it with what it is in fact becoming" (Schroyer, 1975, pp. 30–31). The fact is that higher education is less and less about education or, for that matter, about things that are higher. A parallel location for criticism is in the tensions and contradictions that emerge between what one takes oneself to be as a person, teacher, and teacher educator and the forms of life and activity one is expected to portray when enacting institutionally valued roles.

Critique begins with a destructive moment of interrogation followed by a constructive moment of loving action — a call to recall oneself, a reminder of our deepest human longings and our desire for connectedness and for mercy. Critics ask what sort of people we are and what sort of people we ought to be. Questions like these invite moral deliberation (Johnson, 1993). The charge is also to consider how institutions shape people and how good the people are who are being shaped. Here, a comment from the past about teacher quality comes to mind: "To be a good teacher one must be first of all a good human being" (Giles, McCutchen, & Zechiel, 1942, p. 231). The appeal to criticism and to conscience, as Green (1999) argued, speaks with many voices, each requiring support within the university community and experience to flourish: the voice of craft, memory or tradition, and membership, as well as duty and service.

The neoliberal university values people who work very hard, but its other values that bring significant institutional rewards may give pause. Are good people rootless and for sale: lacking focus; always holding a finger in the air to test the winds hoping to catch a market opportunity, an idea that will sell; lack conviction and the ability to make strong evaluations, an inability that is dressed up as an urbane and principled and sometimes aggressive open-mindedness? Does the frenzy of fast time that urges indifference with blindness to moral blindness, even as it supports a kind of professional speed dating — racking up connections that might lead somewhere — motivate a person to become a professor? Do university faculty look forward to a lunch — when getting ahead means being disconnected from place, working surrounded by strangers but linked to a network of like-minded scholars spread across various time zones all of whom are looking at a computer screen — alone? Knowing they are always being judged, do university faculty gain in confidence, competence, and commitment, by checking every day, and sometimes multiple times a day, to see if their H-index is up or visit ResearchGate, a social networking site for researchers, to see if anyone important is following their work? Finally, do university faculty enter higher education because of a love of grant writing that, if successful, promises even more time spent grant writing and less time studying and teaching?

Viewing higher education through the paired lens of issues and troubles and in relation to neoliberal imperatives reveals a deep disjunction. Like teachers, mostly university faculty came to their work because of the work itself. Mostly, they enjoy teaching. They value ideas and delight in talking about them with interesting and interested people. They like pursuing projects that they have a hand in designing and delight when a project produces an interesting or surprising result. Autonomy is important to them as are relationships, including and sometimes especially, with students. And again like teachers, they hope their lives will add up to something, a positive difference of some kind, for someone, somewhere. Many faculties also value slow time, knowing that "truth, be it the ancient truth of Being or the Christian truth of the living God, can reveal itself only in complete human stillness" (Arendt, 1958, p. 15). And mostly, faculty know that the "university needs to be understood as engaged in forms of individual and collective development that cannot be captured in economic terms. Education cannot pay in this way" (Newfield, 2008, p. 273).

Often it is said that the "price of liberty is eternal vigilance." Some years ago, philosopher Maxine Greene (1977) made the parallel point that a morally meaningful life requires "wide-awakeness" which sets for educators the terrible task of actually making "things harder for people [by] awakening them to their freedom" (p. 120) and to their responsibility to protect that freedom. Under neoliberalism, decision making in many of life's most important arenas, including education, is being or has been relegated to markets which is, as Harari (2017) warned, "dangerous [...] because these forces do what's good for the market rather than what's good for humankind or for the world" (p. 382). By displacing reason, the worship of markets, a form of idolatry, leaves humanity crippled, hobbling along without full use of its most powerful survival tool. And it is to public education and higher education that we rightly look to cultivate and protect the reasonableness of reason. It is in such institutions where the young should be able to find what they so desperately need: wide-awake educators who offer "reliable orientation points and [stand as] trustworthy guides" (Bauman, 2008, p. 24).

CHAPTER 2

LOOKING BACK ON 40 YEARS OF TEACHING EDUCATION: A PERSONAL ESSAY

INTRODUCTION

In the fall of the 1973–1974 school year, I began graduate school at The Ohio State University. While driving to Columbus, Ohio, I stopped to visit friends at the University of Missouri, where I received a phone call from Columbus informing me that I needed to attend a meeting that was part of an effort to shift the teacher education program to a competency-based model. I was stunned. I had been teaching in an alternative public high school program, a school-within-a-school, designed for 14- to 18-year-olds who, for a variety of reasons, found themselves disconnected from what went on in schools. Drawing on Freire's then recently published *Pedagogy of the Oppressed* (1970), my students and I, along with a small group of student teachers from the university, planned thematic interdisciplinary units, built a recycle center, studied events unfolding in Southeast Asia and planted and tended a large garden, among other activities. As I drove to Columbus, I wondered what I had gotten myself into.

What follows is a personal essay. The formal essay is concerned with argumentation, the making and defending of a point of view. The essays in the chapters that follow are formal. In contrast, the personal essay focuses on discovery. In writing personal essays, one discovers where one stands on complex issues, problems, questions, and subjects. In writing such essays, one's feelings, instincts, and thoughts are tested in the crucible of composition (Epstein, 1997, p. 15). The hope embedded in the personal essay is that an author will discover what he or she thinks about a topic, and through writing "learn perhaps something new about [himself] and the world" (p. 16). Unlike fiction, the personal essay is "bounded – some might say grounded – by reality" (Epstein, 1997, p. 14) – in this instance the reality of some 40 years lived in teacher education.

My time in Columbus began what I then could not possibly have imagined, a long, mostly interesting, but sometimes tiresome, encounter with the people, literature, language, and ideas of teacher education. Several publications scaffold the essay and move the narrative along. Most of these are works that demanded my sometimes unwilling attention and sometimes shaped my thinking about and practice of teacher education. Thus, the essay portrays one person's evolving participation in the discursive community and practice that is teacher education.

TECHNICAL VIEWS OF TEACHING AND TEACHER EFFECTIVENESS: THE 1970s

When I arrived at Ohio State, a major reform effort was underway there and across much of the teacher education landscape to address a set of troubling and, as I was to learn, persistent, issues. The curriculum of teacher education was badly fragmented. There was duplication in course content, and students spent little time in schools outside of student teaching. For the most part, field experiences were simply left to school teachers to do what they thought best. Cooperating teachers and university faculty seldom interacted. As I recall, the curriculum included an introduction to education course; a general methods class of the sort I would teach; special methods classes on how to teach one subject or another; "foundations" (educational psychology, history, or philosophy) and a media class, among others — as well as student teaching.

The plan for improvement involved identification, with significant faculty involvement, of program goals; agreement on course aims and content; and improvement in the number and quality of field experiences. Reducing the aim of reform to bare essentials, the faculty developed a list of specific teaching competencies. The dean wrote: "We must face straightforwardly the task of defining exit criteria, literally spelling out those skills we expect our teachers to possess when they seek certification" (Cunningham, 1973, p. 152). The dean's views of the future of teacher education were widely shared. In the same publication, for example, Howe (1973) of the Ford Foundation made a similar point, suggesting that teaching is like learning to play tennis and that the good teacher "comes somewhat near to solving his multifaceted problems by getting into a classroom, contending with reality, and getting immediate feedback on his performance from someone more skilled than he is" (p. 55).

The question was, of course, what competencies did effective teachers actually possess? What skills and, using current jargon, *dispositions* characterize an effective teacher? The promise then offered by process-product researchers to teachers was deceptively simple and certainly misleading: Be this or do that and you will get this. The aim was to identify "what works." Context differences mattered little. Teacher beliefs mattered not at all. A year prior to the publication of Dean Cunningham's chapter, Gage published his much-anticipated book, *Teacher Effectiveness and Teacher Education* (1972). Gage's ambition was clear, and is still with us, to develop a robust science of education (see Chapter 3). The pathway to science was assumed to run directly through studies that linked specific teaching skills and teacher qualities to student learning:

> The development of paradigms [for research on teaching] should lead to analysis of the teaching process into various component activities, as independent variables, and kinds of criteria, such as types of achievement, as dependent variables. Such an analytic approach may be contrasted with the global criterion approach that led to gross ratings of ill-defined teacher characteristics without clear referents in classroom teacher behavior. (Gage, 1972, pp. 20–21)

A goal was to tighten things up, identify what specific teaching skills promised the desired student performance, and develop those skills in teachers, just as Cunningham and Howe suggested. Gage was well aware of the difficulties ahead and noted others' pessimism: research had not delivered what teachers and teacher educators needed. But, he said, the reason for optimism could be found in studies offering evidence of the positive influence of a few teacher behaviors on student learning. Examples included teacher "warmth" (pp. 34–35), "enthusiasm" (p. 38), and cognitive understanding of what was being taught (p. 37).

Sharing Gage's ambition, Rosenshine, and Furst (1971) identified clarity, variability, enthusiasm, task-oriented behaviors, and student opportunity to learn as the five most powerful teacher variables affecting student behavior. By 1973, these concepts had made their way into methods textbooks. That year, for example, the first of 10 editions of the best-selling *Looking in Classrooms* (Good & Brophy, 1973) introduced the importance of clarity in teaching: "If students are to become involved in their work, they must clearly understand what they are to do" (p. 317). Linked to student motivation, enthusiasm captured the commonsense conclusion that people "are more likely to try things or to want to do what [they] see others enjoying" (p. 300). But enthusiasm is, as Good and Brophy noted, a rather slippery concept. Nevertheless, they argued, "Although it is impossible to specify the behaviors of an enthusiastic teacher with precision, certainly these terms are important predictors: alertness, vigor, interest, movement, and voice inflection" (p. 301).

Good and Brophy's statement that it is "impossible to specify the behaviors of an enthusiastic teacher with precision" proved telling. Later studies demonstrated that differences between what effective and ineffective teachers supposedly did in the classroom were not easily determined, forcing the conclusion that ultimately such studies are "not really about teaching at all but about indicators [...] [S]uch indicators are not skills, processes, or practices. They are, instead, arbitrary fragments stripped of the particulars of purpose, subject matter, context, and understanding" (Doyle, 1990, p. 19). Nevertheless, seeking up-to-date content, teacher educators like me taught that effective teachers are enthusiastic (whatever that meant), vary their instruction, and are clear in their directions. But they are not "so enthusiastic" they would be obnoxious, not "so variable" that the value of routines to managing a classroom would be lost, not "so clear and precise" that responsiveness and openness to unexpected opportunities to support student learning would be missed. I recall wondering if the curriculum of my course really was only about straw men. Who would argue for the value of lifeless, rigid, and confused and confusing teachers? Concepts offered by Kounin (1970) would prove more helpful, but *with-it-ness, overlapping, momentum* and *slowdowns, group focus,* and *intellectual challenge* only became part of my vocabulary somewhat later.

A key element of the reform then underway was increasing the amount and quality of the time teacher education students actually spent teaching and talking about teaching. More field experience was added to student teaching, and microteaching was required (Allen & Ryan, 1969). The centerpiece of the methods class I taught was a "short course" designed to place beginning teacher education students into teams to plan, execute, and evaluate a unit taught in a local Columbus school. Among the books used to support the short course and to prepare candidates for student teaching was the trilogy of Popham (1973) and Popham and Baker (1973a, 1973b). Each book was organized into "programs," which would currently be thought of as self-instruction "modules" (discussed in Chapter 1) and complete with built-in assessments of understanding. Rather than being research-driven, most of the programs reflected what the authors thought was the best of current teaching practices.

Reflecting the priorities of Popham and Baker, and others, the content of general methods courses emphasized learning terms — *teaching unit, lesson plan, needs assessment* — and developing knowledge about the skills associated with planning, instructional tactics (Popham & Baker, 1973b), classroom management, student "discipline," and evaluation, including an emphasis on student performance and measurable goals as proof of effective teaching. Practice of those skills typically came later.

Echoing business influences in public schools that had embraced "management by objectives" and its underlying grounding in behavioral psychology, the aim was to make instruction more systematic. Writing clear performance objectives that specified what students would be able to do as a result of instruction was thought to be the most promising move toward better quality teaching and learning. Bloom's Taxonomy (Bloom, Engelhart, Furst, Hill, & Krathwohl, 1956) was used to make certain that objectives covered what were thought to be the most valued cognitive outcomes. Linked closely to evaluation, the quality of objectives and goals was thought essential to the quality of assessment. Accordingly, methods course instructors commonly spent an inordinate amount of time teaching and testing to make certain students knew how to write "proper" behavioral objectives. No one I recall ever believed teachers actually planned for instruction this way (and they do not), but it was claimed that the exercise had value for focusing teachers' attention on student learning (see Clark, 1983).

Given my background, even though I enjoyed teaching and appreciated my students, I struggled to adjust to life within an evolving competency-based program. In contrast, my studies were engaging. My major professor, Paul Klohr, the grandfather of the reconceptualist movement in curriculum studies, was very much interested in alternative states of consciousness, education for critical consciousness, hermeneutics, thematic units, and interdisciplinary studies — ideas that stirred my own and others of his students' imaginations. But teacher education was moving elsewhere and in some ways back to its roots in the earlier part of the century in the emerging social sciences with their instrumental versions of rationalism and their interest in predication and control (see Clifford, 1973). In the quest for a science of education, the values of training were ascendant, showing signs of displacing those of education with its inherent messiness and unpredictability (Bullough & Gitlin, 1994). Enough of 1960s romanticism — teaching needed a tough-minded tidying based on robust data: real data from real research, not the soft stuff. Learning outcomes needed identification, precise statement, and ordering for measurement.

TEACHER EDUCATION AT RISK: THE 1980s

Graduating, I stumbled into a position as an assistant professor at the University of Utah and got about the business of making a career. Meanwhile, on August 26, 1981, the US Secretary of Education, Ted Bell, who later became a faculty member in my college, appointed the university's president, David Gardner, chairman of the National Commission on Excellence in Education. When appointed by President Reagan, Secretary Bell's charge had been to abolish the federal Department of Education (Bell, 1988). Instead, he saved it. Released on the heels of recession, the Commission's report *A Nation at Risk* was front page news in the US in the spring of 1983. The apocalyptic prose of the report touched a nerve within the wider public and, much to the president's dismay, a sudden urgency for educational reform swept the nation.

Educators faced a perfect storm: then as now, policy-makers were seeking quick and easy solutions to intractable social and economic problems, and were looking to deflect responsibility for them by placing blame. Educational reform leaped to the center of the national political agenda where until recently it has remained. Driven by the simple-minded assumption that school quality was directly linked to national economic competitiveness, in biting prose the report imposed causality for the economic threat posed by Japan and other challenges: the nation was at risk because of mediocre education.

The report called for elected officials to take charge of educational reform and the federal government to get much more involved in education. Within months of its release, across the nation high school graduation requirements were raised, as were college admission requirements. Courses were refocused and the curriculum narrowed to reflect commission priorities, including technology, foreign language, science, and mathematics. Teachers and teacher educators were called to task, implicitly blamed for the apparently sorry state of affairs. Recommendations for teacher education included placing greater emphasis on academic learning and strengthening teacher evaluation systems to reward "superior teachers" (p. 30). Career ladders were recommended and over time tested, then faded. To solve shortages of mathematics and science teachers, greater flexibility was urged in the routes to teaching. Finally, a call was made for master teachers to be involved in "designing teacher preparation programs and in supervising teachers during their probationary years" (p. 31).

The year *A Nation at Risk* was published also produced Ernest Boyer's *High School: A Report on Secondary Education in America* (1983). As President of the Carnegie Foundation for the Advancement of Teaching, Boyer was deeply concerned about the status and work conditions of teachers, and he located several troubling trends. "This nation has always been ambivalent about teachers," he wrote.

> Today, teaching occupies [a] "shadowed place" in the public's esteem. In just twelve years, from 1969 to 1981, the number of parents who said they would like to have their children become teachers in the public schools dropped from 75 to 46 percent. (p. 154)

He then pointed to a simple fact often overlooked by critics:

> Whenever schools are discussed, teachers are blamed for much of what is wrong. [But] concentrating only on the weakest teachers misses an essential point. Whatever is wrong with America's public schools cannot be fixed without the help of those teachers already in the classroom. (p. 154)

Boyer had much to say about teacher education, which included recommending a fifth year of professional studies to replace the typical four-year program and an "apprenticeship experience" (p. 175) that would include assignment of beginning teachers to a teacher team, like a residency in medicine.

Goodlad's monumental study, *A Place Called School: Prospects for the Future,* was published in 1984. Evidencing a rare but measured faith in teacher and school administrator willingness and ability to make wise decisions when given adequate information, support, and encouragement, Goodlad argued for decentralization of decision making, so those closest to educational problems and best positioned to recognize and promote learning opportunities would have the greatest influence over the actions taken. This simple but still powerful idea for a time inspired considerable interest, which included some policy-makers and teachers who liked the idea of being trusted. The individual school and building faculty, as part of a linked community of concern, was, he suggested, the most effective and, ultimately, efficient unit for thinking about and planning for change. Later, Goodlad would use the phrase *educational renewal* to capture the idea (1994). On this view, school improvement principally is a matter of learning.

To transcend discredited conventional wisdom required re-imagining schooling. Among the many concerns Goodlad identified were differences in the quality of schooling offered to high- and low-track students: "Minority students were found in disproportionately large percentages in the low track classes of the multiracial schools in our sample" (1984, p. 156). Over time, this and related issues grew dramatically in importance and influence in teacher education policy and practice, giving rise to a growing concern for social justice. Goodlad thought the most promising strategy for improvement might be development of "exemplary models" of teaching in demonstration or "key schools" that "should be linked to universities and to one another in a communicating, collaborating network" (p. 301). Recalling elements of an earlier generation of university laboratory schools, key schools were to help create "preparation programs of such length, depth, and quality that they [would] be effectively separated from most of the conventional ways of teaching" (p. 314). "Teacher preparing institutions must join with school districts in identifying and subsequently working with schools to be designed as key and demonstration schools" (p. 316). Within key schools, "outstanding career and head teachers [would] be drawn. Beginning teachers [would] be interned only in these schools" (p. 316). Finally, within key schools, university faculty members would "carry on their scholarly inquiries, sharing their expertise with the school faculty" (p. 316).

Consistently overestimating the power of schooling to fix things and ignoring the nature of education as primarily a long-term investment in human capital, many dozens of reports were published between the release of *A Nation at Risk* and the end of the decade. Outside of works like those written by Boyer and Goodlad, who were not politicians, businessmen, nor free-market enthusiasts but educators, a consensus on teacher education emerged, largely echoing an old refrain:

> More stringent admission standards, better screening of teacher applicants, an increase in the number of academic courses required, more—or, alternatively, fewer—prescribed professional education courses, a beefing up of the number and quality of clinical experiences, and, possibly, standardized testing of teaching and subject matter competence prior to certification. (Lucas, 1999, p. 90)

These recommendations initially shaped my faculty's discussions about the future of our program at the University of Utah. Our conversations, however, took a turn when the college embraced the Holmes Group, then organizing under the leadership of Dean Judy Lanier of Michigan State University to articulate a response by leading research universities to the attacks on teacher education. My dean, Cecil Miskel, who went on to the deanship at Michigan, joined 12 other deans and a college president on the executive board. Along with 35 deans and a few faculty members, I am listed as one of the "participants in the development of the reform agenda" (Holmes Group, 1986, p. 79). The first two paragraphs of the first Holmes Report began with two remarkable sentences: "America's dissatisfaction with its schools has become chronic and epidemic" and "Teaching must be improved, but plans for improving teaching also must be improved" (p. 3). Speaking with "exceptional candor" (Lucas, 1999, p. 90), this highly controversial report laid out what were thought to be the problems with teacher education and then offered a set of five corrective goals (Holmes Group, 1986, p. 4):

(1) "To make the education of teachers intellectually more solid."
(2) "To recognize differences in teachers' knowledge, skill, and commitment, in their education, certification, and work."
(3) "To create standards of entry to the profession – examinations and educational requirements that are professionally relevant and intellectually defensible."
(4) "To connect our own institutions to schools."
(5) "To make schools better places for teachers to work, and to learn."

Given the prominence of group membership and with the support of various granting agencies, a flurry of activity followed.

PROFESSIONALISM, REFLECTION, AND A CHANGING CONTEXT: TOWARD THE 1990s

A tradition of autonomy as the essence of teacher professionalism had longdominated teaching and teacher education, a vision supported by the quest for teacher competencies. As Hargreaves (2000) stated, "The words 'professional' and 'autonomy' [had become] inseparable among educators" (p. 159). But individualism got in the way of teacher learning. By the mid-1980s, "the world in which teachers worked was changing, and so was their own work. More and more teachers faced the prospect of having to teach in ways they had not been taught themselves" (p. 162). A more collaborative form of professionalism began to emerge in response to rapid change and pressures to reform, the seed of what eventually became professional learning communities (Stoll, Bolam, McMahon, Wallace, & Thomas, 2006).

The Reflective Practitioner (Schön, 1983) offered a promising lens for transcending the conventional wisdom of teaching. Representing an understanding of teaching, among other forms of practice, as extraordinarily complex, Schön called attention to the "epistemology of practice implicit in the artistic, intuitive processes [including teaching] which some practitioners bring to situations of uncertainty, instability, uniqueness, and value conflict" (p. 49). "Knowledge-in-action," he asserted, is inherent in practice and is grounded in large measure in the experiences and tacit knowledge of practitioners. Such knowledge is not easily identified, and changes and grows as situations shift, rules fail and new problems emerge that demand an "on the spot experiment" (Schön, 1987, p. 28). Schön explored how such knowledge arises from "reflection-in-action" and how its cultivation presents extraordinarily complex challenges for educators. Such knowledge does not easily translate into teacher education content or skills. Instead, underscoring an insight offered by Dewey (1916) that, "we never educate directly, but indirectly by means of the environment" (p. 22), Schön saw the educational challenge as developing social processes that encourage the kind of human experience that, again echoing Dewey, would, upon reflection, tend toward the desired learning. Teachers needed "coaches" (Schön, 1987, p. 40). Concomitantly, interest in action research was rekindled (Carr & Kemmis, 1986; Elliot, 1991).

Several additional developments urged enriching the curriculum and the instruction of teacher education. Interest increased in better understanding teacher development, which included identifying differences between expert and novice teachers' thinking and problem-solving (Berliner, 1986). Studies of teacher development connected teachers' learning and development to biography and to cultural and social influences including the nature of the work of teaching (e.g., Bullough, 1989; Connelly & Clandinin, 1988; Elbaz, 1983; Nias, 1989). Staged models of development emerged, extending and reconfiguring early insights of Frances Fuller (Fuller & Bown, 1975; see Huberman, 1989). Recognition that teacher knowledge was storied and episodic increased, teacher narratives were more frequently used for rethinking teacher education practices and teacher learning (see Clandinin & Connelly, 2000; Connelly & Clandinin, 1990). Drawing on insights from medicine, analysis of teaching cases was offered as a promising means for developing pedagogical knowledge (Shulman, 1986a). Under Shulman's influence, rethinking of the content of teacher education was begun, leading to a widely shared conclusion that pedagogical content knowledge perhaps offered a distinctive form of knowledge sufficient to support professional claims (Shulman, 1986b; see Bullough, 2001b).

Several story forms, including autobiographies of being a student and of being taught and learning a discipline, found their way into teacher education, including my classes. Although like other teacher educators, I had previously engaged students in analyzing portrayals of complex and sometimes troubling classroom events including videotaped teaching episodes, I expanded the curriculum to include written teaching cases. Given the personal nature of teaching, biography and the emergence of a teaching self, currently thought of as teacher identity, also became part of the curriculum. To get at conceptions of self-as-teacher, I invited students to generate and analyze personal teaching metaphors (see Bullough, Knowles, & Crow, 1991, Chapter 10). Journaling became commonplace. Recognizing that identity is shaped by practice and by the communities within which we practice (Wenger, 1998), I had students conduct classroom ethnographies and, during practice teaching, conduct action research projects.

As content changed, program structures also were changed. Recognizing the importance of a "shared ordeal" (Lottie, 1975) in professional learning and acknowledging that learning to teach is a social practice in 1982–1983, my faculty organized students into cohorts: groups of teacher education students who proceeded through the program as a class. As in many institutions, cohorts remained together for a full academic year or two. Supported by the Holmes Group, among others, across the nation cohorts became common in teacher education. Many institutions also developed fifth year and graduate certification programs, several of which endure. Additionally, portfolios were introduced to document teacher learning (Bullough, 1993). As noted in Chapter 1, in the intervening years, portfolios, which evolved from paper to online documents, e-portfolios, and into teacher work samples (Girod, 2002), gained a prominent place in beginning teacher assessment for licensure (see Bullough, 2010).

This was a heady time for teacher education, a time characterized by remarkable experimentation, but perhaps no change was of greater potential consequence than work done to rethink the relationship between teacher education and schooling, a central item of the Holmes' agenda and of Goodlad's vision.

CHANGING FIELD EXPERIENCE: THE 1990s

Involvement with the Holmes Group strengthened interest in an idea that my faculty had been quietly developing from the late 1970s, professional development centers (Nutting, 1981). Within the Holmes Group institutions, large research universities, and teacher education institutions across many nations (see Furlong et al., 1996), the idea of the professional development school (PDS) gained momentum as teacher educators began to reimagine the nature of practicum experiences and beginning teacher induction.

In this effort perhaps no influence was of greater consequence than John Goodlad and the Southern California School–University Partnership he formed (see Sirotnik, 2001) and later his Center for Educational Renewal (CER) in Seattle. Goodlad considered it impossible to have high-quality teacher education without high-quality schools. From these bases, Goodlad fleshed out the concept of "key" or "demonstration" schools. CER was founded with two purposes, the second being to "build, support, and sustain a network of school—university partnerships in diverse settings around the country" (Sirotnik, 2001, p. 13). Thus, the National Network for Educational Renewal (NNER) began in 1986 with 10 partnerships in 10 states. Reorganized to support a shared Agenda for Education in a Democracy, the NNER expanded to more than 20 partnerships, each committed to a social vision of public education that reached well beyond instrumental, economic, ends. Four "moral dimensions of schooling" framed the mission: "Enculturating the young in a social and political democracy; Providing access to knowledge for all children and youths; Practicing a nurturing pedagogy [...]; [and] Ensuring responsible stewardship of schools" (Sirotnik, 2001, p. 28; See Bullough & Rosenberg, 2018).

Recognizing a dramatically changing social and economic landscape, the Agenda represented an effort to rethink fundamentally the purposes of teacher education. Rapidly changing immigration patterns and rising student body diversity, along with issues related to poverty leading to radical inequality of school performance across racial and ethnic groups, encouraged teacher educators to engage in a variety of changes. Increasing numbers of immigrant children came to school needing to learn English and representing cultures quite foreign to the experience of their mostly white and middle-class female teachers. Initially, courses in multicultural education were added and method course content was adjusted to be more attentive to students' differences in background and patterns of learning. Greater effort was directed toward developing field experiences for beginning teachers that increased their opportunities to work with and learn from diverse student populations.

Not all was rosy, however. From the vantage point of the mid-1990s and in full recognition of the persistent difficulties associated with re-forging long-established and habitual school—university relations, Goodlad concluded that much of the initial flurry of activity around partnerships and many published reports of progress represented a lot of "rhapsodic twiddle that confuses paradise envisioned with paradise gained" (1994, p. 116). Similarly, the Holmes Group warned of "cheap copies" of genuine partnerships (1990, p. 79). My partnership work at the University of Utah and that of my colleagues in the 1980s and 1990s was sincere, demanding, politically complex, and very seriously underfunded. Partnerships are expensive when done well. To soften the burden, some faculty lines were redefined as *clinical*, a development common across teacher education institutions that actually enabled the flight of some faculty from schools. The result was a "clinicalization" of teacher education, a trend that is now well established (Bullough et al., 1997). Although field experiences were improved, neither resources, nor institutional and faculty commitments, were sufficient to sustain the work — particularly of developing shared lines of research (see Winitzky, O'Keefe, & Stoddart, 1992).

By the late 1990s, so many teacher education institutions claimed partnerships that the National Council for the Accreditation of Teacher Education (NCATE) stepped in and, hoping to provide order, developed a set of standards that was released in 2001. NCATE believed that the standards would support

PDS development and encourage partnership research, but these were mostly unrealized aims. PDS research proved astonishingly complex and difficult to sustain (Castle, Fox, & Souder, 2006, pp. 65–66). Accordingly, in the intervening years, writing about PDSs diminished. Unlike the first two editions of the *Handbook of Research on Teacher Education*, the third (Cochran-Smith, Feiman-Nemser, McIntyre, & Demers, 2008) does not include a chapter on PDSs, and "partner schools" and "partnership" are not even listed in the index. Nevertheless, partnerships of various kinds exist across the country, many are robust, and the quality of fieldwork is arguably much improved. The university–public school partnership sponsored by my current institution, Brigham Young University, is both large and vibrant. Significant support for PDSs came in 2005 with founding of the National Association for Professional Development Schools.

TEACHER KNOWLEDGE AND ACCREDITATION: MOVING THROUGH THE 1990S

Over the years, numerous attempts have been made to detail what teachers ought to know and be able to do, just the sort of task that guided the teacher competency reform effort at Ohio State. As part of the reform mania of the 1980s, in 1987 the National Board for Professional Teaching Standards, mentioned in Chapter 1, was established to develop standards for advanced certification thought essential to strengthening teacher professionalism. During the same year, the Interstate New Teacher Assessment and Support Consortium (InTASC) was established by the Council of Chief State School Officers (CCSSO), an organization that was primarily responsible for teacher licensing and program approval. InTASC promoted collaboration among the states to rethink teacher assessment for initial teacher licensure. By 1992, InTASC had identified 10 National Board "compatible" core standards for content and pedagogical knowledge expected of beginning teachers which, among other outcomes, gave a prominent place to teaching issues related to student diversity. Each standard involved statements of desired teacher *knowledge, dispositions*, and *performances*, detailing what was to be known and then demonstrated by beginning teachers – knowledge first. Importantly, the most recent update of the standards puts "performance" first (see CCSSO, 2011).

The 10 InTASC standards and dimensions quickly found their way into teacher education accreditation, framing institutional responses to NCATE visits. Founded in 1954, for most of its history NCATE dominated teacher education accreditation in the US, complementing state approval. A threat to NCATE dominance arose in 1997 when the Teacher Education Accreditation Council (TEAC) was formed and then certified by the US Department of Education. In contrast to NCATE's standards model of accreditation and echoing some elements of teacher professionalism championed during the 1980s, TEAC embraced an accountancy model. The TEAC model allowed institutions considerable program flexibility when setting aims, but required evidence of accomplishment of intent. Signaling a shift in historic accreditation priorities, both organizations came to emphasize "*outputs*," proof of student learning, over "*inputs*," opportunities for learning and quality of program resources, in program evaluation, a change that came in 2002 for NCATE. While in much of the country, teacher education accreditation had been voluntary, for the most part this also changed. With the merger of TEAC and NCATE to form the Council for the Accreditation of Educator Preparation (CAEP), completed in the summer of 2013, NCATE's model (which embraces the InTASC standards to define its first of five program standards) was strengthened, and the openness and flexibility that characterized TEAC diminished dramatically.

That "knowledge" was initially placed before "performance" in InTASC guidelines appears to have been based on belief that research "findings are valuable not because they yield rules for teaching but rather because they help teachers to assess the likely consequences of alternative strategies and thus to make more informed decisions" (Good, 1990, p. 64). Put differently, knowledge was intended to support reflective action in pursuit of further knowledge, a view well understood by action researchers. Good (1980) offered an early and especially apt warning about what happens when performance is placed first: "We should be suspicious of simple models of teaching that offer universal solutions to classroom problems" (p. 55). Despite such cautions, teacher education students and, facing continuing sharp criticism, many teacher educators have sought in research greater and more detailed direction, an ambition now strongly supported by CAEP; what was and perhaps is wanted were rules, techniques, and best practices (see Chapter 4). InTASC's elevation of "performance" over "knowledge" strengthens reliance on techniques and procedures while discouraging development of the complex understanding of teaching valued by Schön, among many others.

Efforts to establish the knowledge base of teaching, particularly for beginning teachers, have a long history in the US and elsewhere, in recent decades closely associated with licensure standards. To this end, standards involving scores on standardized student achievement tests have dramatically increased in importance. Numerous and often critical publications seek to lay out what beginning teachers ought to know and be able to do (Cochran-Smith & Zeichner, 2005; Darling-Hammond & Bransford, 2005; Reynolds, 1989; Smith, 1983). *Preparing Teachers: Building Evidence for Sound Policy* (2010), written by the Committee on the Study of Teacher Preparation Programs in the United States, a committee established by the National Research Council, is a recent and especially important contribution (see Chapter 3). Dismissing the value of local studies to teacher education program quality while seeking generalizable best practices through large-scale quantitative studies, authors of this report found little to praise and much to criticize in education research. Like Gage, championing creation of a science of education with its promise of clear teacher directives and seeking a tightly aligned system of education, the authors argue for greater emphasis on random trials and for funding of a national data network for teacher education, among several proposals.

A FULL-SCALE FEDERAL INVASION: INTO THE TWENTY-FIRST CENTURY

Following creation in 1990 by the first President Bush and the nation's governors of a set of national education goals with year 2000 as their achievement date (see National Education Goals Panel, 1995), on March 31, 1994, President Clinton signed into law The Goals 2000: Educate America Act. Driven by an outcomes model reminiscent of early competency-based reforms, the act provided modest financial incentives to states to achieve a specific set of lofty goals. (By default, in the US, the states are responsible for education under the Constitution.) The act proclaimed that by 2000 all children in America would enter school ready to learn; high school graduation rates would reach at least 90%; all children would demonstrate proficiency in English, mathematics, science, and foreign languages; and every school would be illegal drug- and violence-free. That anyone would have believed these standards would be met in six years after the announcement underscores a deepening and almost total disconnect between policy-makers and educators. No surprise − in their pass-a-law, make-it-happen!, top-down, managerial view of institutional change − policies typically have been set with rather little educator input.

On another front, two years later, on 26 March, the president "joined business leaders and educators in a National Education Summit to reaffirm their commitment to achieving higher academic standards for America's schools and students" (National Commission on Teaching and America's Future, 1996a, p. 3). Summit participants concluded that "America's future depends now, as never before, on our ability to teach" (National Commission on Teaching and America's Future, 1996a). Under the leadership of the governor of North Carolina, the National Commission on Teaching and America's Future was formed. The Commission developed an ambitious reform agenda written primarily to influence state policy-makers. Five "interlocking changes" were recommended:

(1) "Get serious about standards, for both students and teachers."
(2) "Reinvent teacher preparation and professional development."
(3) "Overhaul teacher recruitment and put qualified teachers in every classroom."
(4) "Encourage and reward teaching knowledge and skill."
(5) "Create schools that are organized for student and teacher success" (National Commission on Teaching and America's Future, 1996b, p. 7).

To "reinvent teacher preparation," specific goals were set for 2006: all teacher education programs were to be organized around standards, and all teacher education programs were to be accredited by NCATE or closed; graduate-level teacher preparation programs that included year-long internships in PDSs were to be created; mentoring of new teachers was to become universal; "new sources of professional development" were to be created; and professional development was to become an "ongoing part of teachers' daily work through joint planning, study groups, peer coaching, and research" (p. 20). Given the status of the members of the Commission and its origins, *What Matters Most* was released with fanfare. More than two dozen states signed on to support the agenda. Shortly after its release, Edgar Stones, the founding editor of the *Journal of Education for Teaching*, asked if I would convene a panel discussion of *What Matters Most*, offering the possibility of publication. Fatigued by the endless flow of reports, I hesitated, but then agreed. The dean and three of my colleagues and I met and recorded our conversation about the report, which Ed later published (Bullough, Burbank, Gess-Newsome, Kauchak, & Kennedy, 1998).

Recently, I reread our response to *What Matters Most*. We were prescient on many accounts, but not all: we thought Americans would be more protective of local traditions of public school governance than they at least initially proved to be. As part of an aggressive neoliberal political agenda supported by virtually every recent American president regardless of political affiliation, development of charter schools (i.e., publicly funded but essentially private schools) and strong encouragement of school vouchers appear to have syphoned away many parents who might otherwise have been actively engaged in efforts to recreate public education and strengthen teaching. We predicted much greater standardization of public education and of teacher education; correctly doubted resources would be adequate to support Commission recommendations; believed the Commission put far too much faith in the power of standards to drive change and in the durability of imposed reforms; feared that greater centralization and bureaucratization would lead to less educational experimentation; and lamented, when thinking of the promising work undertaken over the previous decade, that so much good work had already been forgotten. We knew our institution's programs were substantially better, and had conducted a number of studies that supported this conclusion.

The report was written as though nothing had been done to improve teacher education since the publication of *A Nation at Risk*. The message was beginning to sink in: there was no way to satisfy the critics of teacher education who, by exploiting a deep-seated historic American faith in the reformative and restorative powers of education, shifted onto teachers and teacher educators the blame for the results of poorly conceived and sometimes mean-spirited social and economic policies that encouraged all sorts of mischief for children, families, schools, and the wider society (Bullough, 1988; Kantor & Lowe, 2013). No surprise — one result has been the weakening of public education, the last and only social institution that still honors America's democratic aspirations. Attending to election cycles, a half-awake observer could predict when and in what form the attacks on public education and teacher education would come. Not surprising, with the signing of the No Child Left Behind (NCLB) act authorization of Goals 2000 was withdrawn.

For me, the 1990s represented a time of consolidation of my thinking about teaching, learning, and teacher education, the result of which lead to two books, the first edition of *Becoming a Student of Teaching* (Bullough & Gitlin, 1994) and *First-year Teacher: Eight Years Later* (Bullough & Baughman, 1997). This was also a time for rethinking the future. In 1999, I assumed a position at Brigham Young University where I work in the Center for the Improvement of Teacher Education and Schooling (CITES), the center of pedagogy that supports Brigham University's partnership with five school districts. Shortly after I arrived, BYU underwent a trying NCATE accreditation. NCATE was shifting standards to outputs and no one associated with the Council seemed able to give clear answers to our questions (Bullough, Clark, & Patterson, 2003). The lesson learned then was to avoid risks and color within the lines. More challenges followed after the NCLB act was signed into law on January 8, 2002.

NCLB: THE NEW CENTURY

Terribly underfunded, NCLB required all public schools receiving federal dollars to annually test all students in select grade levels or risk loss of federal funding. Schools were to make adequate yearly progress (AYP), which required increasing standardized test scores year after year across several specific groups including economically disadvantaged students, limited English speakers, and students with disabilities. Of these groups, at least 95% of the students were required to be tested. Failure to meet standard by any one group meant school failure. Schools that did not meet AYP over time were to be punished, potentially involving replacement of the entire staff and even closure. States were charged with developing statewide measurable objectives and tests. In addition, "highly qualified" teachers were to be provided for each classroom. Definitions of highly qualified varied widely, but in a direct slap at teacher education, the then US Secretary of Education, Rodney Paige, determined this meant merely having passed a test of academic competence and having demonstrated verbal ability. The act also required embrace of "scientifically based research," a phrase used dozens of times in the text of the law when addressing the law's requirements. Scientifically based research meant "research that involves the application of rigorous, systematic, and objective procedures to obtain reliable and valid knowledge relevant to education activities and programs" (No Child Left Behind Act, 2002, subpart 37 of section 9101).

Criticisms of NCLB abound, but the law did call much-needed attention to groups with histories of poor school performance who needed help. However, the law led to a national test fetish that persists despite the failure of reauthorization of the legislation, severe narrowing of school programs especially helpful to poor children in favor of time spent on mathematics and reading (Berliner, 2009), and system gaming. Tremendous discouragement followed as teachers and school administrators struggled to implement the law, even as they doubted the possibility of meeting its goals. On the whole, NCLB appears to have accomplished rather little and has done a good deal of harm, as Diane Ravitch, once a Washington insider and champion of NCLB, concluded, by offering "promised miracles that would shame snake-oil salesmen" (Rich, 2013; see Ravitch, 2013). Over the years, policy-makers have learned very little about the challenges of successful educational change or about the strategies that support innovation. No surprise, as the 2014 deadline approached, teacher job satisfaction levels fell to a 25-year low (Metlife, 2013, p. 6), and currently, there is a massive teacher shortage and signs of growing anger and frustration. After years of flat or falling salaries, teacher and parents are organizing and protests have popped up in several states (Goldstein & Casselman, 2018). In a 2016 survey, about half of all teachers reported that state and district policies actually get in the way of teaching (Center for Education Policy, 2016).

The ideology of neoliberalism underpinning NCLB continued in President Obama's administration, as evident in the federal Race to the Top initiative, a US$4.35 billion "competitive grant program designed to encourage and reward States that are creating the conditions for education innovation and reform" (US Department of Education, 2009, p. 2). By 2009, no one was guessing what was meant by *innovation* and *reform*: simply raise test scores and keep raising them year after year after year. Initiated at a time of severe economic recession, states rushed to enter the race. To win states submitted grant proposals that had to meet stringent selection criteria, which included: (1) "Improving teacher and principal effectiveness based on performance," (2) "Improving the effectiveness of teacher and principal preparation programs," and (3) "Providing effective support to teachers and principals" (US Department of Education, 2009, p. 3). Only four states did not apply; eager to win, some state legislatures changed long-established education policies just to enter the race. Standardized testing and value-added measures for determining teacher quality were prominent in the winning proposals. Stakes were high: Tennessee was awarded US$400 million; Ohio, US$400 million; Florida, US$700 million; and New York, US$700 million.

Beginning in the 1980s, interest grew in alternative routes to teacher certification, initially as means for staffing challenging schools. With the increasing influence of neoliberal reforms emphasizing markets and provider competition, at the same time as efforts were underway to standardize teacher education programs associated with colleges and universities, the federal government began funding a variety of licensure programs that offered greater program flexibility. As Darling-Hammond and her colleagues (2018) noted, in the US responses to teacher shortages are usually met by "reducing standards rather than increasing incentives" (p. 9). By 2016, about a fourth of all new teachers entered teaching through one or another alternative route; some estimates run higher (Feistritzer, 2011). Many of these programs have been less selective and less rigorous than university-based teacher education programs, and many offer little opportunity to gain significant pedagogical knowledge or school experience or provide consistent support from experienced teachers and informed feedback. Turnover for alternatively certified teachers is substantially higher than for their better-prepared peers (see Boyd et al., 2012; Ingersoll, Merrill, & May, 2014; Redding & Smith, 2016).

From a teacher educator's perspective, the effects of NCLB, and its aftermath, along with generous federal funding of alternative certification, complicated by greater standardization through accreditation of college- and university-housed teacher education offerings, have had shattering results. Aside from those few teacher educators who have found work and a measure of fame in the businesses of testing, evaluation, and teacher and teacher education criticism (areas where product development and academic capitalism are flourishing), most find themselves working under an ever-present and threatening regulatory gaze. On the whole, what counts as innovation in teacher education is reactive, not forward-looking nor often very imaginative. One of my professors, Harry Broudy, once quipped that "to be progressive is to get ahead of what is going to happen anyway," which seems to be the case in teacher education. Worldwide, comparing student test scores is now sport, and as in sport, coaches live and die by the tables (see Chapter 6). As competitive sport, test scores distort more than illuminate student (and teacher) performance (see Berliner & Glass, 2014, pp. 12–17). Students, and their teachers, simply must "measure up" and so must teacher education and teacher educators. A 2016 study reported that more than half of public school teachers have student test scores included in their performance evaluations (see Center on Education Policy). Gaming is inevitable when everyone is subjected to constant measurement, ranking, and rating and especially when those being measured, ranked, and rated have absolutely no influence over the criteria used. As Boyer knew, quality suffers in systems driven by distrust of those charged with doing the work, and it suffers when that work loses its joy and attractiveness. No surprise, in the US, fewer and fewer college students any longer consider teaching a viable career option (US Department of Education, 2012, Table 1.1). Filling up expensive and rapidly evolving data management systems to document quality is no substitute for pursuing quality. Ironically, one cost of such systems is efficiency.

CONCLUSION

Personal essays, as mentioned, focus on discovery. Thus, the personal essay ends when the pen drops, signaling more a resting place than a conclusion, a pause rather than a denouement. So, what has been discovered? The question that presses for an answer is "Why, other than tenacity and the possibility of a paycheck, do teacher educators teach? Why do we persist in a work that is so deeply misunderstood and so seldom appreciated?" This question, of course, is but a variant of another question: "Why does anyone desire to teach?" The answer is the same. We teach because the work morally matters and mostly interests us. And we teach because of the people we serve. Despite all of the challenges, teaching continues to attract smart, interesting, and dedicated people (see Chapter 5) – good people, although currently not enough of them. As teacher educators, we do our best to help teachers to realize their dreams as we struggle to maintain and realize our own. This is what we do.

CHAPTER 3

TOWARD RECONSTRUCTING THE NARRATIVE OF TEACHER EDUCATION: A RHETORICAL ANALYSIS OF *PREPARING TEACHERS*

INTRODUCTION

When in 2013 the self-proclaimed National Council on Teacher Quality (NCTQ) released the first of its annual *Teacher Prep Reviews*, a 105-page report on the quality of teacher education in the US, and only four institutions made the "Dean's List," a shutter went through the teacher education community. The vast majority of the programs that participated in the review (and many did not) were judged marginal at best. Feeling rather smug, the Council warned potential consumers of teacher education, "It is not just conceivable, but likely, that many aspiring teachers and school districts will not be able to locate a highly-rated program anywhere near them" (2013, p. 57). Funded by the US Department of Education and an abundance of tax-exempt foundations committed to educational entrepreneurialism, including the Walton Family Foundation and the Edythe and Eli Broad Foundation, the Council has grown in influence since its founding even as criticism has sharpened about the methods used to rank teacher education programs, including the data used (and missing) and the lack of strong relationships between program ratings and actual teacher performance (see Educational Policy Initiative at Carolina, 2015). The Council engages in politically inspired advocacy research.

In addition, during the summer of 2013, the merger of National Council for the Accreditation of Teacher Education (NCATE) and Teacher Education Accreditation Council (TEAC) quickened pace. That spring, the new Council for the Accreditation of Educator Preparation (CAEP) unveiled its recommendations, revealing what has become a very complex and very costly system of program review. CAEP's initial message meant to justify the merger was proclaimed crisis, a demand for "urgent changes in educator preparation" (Council for the Accreditation of Educator Preparation Commission on Standards and

Performance Report, 2013, p. 5). CAEP offered a vision of an "ideal system" of teacher education, suggesting that the Council's aim was to produce a single, national, model of teacher education with rather few variations. Diversity of programs and practices was viewed as a serious weakness, not a strength. Throughout the report, this message was forcefully articulated from urging the establishment of "specific and common cut-score[s] across states" (p. 18) on a set of common tests to developing, with federal funding, a single "national information [data] base" (p. 33) to locate problems in programs.

Both CAEP and NCTQ drew support for their assertions from *Preparing Teachers: Building Evidence for Sound Policy*, an important publication of the National Research Council (NRC), Committee on the Study of Teacher Preparation Programs in the United States (NRC, 2010). Extending conclusions drawn from other Council publications, particularly the highly influential volume, *Scientific Research in Education* (NRC, 2002), *Preparing Teachers* set the outlines of a vision for the future of teacher education that CAEP embraced, a vision that presumably would answer teacher education's critics while putting teacher education on a solid — scientific — footing. The authors who wrote *Preparing Teachers* were charged with answering questions related to (1) characteristics of teacher education candidates, (2) instruction and experiences offered in teacher preparation programs, (3) the scientific standing of that instruction and those experiences, and (4) identification of a model for data collection that would produce "valid and reliable information about the content knowledge, pedagogical competence, and effectiveness of graduates from the various kinds of teacher preparation programs" (NRC, 2010, p. 1). Tapping expert opinion and reviewing a large body of published literature, the Committee stuck close to its charge.

Given the prestige of the NRC, including the influence of its publications as they contribute to and shape public policy, teacher educators need to thoughtfully and critically engage with *Preparing Teachers* and its vision for the future of teaching and teacher education. To promote critical engagement, the beginnings of a rhetorical analysis of *Preparing Teachers* follow a deconstruction in anticipation of a much-needed reconstruction of the narrative of teacher education, of how teacher education is understood, and what sort of future is anticipated and desired for it. The importance of work of this kind was underscored by Feyerabend (1994) in noting that

> languages and the reaction patterns they involve are not merely instruments for describing events, but that they are also shapers of events, that their "grammar" contains a cosmology, a comprehensive view of the world, of society, of the situation of man. (p. 164)

In framing the task, insights are drawn from literary theorist and critic Kenneth Burke, including elements of his "dramatistic" conception of the role of language as symbolic action with suasive intent. Rhetoric, Burke (1950) argued, induces cooperation — that is its aim. From this view, textual analysis is a form of social analysis, a matter of identifying and explicating motives: "Since language, however manipulated by the individual user, is essentially a collective or social product, the powers of the social order will inevitably be manifested in it" (Burke, 1955, p. 288).

AGENTS AND ACTS

A dramatistic conception of language is embedded in a set of foundational assumptions beginning with the claim of a "pragmatic distinction between the 'actions' of 'persons' and the sheer 'motions' of 'things'" (Burke, 1989, p. 124): Having intentionality, persons act; things move. Action, Burke stated, is the "key term" (p. 125). For making sense of an act, Burke developed the "Pentad," a set of five concepts that focus analysis:

> For there to be an act, there must be an agent. Similarly, there must be a scene in which the agent acts. To act in a scene, the agent must employ some means, or agency. And it can be called an act in the full sense of the term only if it involves a purpose. (Burke, 1989, p. 135)

Relationships and changes in relationship among the concepts – act, agent, scene, agency, and purpose – illuminate motives. The following analysis focuses attention on scene: the backdrop against which the problems of teacher education are understood and the boundaries set for how they may be addressed.

"Terministic screens" frame action and represent authorial worldviews: "Even if any given terminology is a reflection of reality, by its very nature as a terminology it must be a selection of reality; and to this extent it must function also as a deflection of reality" (Burke, 1989, p. 115). Commenting further about deflection, Burke (1989) stated, "Here the kind of deflection I have in mind concerns simply the fact that any nomenclature necessarily directs the attention into some channels rather than others" (p. 115): We see what our language allows us to see. A related insight from Robert Coles (1989) is that the "critical root" of the word theory is "'I behold,' as in what we see when we go to the theater" (p. 20). We behold the world richly or poorly through our theories and our theories are language-embedded screens directing and limiting our attention. As Burke argued,

> [O]ur terms affect the nature of our observations, in the sense that the terms direct the attention to one field rather than to another. Also, many of the "observations" are but implications of the particular terminology in terms of which the observations are made. In brief, much that we take as observations about "reality" may be but the spinning out of possibilities implicit in our particular choice of terms. (Burke, 1989, p. 116)

Different terms, including different metaphors, or "perspectives" (Burke, 1989, p. 247), produce different realities (Burke, 1955, p. 289) and also supporting logics. The challenge is to reveal the realities opened and closed by the language of terministic screens, a challenge I take up here.

For this purpose, Burke developed "cluster" analysis. Key symbols or terms foundational to the structure of an argument are identified within a work, and around these terms, others are clustered, often revealing what for the author are implicit equations that function as preunderstandings:

> Now, the work of every writer contains a set of implicit equations. He uses "associational clusters." And you may, by examining [an author's] work, find "what goes with what" in these clusters—what kinds of acts and images and personalities and situations go with his notions of heroism, villainy, consolation [and so on]. (Burke, 1957, p. 18)

Close reading of a text reveals terms thought most significant to the writer. The most powerful words function as god or devil terms, words "from which a whole universe of terms is derived" (Burke, 1989, p. 135), representing the good and the evil within a given lens. Term selection is guided by textual placement, prominence, frequency, and intensity. As terms are linked, clusters are charted indicating one form of relationship or another. Relationship includes proximity, cause and effect, and other patterns of connection or association. Patterns are revealed by use of conjunctions (*and; but*) and, as noted, may be expressed as equations (one term equaling another), or as opposition. Opposing terms involve agon analysis: identifying paired but contrasting terms whose meaning is linked as antitheses and in negation (*light/dark; hot/cold*).

As action, language has purpose, and this purpose is, fundamentally, to get others to see reality as the author sees it and to get readers to do what is wanted; screens define reasonable action. Accordingly, a final step in text analysis for Burke involves teasing out authorial intent. What does an author want to be done? What is the author's motive?

On terms, Burke (1989) argued, "Basically, there are two kinds of terms: terms that put things together, and terms that take things apart" (p. 120). The first emphasizes continuity; the second discontinuity; or difference. This distinction is often seen in "*differences of degree and those based on differences of kind*" (p. 120). Continuity and difference support a tendency to either/or thinking: taking sides and distinguishing enemies from like-minded friends. Authors set up and then choose sides and invite others to identify with them and accept their choices. Burke, however, sought more complex relationship: "[W]here two opposed principles are being considered, each of which has the 'defects of its qualities,' what we want is something that avoids the typical vices of either and combines the virtues of both" (Burke, 1955, p. 293). This insight is important to the analysis that follows.

Concerning terministic screens, Burke (1989) argued for a kind of "terministic compulsion" present in screens, a push to "carry out the implications of one's terminology" (pp. 73–74). Representing an insistent logic, screens are stretched and pushed beyond their limits until, by becoming unreasonable, they reveal an inevitable one-sidedness and excess: Something is gained, something is lost. As Burke stated, being always partial, screens produce "excesses" (p. 122) and "embarrassments" (p. 120). The task, he suggested, is to "*try, at least within the limited orbit of theory, or contemplation,* to perfect techniques for doubting much that is now accepted as lying beyond the shadow of a doubt" (Burke, 1955, p. 272). Hence, locating excesses and embarrassments has value for criticism. Finally, a Burkean analysis of terministic screens involves uncovering the "magic of the social order [as it] infuses men's judgments of the beautiful [and the good, true and right]." This requires that "we watch everywhere for the manifestations of the 'hierarchical' motive [of] degree" (Burke, 1955, p. 295). Degree produces distinction and, in Burke's (1989) dramatistic formula, conflict and "victimage" follow (p. 125).

TEACHER EDUCATION: THE SCENE

Peopled by a large and diverse community of practitioners and scholars, teacher education is under attack on many fronts, not just from the NCTQ and the US Department of Education. Over the past century, and more, virtually every social problem facing America has been defined — reduced — to an educational problem (Kantor & Lowe, 2013). Trying to make a case for the value of their work, educators have often responded by optimistically over-promising, assuring disappointment would follow.

Written in response to a growing sense of crisis, *Preparing Teachers* nicely captures the rise and dominance of neoliberal solutions to educational problems emphasizing "the economy, individualism, and free markets" in policy debates (Cochran-Smith et al., 2013, p. 11; see Chapter 1). Presumably, cutting through the thick walls of partisan politics to reveal better, more "scientific," knowledge, the Committee held, would lead to better policy and better programs of teacher education: "Federal and state policy makers need reliable, outcomes-based information to make sound decisions" (NRC, 2010, p. 7). So the Committee was given the charge to review "the scientific evidence that pertains to teacher preparation and to consider the data collection that will best support improvements to this critical element of the public education system" (p. 10).

As with most education reform efforts of the past, this one grew out of and stood in the shadow of business, most recently the attempt to more effectively manage and respond to the challenges of "high causal density and holistic integration" (Manzi, 2012, p. 59) exacerbated by globalism. The aspiration for education is formation of data systems somewhat like those now in place within many large corporations such as Capital One (Manzi, 2012, Chapter 1), but much larger, that locate consumer preferences and seek to maximize efficiencies. "[Capital One] tests everything: product offers, the color of the envelopes the product offers are mailed in, procedural changes, employee selection, and so on. Testing is integrated with normal business operations in an automated or semi-automated way" (p. 145). In education, rather than thinking about individual business data systems, a level of organization roughly analogous to school district or state systems that are currently in place, many reformers long for a single integrated federally funded data network, a "comprehensive data collection system" (NCR, 2010, p. 182). Such a system would support large studies in education and the social sciences by enabling random trials and natural experiments while enabling a quick read to locate trouble spots. This is an education version of "big social science."

Despite seeming to be overly sanguine about the power and promise of social science research to provide clear and valid directives for practice, authors of *Preparing Teachers* were well aware of the difficulties of achieving "scientific evidence" in education: they identified problems related to defining constructs and developing reliable empirical measures, "accounting for the heterogeneous behavioral responses of individuals," as well as difficulties associated with conducting random experimental trials (p. 23). There are, as the Committee noted, many sources of variation among people, but also variations across states in policies and accreditation practices. Causal connections are illusive and generalizations weak. The most serious difficulty, however, was thought to be system size: "Given the size of the teaching force, it is likely that there is no one best pathway to high-quality preparation for teachers" (p. 61). Nevertheless, the Committee argued for a unified data system on which to base "recommendations for the composition of teacher education programs and pathways" (p. 61).

With or without a unified system, the problems of variation and complexity will remain to say nothing of politics and the conflicting purposes commonly held for schooling and teacher education. The authors may have seriously underestimated the difficulties of the task, a point evident, for example, in Smith and Colby's (2010) analysis of research related to the rather "clean" and presumably simple comparative studies of National Board Certified teachers with their unsuccessful colleagues (p. 145) and in Radford's (2008) analysis of the nature of research in education:

> Within complex systems, there are too many variables to account fully for any event. Even if we could take account of all internal operational variables or elements within a system, complex systems have "fuzzy" or open boundaries, and there may well be other influential factors at those boundaries that could not have been foreseen [...]. [Also], the information that is contained in a system is as much invested in the relationships among variables as in the variables themselves. The relationships among variables are non-linear: in other words, the impact of any one set of variables upon any other is disproportionate and variable, depending on local and temporary conditions. Relationships among variables are weighted in such a way as interactions among them may excite or inhibit the impact of the interactions. [Additionally], interactions are rarely reducible to an observable set of variables [...] Finally [...] interactions among variables give rise to emergent properties that could not have been identified from analysis prior to the interaction. (p. 144)

Even if strong links can be formed among variables of interest, knowing how to work with them and making a case for what ought to be done often inspire intense disagreement even among well-informed and interested parties. Better knowledge does not resolve differences in values, opinions, or beliefs – differences in what information means and of what ought to be done with it and why. Recognizing such limitations surely should inspire patience and humility, encouraging the development of more reasonable and perhaps modest expectations, but it has not.

In contrast, Manzi (2012), in reviewing recent developments in business flowing from globalism, noted the importance of lowering expectations for businesses to prosper and of actually reducing scale to better attend to local contexts and respond to individual clients' preferences:

> Though social scientists sometimes look upon the era of largescale social experimentation from the late 1960s to the early 1980s as a golden age, this is pure nostalgia. What really happened was that unrealistic expectations about our ability to develop unconditional evaluations of programs were dashed. It has become clear that the problem is more complex. We need to find an array of causal rules for the effect of programs that are localized in many ways—for particular implementations in particular social contexts, for particular kinds of recipients, at particular times, and so forth. (p. 170)

Even when reduced to the aim of raising standardized test scores, education is more complex by magnitudes than business, with its goal of increasing sales and profits and its comparatively clear and simple patterns of human relationship and interaction, lines of authority, standards of quality, and systems of reward. Parents are not merely consumers or stockholders but citizens and neighbors. And children, drawing on Burke's thinking, are not merely material to be molded or shaped or creatures to be trained to perform like "things." They too are citizens and neighbors, and they are future parents: people who have aspirations and dreams for the future. Like their parents, children are actors with purpose, will, and desire, and are also citizens with rights, social obligations, and responsibilities that must be learned to be adequately understood and appropriately expressed. This is the scene.

CLUSTER ANALYSIS

Following Burke's model for rhetorical analysis, this section begins by identifying term clusters with associated equations and term pairs drawn from *Preparing Teachers*. Each cluster will be described and then unpacked for potential implications. Words that rise to the status of god or devil terms will be noted. Motives will be explored in the section that follows.

Science, Research, and Researcher

Given the scene, including the origins of *Preparing Teachers* and the Committee's charge, perhaps it should be expected that the first cluster coalesced around the key term *science* and the related term *researcher*. *Science*, a god term, is tightly linked to the second key term, *research*. The related equation reads as follows:

> Science = research = quantitative research methods (e.g., "randomized trials" and "quasi-experimental designs") = "systematic information" = replicable and generalizable results = "strong empirical evidence" (p. 30) = "responsible scholarship" (p. 10) = more "effective pathways" to quality teaching and teacher education.

The logic becomes clear when all but the first and last terms are removed: science = more effective pathways. Here I am reminded of William James' (1899/1922) warning about what educators can reasonably expect from social science research:

> I say [...] that you make a great, a very great mistake, if you think that psychology, being the science of the mind's laws, is something from which you can deduce definite programs and schemes and methods of instruction for immediate schoolroom use. Psychology is a science, and teaching is an art: and sciences never generate arts directly out of themselves. An intermediary inventive mind must make the application by its originality. (pp. 7–8)

The space separating science from "more effective pathways" is wide, bridged only when occupied by genuinely inventive minds that know how to produce and then sustain a transformative tension between generalizations and teaching within specific classrooms and institutions.

A researcher is one who accepts the equation, finds place within it, and exercises the ambition to further its realization. An honorific term, *researcher* invites readers' positive identification, thereby emphasizing continuity and supporting the presumption of special status. Simultaneously, the term excludes others, including teachers but also many handmaidens, many of those "intermediary inventive" minds as James discussed, whose work or professional commitments reflect a different subject position and professional identity – field supervisor, mentor, methods course instructor, and case or narrative "inquirer." The division is hierarchical, reflected in differences in status, privilege, and job security (see Nuttall, Brennan, Zipin, Tuinamuana, & Cameron, 2013). Teacher educators – including field supervisors, mentors, methods course instructors, and qualitative researchers of many sorts – are occupied with tasks associated with supporting pathway trials and assuring treatment fidelity, "faithful implementation" (p. 29), a matter of local knowledge associated with the consuming task of relationship maintenance (Ellis et al., 2013, p. 270). Departmental divisions emerge between teacher educators who engage in field-intensive work and other faculties who successfully distance themselves from mere practitioners by locating themselves as knowledge producers. Conception (of ends) is separated from execution (of means) (Braverman, 1974), yet ends are ever and always wholly dependent on those charged with execution (Dewey, 1916).

Order/Disorder

The science cluster equation is bound to an opposing pair of terms: *order*, found inherently "beautiful," and *disorder*, a devil term. Ironically, as with all educational research, order can take many forms and is always but seeming: A shift in terministic screens produces a different order and supporting logic. Those who do not identify with the science term cluster find themselves linked to disorder. By implication, their studies are trivialized as disconnected or as merely a matter of local knowledge (see Chapter 4). The call to order evident in *Preparing Teachers*, according to the Committee, is in response to "patchy" (p. 10) data, data that are weak, not strong (p. 21), "extremely diverse" (p. 43), "surprisingly" (p. 70), or "relatively thin" (p. 109), thus mostly or merely local, and concerned with improving practices characteristic of specific programs.

When viewed through a dramatistic lens, disorder is an implication, an observation outcome, of order. The choice offered is order or chaos, a false dichotomy. Dismissed is the possibility argued by complexity theorists that there are other origins, forms, and levels of order than those born of imposition and hierarchy, including interrelatedness and shared local practices. Morrison (2008), for example, argued that "order is not imposed, it emerges" (p. 18) over time. Haggis (2008) extended the point:

> The concept of open, dynamic systems, embedded within and partly constituting each other, whilst at the same time maintaining their own coherence, allows for different ways of thinking about context, and provides a rationale for the investigation of *individuals, difference* and *specificity*. (p. 165, italics in original)

Accordingly, there is a geography and geometry of order/disorder. Ordered systems are located within ordered systems with relations loosely or tightly bound in varying degrees. The intent of the report is to rationalize relations by encouraging a vigorous tightening and tidying of bonds and ranking of the connections to create greater system-wide efficiencies. The more likely result, however, is homogenization (sameness), with a narrowing of the range of experimentation and, probably, greater inefficiency (see Newfield, 2003).

From a dramatistic perspective, order is embedded in the first term of multiple oppositions: for teacher education programs, *accountable* versus *unaccountable* the first term implying the meeting of an order-imposing external set of standards in which internal coherence either does not count or is thought a problem to be overcome, and the second term suggesting lack of professionalism, irresponsibility. "Accountability systems now in use are haphazard" (NRC, 2010, p. 169), disordered. Needed is an "accountability system that is based primarily on the evaluation of program graduates' ability to use instructional practices that facilitate K-12 student learning in core subjects" p. 171), a point with which no teacher educator would disagree. But what does this mean? Accountable to whom and for what? One wonders. The "to whom" is clearly indicated by the authors of *Preparing Teachers*: "responsible" scholars (p. 10).

Training/Education

Training versus *education*, a topic introduced in Chapter 1, is a second opposition: The values of training — "program graduates' ability" — are linked to order and implicitly elevated over those of education. The distinguishing characteristic of training — a service or product — is a high degree of predictability, a promise that certain actions will lead to targeted responses or prespecified outcomes, and that proof of achievement is direct, involving a specific demonstration. In contrast, education — a process — is messy, and highly context sensitive, with outcomes uncertain and proof of accomplishment always indirect and usually long delayed. On this point, consider the difficulty of creating an operational definition of *wisdom*, a widely valued education aim: a set of measures and an accompanying test as proof of being wise (see Hall, 2010). An echo of neoliberalism sounds: Services and products can be packaged and sold, processes cannot.

Training versus education is portrayed as a difference in degree, when primarily, it is a difference in kind, as illustrated by the analogy of beginning teacher to physician offered in *Preparing Teachers*:

> Ensuring that novices will be able to apply the knowledge they have gained in a classroom to real situations is a key challenge in any field. Whether for a doctor learning how to insert a needle or make an incision or for a teacher learning what to say to a disruptive student or how to encourage student participation in class discussions, professional preparation must provide opportunities to practice new skills and apply new knowledge. (NRC, 2010, p. 50)

Placing learning how to insert a needle into or make a cut in a single, passive, body appears remarkably simple alongside the skills needed to encourage the simultaneous and ongoing engagement in a lesson of 30 students, some of whom are unwilling participants, over an extended period of time. This linkage discounts the dramatic differences in predictability of outcomes of these actions. Both problems seem intended to represent a training challenge, but the example from teaching is infinitely more complex than the application of training, with the results not only highly unpredictable but also much more a matter of interpretation (judgments) based on knowledge of a unique context, particular persons, situational possibilities, of self, shared history (perhaps of goodwill), and maybe luck.

Indeed, to encourage beginning teachers to practice single teaching skills presents a major conceptual and practical problem. Teaching skills are clustered; they do not march in single file rows. Despite recent pleas to strengthen and focus teacher education on skills training (Ball & Forzani, 2009), as the Commonwealth Teacher-Training Study (Charters & Waples, 1929) demonstrated, determining what constitutes a discrete teaching skill is far from a simple matter, as much a challenge to philosophy and theory as it is of job or task analysis. Burke's warnings about the shaping powers of opposing principles and the dangers of taking sides that lead to the problems of "terministic excess" stand as reminders that training is not a substitute for education, but teacher education without attention to training brings its own serious defects.

Aligned/Unaligned

Aligned versus *unaligned* represents yet another set of opposing terms associated with the order versus disorder pairing. *Alignment*, which involves prescription of practice and coordination of levels of action, is driven by presumption of a shared understanding of priorities and purposes. In *Preparing Teachers*, purpose is assumed and expressed indirectly, capturing a commonly held assumption. Schooling is mostly about jobs—"U.S. students' performance in science on international comparative studies has remained stagnant and is below that of many of the nation's economic competitors" (NRC, 2010, p. 127). Much of the urgency in the scene arises from economic concerns about the future and belief in a strong connection between test score rankings and national economic prosperity, an echo of *A Nation at Risk* (1983).

Sharply focused on test scores, the curricula of schooling and teacher education are both to be driven by specific outcomes. Put positively, the curriculum in both arenas is to be sharply focused; put negatively, it is to be dramatically narrowed, a trend evident following passage of No Child Left Behind (NCLB). Within a corporate culture, evaluation drives curriculum and instruction, not the reverse; as with money, common metrics enable direct but distorted comparisons of the worth of the individual performances of students, teachers, and teacher educators for the purpose of ranking, rewarding, and punishing. Focusing on a common quantitative standard for measuring performance, assessing academic output, and establishing departmental standing of the sort now used in England (the Research Excellence Framework (REF), see Ellis et al., 2013), the personal, social, cultural, and historical embeddedness of quality performance and differences in purpose are denied. What is left is the totalism of "sameness" (Levinas, 1969).

Within a tightly aligned system, information related to legislatively mandated outcome sets is to be gathered and stored in a national data network. Generated but also sifted and shaped at each level by use of common forms, definitions, metrics, scoring rubrics, and content categories – a strong taxonomy and institutional screen – data will be further checked, pasteurized, and then passed along: school to district, district to state, and state to the federal database. In principle, problems could be sent upward for clarification and illumination, but they too would need to take recognizable forms. The flow of problems would seem inevitably to be most robust downhill, coming as alerts, perhaps warnings born of anomaly, of the sort implied by CAEP in describing an ideal world for teacher education and by the authors of *Preparing Teachers* when calling for a "short-term national indicator system to monitor the status of teacher education" (NRC, 2010, p. 186). Flowing upward and downward, problems and information morph so that what would be offered as a problem or a solution may or may not either speak to each other or be sensitive to local concerns. Once set, systems define what counts as a legitimate problem and reasonable solution.

Issues of data ownership become troubling. Are data owned by the network, the individual data-generating institutions, or a corporate and university consortium committed to developing products for sale – such as a tool for assessing beginning teachers? From the perspective of teachers and teacher educators, with manifestation of the "hierarchical" motive come distinction and the accompanying conflict that produces "victimage" (Burke, 1989, p. 125): losers and winners, those marginalized and those with power and privilege within the academy and academy-corporation partnerships. Whatever its shortcomings, once formed, a "national indicator system" of monitoring is difficult to anticipate being "short term." The investment will be too great, and for some, the rewards for system maintenance will be too high.

Large Scale/Small Scale

Throughout *Preparing Teachers*, scale is a central term, and yet, another oppositional pairing emerges: *large scale* versus *small scale*. Large is much better than small. *Large*, like researcher, is an honorific term, one supported by a narrow definition of the term *empirical,* whereas *small* is linked with *non-empirical,* with studies portrayed as being of little consequence because local (hence small). Given the Committee's charge and purpose, the lack of strong empirical generalizations is a source of genuine disappointment and frustration: "Unfortunately, we found that the existing studies have generally been insensitive to the details of teacher preparation that are most likely to result in differences in quality" (NRC, 2010, p. 178).

In response, among the Committee's appeals is one for a "longitudinal, nationally representative study of teachers' career pathways beginning with their undergraduate education" (p. 186). Committee disappointment cuts across the board to include studies of classroom management, methods for teaching diverse students, and examination of educational foundations. *Preparing Teachers* laments, "Most of the available studies are small in scale and cannot provide answers to questions about how teachers might best be prepared" (p. 49). Of studies of field and clinical experiences, the authors similarly conclude that "little systematic information is available about how much time aspiring teachers spend in field experiences or how those experiences are structured, or about differences across pathways in what is available or required" (p. 51).

The Committee was probably correct that the studies reviewed and dismissed could not provide answers to the questions posed by its charge. Presumably, policy-makers are interested in the "big picture" of teacher evaluation and in the performance of all 3.2 million American teachers and small studies do not have much to say about this. In her discussion of seeing things "small" and things "big," Greene (1995) sets the issue on its head, reversing priorities:

> To see things or people small, one chooses to see from a detached point of view, to watch behaviors from the perspective of a system, to be concerned with trends and tendencies rather than the intentionality and concreteness of everyday life. To see things or people big, one must resist viewing other human beings as mere objects or chess pieces and view them in their integrity and particularity instead. One must see from the point of view of the participant in the midst of what is happening if one is to be privy to the plans people make, the initiative they take, the uncertainties they face. (p. 10)

Greene's aim is to see people as "big," not "small," and from her view, it does not follow that small-scale studies "cannot provide answers to questions about how teachers might best be prepared" as asserted by the Committee. To the contrary, among the virtues of well-conceived small-scale studies, ones that make persons "big" and populations "small," is that they can and often do provide answers to how teacher education students are faring within specific contexts. Thus, they have the potential of opening for consideration a wide range of variables of the sort large-scale studies inevitably miss or neglect.

Contrary to the Committee's conclusion, a counterclaim seems nearer the truth: the large-scale, randomized, studies longed for cannot provide answers to how teachers might best be prepared, nor is it likely they can achieve the "sensitivity" promised for the "details of teacher preparation most likely to result in differences in quality." What generalizations can do, even the weak ones of the sort most likely to emerge from large-scale studies that see "small", is provide helpful orientation, a place from which those intermediary inventive minds charged with designing and improving teacher education think about and work on their problems that are mostly managed and seldom solved (see Chapter 4). From this perspective, perhaps the greatest value of large-scale studies will be found in the local studies they may encourage.

MOTIVES: SCIENTISM AND A DIFFERENT NARRATIVE

As noted previously, as a form of social criticism, Burke's model for rhetorical analysis seeks to reveal the reflections and deflections of reality formed by terministic screens, including how screens shape actors and influence their actions.

Reviewing the results of the cluster analysis in relation to the scene described above, in particular, the rhetorical excesses and embarrassments found in *Preparing Teachers*, the values of a strong scientism are readily apparent. As Baez and Boyles (2009) noted, the federal government is intent on creating a "science *for* education" (p. 5) that "privileges scientism over scientific inquiry, establishing experimental methods as providing the best evidence of educational effectiveness" (p. 7), with a strong preference for large-scale random trials.

These values and associated motives, which run throughout the term clusters identified in this analysis, are tightly associated with the quantification of human experience and performance for purposes of categorizing and then rating and ranking them (see Hacking, 1990):

- Extended hierarchies conferring higher status to those furthest removed from local practices and concerns.
- Celebration of externally imposed order.
- Trivialization of teaching evident in the separation of conception from execution of labor.
- Tightening and narrowing of job specifications and a need for high levels of conformity to achieve greater outcome predictability and fidelity of prescribed "best practices".
- Devaluation of processes and relationships in favor of products and things (including test scores).
- Fear of human agency and of the goodness of human intentions in favor of faith in markets and systems and in those few experts who interact directly with those systems to produce what are thought to be the most reasonable decisions about what teachers and teacher educators ought to do and therefore "be."

Lost is a vision of a wider public good of the sort that has historically driven college and university-sponsored teacher education and inspired teachers to teach. Performativity raises its ugly head (Ball, 2003), offering a sort of invitation to system gaming that has become part of preparing for accreditation visits. Given such priorities, agency is distorted, narrowed, and increasingly thought to be only self-serving. A narrow individualism embedded in competitive relations replaces collegial relations within and across academic departments. Cross-institutional collegiality and relationship maintenance that consume so much of the work of teacher educators (Ellis et al., 2013) are devalued and passed downward to part-time and comparatively low-salary faculty (Bullough et al., 1997). Program quality likely also suffers as more and more teacher educators find they are unable to meet the research standard offered in *Preparing Teachers*, give up active inquiry, and come to no longer think of themselves as engaged in scholarship at all. And seeing dollar signs a very few privileged institutions of higher education will further strengthen their ties with commercial product vendors (Ball, 2018). Thus, they will gain ever greater control over teacher education practices, including student admissions and quality assessment while furthering an agenda of standardization in the name of quality (see Cochran-Smith et al., 2013).

There is likely real value in creating a national data network of some sort although that case needs to be made, but there is also value in maintaining strong institutional commitments to quality local studies in support of better programs. These are related but quite different actions representing different forms of life and of personal understanding and professional commitment. As Burke argued, taking sides when considering opposing principles encourages hierarchy and victimage when the real challenge and greatest hope come from seeking value and locating weakness in both positions in the hope of combining "the virtues of both" (Burke, 1955, p. 293). *Preparing Teachers* calls for taking sides, as demonstrated. But, the question for universities, as Rhoades (2006) set the problem, ought not involve taking sides: An institution seeking to helpfully frame and effectively address a wide range of fundamental and pressing human ecological problems, educational problems among them, requires a culture characterized by openness, breadth of understanding, and generosity of spirit. Yet, currently, only neoliberal visions seem to hold the floor, and only this side and its worldview are thought reasonable (Weiner, 2007), as argued in Chapter 1. At the policy level, there is no debate: Scientism and its supporting terministic screen lie, in Burke's terms, "beyond the shadow of a doubt" and dominate discourse, constrain action, and narrow vision.

Dialogue is required to dig up "doxa" (Bauman, 2011a, 2011b, p. 171). But, dialogue assumes openness and recognition of viable, although not necessarily compelling, counterpositions − counternarratives (Bullough, 2008a, 2008b). As Burke argued, every position has its own excesses and embarrassments that need to be located, articulated, and confronted, and this is as true of the studies valued in *Preparing Teachers* as it is for local studies. For teacher educators, viability depends on making a compelling case that ours is legitimate academic work of social importance and of institutional and personal significance. Currently, such a case is not easily made, but it may be providing greater willingness to embrace a future ever more closely tied to teachers' lives, their well-being, and their teaching. As suggested, *Preparing Teachers* reveals a consistent underappreciation of how all educational programs, including those that grow out of the most robust of generalizations, are fundamentally and wholly dependent for their livelihoods on the inventive minds described by James: those who work to realize the educational potential of any and all promising ideas proffered by research.

But the issue goes beyond implementation or treatment fidelity. Viability rests on the validity of the data out of which arguments and programs are built, and the quality of these data, like the programs they support, ultimately rests on the involvement, goodwill, and intelligence of these inventive minds: People, among whom are teacher educators, must find and then nurture a welcoming place. Educational and social values are primarily locally determined matters that involve creation and exploitation of at-hand opportunities, "niches," specific points of advantage, and "strategic synergies in the internal and external [institutional] environments" (Rhoades, 2006, p. 401). To take advantage and extend these opportunities, the case for action research and other forms of program study needs to be made in terms of impact on learning, understood very broadly, and in terms of knowledge application *and* production, demonstrating its intellectual rigor and theoretical sophistication (Spencer, 2013, p. 303), as well as its educational value, specially to teachers and children. As virtually every learner knows, the "most effective evaluation for learning is self-evaluation" (Johnston, 1989, p. 523).

A more complex understanding of institutional and cultural change than is allowed by simple competitive business models emphasizing managed orderliness within competitive externally imposed frameworks needs articulation within teacher education and the wider university — models that support the social purposes of education within a democracy. Teacher educators have an important role here. In contrast to competitive models of change that emphasize rewards and punishments, as does the REF in place in England that appears to be undermining the quality of many "new" universities (Spencer, 2013, p. 302), within healthy academic cultures, change is understood as involving renewal (Goodlad, 1994), a matter of learning and growing together within community and of sharing a quest for understanding and growth. With this view, involvement in shared inquiry is understood to be the most powerful form of professional development, a means for strengthening trust and building institutional loyalty through enriching relationships.

Successful change generally involves tinkering — seeking after better, not best practices (see Chapter 4), particularly when those practices are imposed, and persisting in the quest. As the authors of *Preparing Teachers* noted, "The development of expertise is gradual" (NRC, 2010, p. 67). Community-embedded and curiosity-driven inquiry, especially conducted in partnership between universities and schools, produces better programs that are sustainable because they support identity, facilitate learning and competence, and deepen relationships — points supported by self-determination theory (Ryan & Deci, 2000). Finally, accountability should be understood not as a matter of satisfying externally imposed mandates but of forging and articulating institutionally and situationally authentic visions of possibility, and then realizing and defending them with generous data and insisting that these visions be recognized by assessors. Just as parents are increasingly saying "no" to the endless testing of their children for what seem to be doubtful reasons, so do teachers and teacher educators need to challenge the excesses of accountability systems. Rather than quietly going about our business and complaining behind closed doors and feeling forced to respond to yet another mandate or critic, we need to push back and aggressively engage our critics. Moping will not do.

CHAPTER 4

AGAINST BEST PRACTICE: UNCERTAINTY, OUTLIERS, AND LOCAL STUDIES IN EDUCATIONAL RESEARCH

INTRODUCTION

Everywhere one turns, there is talk of "best practice" in education and teacher education, a concept taken as an unqualified good – and always and everywhere an appropriate aim. It is also a source of much mischief, as will be noted. This chapter explores aspects of this ambition, situating it in an admittedly sweeping history and in relationship to a few select insights drawn from the writings of John Dewey, among others. Along the way, I wish to question not just the possibility but also the desirability of the aspiration, while arguing for a more modest ambition – "better practice." Better practice is born of research especially attentive to outliers and to local contexts understood not merely as being research venues but as representing a moral stance. This stance is characterized by humility in facing the complexity of education, a complexity that is not yet fully or adequately appreciated (Mason, 2008), and of profound respect for those whose work researchers seek to understand.

THE ROOTS OF AN AMBITION: THE ROYAL SOCIETY AND POLITICAL ARITHMETIC

To set the context for discussion of best practice, a good place to begin is 1667, when Thomas Sprat published a rather remarkable book, *The History of the Royal Society*. Although in some respects beginning here is arbitrary, the founding of the Royal Society set a clear ambition that played out across the centuries, culminating in a culture-wide belief in, and seductive pursuit of, what we now call in the West "best practice": single, best responses or solutions to complex human problems. The full title of Sprat's book is *The History of the Royal-Society of London, for the Improving of Natural Knowledge*. Described by Wood (1980) as an apology for the work of the Society, then only a few years old, the history gives a glimpse into the values of at least some prominent Society members and into the issues that concerned them as they tried to make the case for the worth of the then emerging forms of inquiry loosely comprising what we would now call science. The history assures potential Society sponsors, most notably the Crown, that its work will be a force for maintaining social stability and order, will strengthen the church by shedding light on God's creations, but will do nothing to challenge the place of the inherited knowledge of the ancients, while creating economically useful knowledge and new technologies, which will increase national wealth. The promise was that Society members would speak the truth both as good and humble Christians and as rational natural scientists.

Seeking to avoid the twin dangers of skepticism and enthusiasm, such knowledge would result from the firm facts of experimentation, presented dispassionately and simply in short declarative sentences devoid of all dogmatism or any hint of speculation. As Sprat wrote:

> There is one thing about which the Society has been most solicitous; and that is, the manner of their Discourse: which, unless they have been very watchful to keep in due temper, the whole spirit and vigour of their Design, had been soon eaten out, by the luxury and redundance of Speech. The ill effects of this superfluity of talking, have already overwhelmed most other Arts and Professions; insomuch, that when I consider the means of happy living, and the causes of their corruption, I can hardly forbear concluding, that eloquence ought to be banished out of all civil societies, as a thing fatal to Peace and good Manners. (Sprat, 1667, 1958, p. 111)

Sprat further warned against the dangers of the passions in discourse, arguing that "they are in open defiance against Reason they give the mind a motion too changeable, and bewitching, to consist with right practice" (p. 112). As is apparent, concern for the dangers of the passions in the social and political life of England was lively following the English Interregnum and the restoration of the monarchy after the death of Oliver Cromwell in 1658.

Sprat argued for forbearance when making truth claims. It was, he thought, the Society's responsibility to make judgments of fact, and once set, the facts would speak for themselves. Setting aside partisan debate, the "redundance of speech," facts were to be verified systematically through "repetition of the whole course of the Experiment [...] never giving over till the whole Company has been fully satisfied of the certainty and constancy; or, on the other side, of the absolute impossibility of the effect" (Sprat, 1667, 1958, p. 99). Consensus was the aim. Note in the above, three phrases: a "mind too changeable" (to be avoided), "right practice" (to be embraced as means for assuring), and "certainty and constancy." Later, I will have a few words to say about "repetition of the Experiment."

As Sprat was writing the history, other developments of interest were unfolding, especially on the continent, that would have a direct bearing on the Royal Society's early concerns. The 1660s, as Porter (1986) has shown, witnessed the emergence of what William Petty came to call "political arithmetic." The purpose of political arithmetic "when not confined to the calculation of insurance or annuity rates, was the promotion of sound, well-informed state policy" (p. 18). Political arithmetic, as Petty wrote, was to bring "puzzling and perplext Matters to Terms and Number, Weight and Measure" so that official policy might be grounded in an understanding of the land and its inhabitants (p. 19). William the Conqueror's *Doomsday Book* of 1086 anticipated this aim, and ever since and through various means, governments have actively sought to know as much as possible about those they govern for various administrative, social engineering, and social and political purposes.

The ambitions of modern statistics have been rooted in political arithmetic. The aim was to gain a clear picture of a nation's lands and its peoples for the purpose of exercising ever more effective control over both. As Porter wrote, the "great merit of statistics was that it eliminated perturbations by ignoring individuals and letting their unpredictable activities average out" (Porter, 1986, p. 152), thus facilitating consistent social planning and policy. A foundational assumption of political arithmetic was the existence of what Porter described as a "common personhood": "statistics tended to equalize subjects. It makes no sense to count people if their common personhood is not seen as somehow more significant than their differences" (p. 25). Hence, the dominating interest of statistics was in averages, understood as offering a human or national type, which now includes even something known as a "proficient fourth-grader" or an "on grade level first-grader." Concern for human variability and diversity came late, very late indeed. Averages (and the human types that presumably portrayed them) came to be linked tightly to conceptions of normalcy, a linkage that has proven both enduring and deeply troubling, as Hacking (1990) argued:

> Words have profound memories that oil our shrill and squeaky rhetoric. The normal stands indifferently for what is typical, the unenthusiastic objective average, but it also stands for what has been, good health, and for what shall be, our chosen destiny. That is why the benign and sterile-sounding word "normal" has become one of the most powerful [of] ideological tools [...] (p. 169)

Stigler (1999) echoed Hacking's concern, concluding that "normal" is a "rare one word oxymoron" (p. 403).

Holding a "cautious optimism for improvement," yet desirous of buttressing social order, by the 1830s statisticians hoped that "the confusion of politics could be replaced by an orderly reign of facts" (Porter, 1986, p. 27). The ambition was utopian: the normalization of individuals for the good of the state and of Society. Underpinning both Sprat's dream for the Royal Society of establishing natural facts and the history of statistics, with its driving concern for social order, was a lively and often desperate quest for certainty.

JOHN DEWEY, UNCERTAINTY, AND A SCIENCE OF EDUCATION

At a much later period of great uncertainty, 1929, Sprat's ambitions were widely thought to be within reach, but not by every thoughtful commentator. In that year, John Dewey published *The Quest for Certainty: A Study of the Relation of Knowledge and Action* (1929a), his Gifford lectures. Speaking to his time (but echoing in ours), Dewey well understood what is felt when life is precarious and outcomes seem arbitrary: "The quest for certainty is a quest for a peace which is assured, an object which is unqualified by risk and the shadow of fear which action casts [...] Perfect certainty is what man wants. (Dewey, 1929a, pp. 8, 21).

For Dewey, certainty in a perplexing, contradictory, and dangerous world was the worst sort of illusion, ultimately requiring disengaging from the world and encouraging a passive acceptance of life's offerings. In contrast, he called for courage in the face of uncertainty, along with engagement, openness, responsibility, moral action and, perhaps ironically, for humility, a recognition that there are many things in life we cannot control, some things we should not even seek to control, and many questions that strongly and perhaps always will resist resolution.

In education, most of the important issues come in the form of dilemmas to be managed, not problems to be solved. On this point, Dewey stated, "intellectual progress usually occurs through sheer abandonment of questions altogether. We do not solve them: we get over them" (Dewey, 1910, p. 19). Ultimately, his call was to move away from relying on others to set life's aims and means: for example, the Royal Society deciding what would count as the facts and the statisticians determining what data would be legitimate for aspiring social engineers and policy-makers. He embraced a wide-ranging experimentalism, taking life as an adventure requiring of each person their full engagement and most honest and skilled thinking and practice. This sort of thinking results in a kind of functional "stability rather than certainty" (Baez & Boyles, 2009, p. 63), a flowing but precarious unity grounded in an acute situational sensitivity that facilitates and also requires consistent and moral action (see Gale, 2010).

The subtitle of Dewey's book is worth noting: "A study of the relation of knowledge and action." His concern was for the sort of knowledge that enables purposeful and effective action, even though in the important matters of life, certainly when confronting the problems of education, that knowledge is always partial, never really fully adequate. Also in 1929, Dewey's Kappa Delta Pi lectures, *The Sources of a Science of Education* (1929b), were published. Connections between his Gifford lectures and the Kappa Delta Pi lectures, which were directed specifically toward educators, are readily apparent. In an uncertain, and in some senses crazy world, what can educators do and where should they look for guidance as they seek to better nurture and educate the young? What, then, are the sources of a science of education?

In this small volume, Dewey had a lot to say about improving educational practice, offering several wise warnings directed to those who primarily taught and those who primarily conducted research on teaching that speak directly to the aspiration for best practices and sure outcomes. Throughout his argument, Dewey assumed the impossibility of certainty in human affairs, suggesting that education is most of all an art, "either a mechanical art or a fine art" that "progressively incorporates more and more of science into itself" (Dewey, 1929b, p. 13). His warnings began with a discussion of the dangers that follow the reduction in educational practice to rules, the deontological and pharisaic stuff of Sprat's right practice:

> When in education, the psychologist or observer and experimentalist in any field reduces his findings to a rule which is to be uniformly adopted, then, only, is there a result which is objectionable and destructive of the free play of education as an art. (p. 14)

Such reductions, he asserted, happened "not because of scientific method but because of departure from it" (p. 14). Contrary to the assumptions of Sprat and his intellectual descendants, Dewey asserted that "laws and facts do not yield rules of practice" (p. 30), but instead invite reflection on "conditions and relationships" which might otherwise be missed. On this view, uncritical fidelity to a practice or procedure (e.g., when teachers seek to precisely replicate a practice) ultimately distorts rather than confirms the value of research, as:

> It is very easy for [the results of research] to be regarded as a guarantee that goes with the sale of goods rather than as a light to the eyes and a lamp to the feet [...] prized for its prestige value rather than as an organ of personal illumination and liberation. (p. 15)

The results of research and theory, he believed, ought to produce a "wider field of observation" p. 20) rather than constrict vision. It is for this reason that Dewey argued, "Theory is in the end [...] the most practical of all things" (p. 17).

While Dewey's specific topic in these lectures was the "sources of a science" of education, his argument grew out of a very generous view of science, methodologically more ecumenical than liturgical, of research and of data. "All thinking is research, and all research is native, original, with him who carries it on" (Dewey, 1916, p. 174). Dewey further warned of the dangers of borrowing research methods from other fields wholesale, noting, remarkably, that "quantity is not even the fundamental idea of mathematics" (Dewey, 1929b, p. 27). Methods must follow problems and respond sensitively to intentions; aims and means are ineluctably linked.

> When means and ends are viewed as if they were separate, and to be dealt with by different persons who are concerned with independent provinces, there is imminent danger of two bad results. Ends [...] become empty, verbal; too remote and isolated to have more than an emotional content. Means are taken to signify means already at hand, means accepted because they are already in common use [and the task is to perfect] the existing mechanism of school operations. (Dewey, 1929b, p. 59)

What was (and is) overlooked, Dewey argued, was a "fundamental issue," of "How far do the existing ends, the actual consequences of current practices go, even when perfected? The important problem is devising new means in contradistinction to improved use of means already given" (p. 60). Representing frozen ideals, in a dynamic and ever-changing culture, all best practices must eventually give way, some to even better practices, others, perhaps unfortunately, to more politically popular or expedient practices.

Expanding on his argument, Dewey issued an oft-quoted warning against over-reliance on quantitative methods of research for seeking guidance.

> That which can be measured is the specific, and that which is specific is that which can be isolated [...] How far is education a matter of forming specific skills and acquiring special bodies of information which are capable of isolated treatment? It is no answer to say that a human being is always occupied in acquiring a special skill or a special body of facts [...] [The] educational issue is what other things in the way of desires, tastes, aversions, abilities and disabilities he is learning along with his specific acquisitions. (Dewey, 1929b, pp. 64–65)

Dewey's distinction suggests what is at stake when education (with outcomes that are always fundamentally, even radically, uncertain) is reduced to training (with outcomes known in advance) (see Chapter 3). But even when training is the aim, students learn both more and less than what is intended, and not all experience is "genuinely or equally educative" (Dewey, 1938, p. 13). Indeed, some experiences are patently miseducative. The question, of course, is: "Better practice towards what ends?"

PROBLEMS OF VERIFICATION AND "BEST PRACTICE"

What, then, of Sprat's and the Royal Society's claim about repetition of experiment to verify the facts? Confidently, Sprat asserted that consensus among Society members achieved through experimental repetition promised natural knowledge, an agreement on the facts of nature. From such agreement about the facts, it was but a short step to rules of practice, a hope and aspiration that have flowed across the centuries and poured into the social sciences. While Dewey did not consider education a social science, he thought that as an art it drew on a range of sciences for insight and support. Notwithstanding Dewey's conclusion that laws and facts do not yield rules of practice, we have witnessed over the past few decades (especially in the US and England) determined government-sponsored effort to forge a science of education due to the belief that specific rules of practice would follow. Randomized sample designs, the gold standard widely held for research, promise reliability, but reliability depends on the existence of three conditions, each of which is at best suspect: (1) a common personhood and comparable life stations, (2) fundamentally simple and similar social systems, and (3) universally accepted educational ends simple enough to be measured.

Another art, roughly of the same sort as education, has been the model for much educational thinking in the US since the 1980s (Holmes Group, 1986): medicine. Considering both programs and practices, educators and teacher educators have looked to medicine for inspiration, often enviously, as a high-status profession with prestige directly linked to funded research (usually randomized controlled trials) and to generation of ever more impressive forms of technology. Randomized controlled trials promise the natural facts that Sprat so admired. Surely, no one would question the power of medical research or its success in reshaping human life, although questioning the similarity of the two practices is certainly wise. Given its many successes and the place of medicine as a model for thinking about education, it is a very good place to test the Royal Society's and now the National Research Council's general research ambitions (see Chapter 3).

Recognizing several highly publicized ethical lapses in published medical research, increasing scrutiny is being directed toward medicine's research-supported claims. In a provocative article, Freedman (2010) described the work of John Ioannidis, described as "one of the world's foremost experts on the credibility of medical research" (p. 78). Ioannidis' research raises serious questions of interest here.

[He] zoomed in on 49 of the most highly regarded research findings in medicine over the previous 13 years, as judged by the science community's two standard measures: the papers had appeared in the journals most widely cited in research articles, and the 49 articles themselves were the most widely cited articles in these journals. (Freedman, 2010, p. 80)

Ioannidis concluded that of the 49 articles, 45 claimed to have found effective intervention: medical best practices. Of these only 34 had been re-tested and 14 "had been convincingly shown to be wrong or significantly exaggerated" (Freedman, 2010, p. 81). Recently, Ioannidis (2017) has called psychologists and "laboratory" scientists to task for defending the "dysfunctional status quo" for their stand on what he described as the "reproducibility wars" (p. 1). The concern is that often "reproducers" of studies, of which there are far too few, are unable to replicate original results. Speaking of cancer research, he investigated producers' claims revealing that rather than reproducing results, "very different experiments" (p. 2) had been conducted. Food and exercise studies present even more serious problems: "Medical experts say the problems with lifestyle studies are so overwhelming and the chance of finding anything reproducible and meaningful so small—that it might be best to just give up on those questions altogether" (Kolata, 2016, A3). Given the vast resources spent on medical research and the comparative simplicity of determining intervention or treatment success compared to education success (except perhaps when success in education is reduced to raising a standardized test score), it is difficult to imagine that educational research can achieve such certitude when medical research has been only somewhat successful.

Ultimately, the problem is with the aspiration to produce *a* or *the* best practice or set of best practices — practices warranted to produce specified outcomes — when the best that can be hoped for is a much more modest, yet more useful, honest, and responsible *better practice* for some, not all, teachers and students. Here, again, I return to Dewey. Rather than encouraging hubris, research should always lead to humility: an expression of an appropriate awe for those who perform well the work of teaching and of a deep respect for the complexity of the challenge.

Consistent with his generous view of the nature of research, a reason for Dewey's optimism about the future of education was the possibility of radically expanding who should be considered a researcher.

It seems to me that the contributions that might come from class-room teachers are a comparatively neglected field. It is to be hoped that the movement [toward educators becoming involved in research] will not cease until all active class-room teachers, of whatever grade, are drawn in. (Dewey, 1929b, pp. 46–47)

Recognizing that research results arising from practice can flow directly into practice, Dewey went even further with his argument: "As far as schools are concerned, it is certain that the problems which require [research] arise in actual relationships with students" (p. 48). On this view, teachers simply must be included in the research enterprise.

Remarkably, a similar conclusion follows from studies of failed modern business practices, from researchers who are coming to appreciate a robust conclusion arising from complexity theory: "Complex systems are, in some special sense, 'individuals,' whether or not they are also members of some species" (Lemke & Sabelli, 2008, p. 121). Reporting on a study of the attempt to impose "best practices" in training courses for Xerox technical representatives (reps) who serviced and repaired copiers, Brown and Duguid (2000) wrote,

> tasks were [not] so straightforward, and machines, despite their elegant circuit diagrams and diagnostic procedures, exhibited quite incoherent behaviors. Consequently, the information and training provided to the reps was inadequate for all but the most routine of the tasks they faced. (p. 100)

The machines' behavior was not quite predictable as the same machine "errors" resulted from different causes. "So, while everyone else assumes each machine is like the next, a rep knows each by its peculiarities and has to sort out general failings from particular ones" (p. 101). To make matters worse, the training focused entirely on what they were to do to solve specific problems, but not why, with the result that, "when machines did something unpredicted, reps found themselves not just off the map, but there without a compass or tools for bushwhacking" (p. 101).

Conclusions like these, supported by Dewey's arguments, point toward the importance of local studies to quality schooling and teaching, the third topic I shall address, where the aim is a progressively more intelligent and responsive practice directed toward achieving ever evolving but valued ends within specific work contexts: *better not best practice*. Before discussing local studies directly, a few words are in order about the place of outliers in educational research, those "non-normal" behaviors and experiences that Porter (1986) suggested have usually been set aside as "perturbations," distortions of "common personhood."

ON OUTLIERS, EDUCATIONAL RESEARCH, AND BETTER PRACTICE

Speaking out of what he described as a "skeptical pragmatism," Toulmin (2001) deepened Dewey's analysis of uncertainty. Noting the complexity of all social and natural systems, Toulmin argued that it is unreasonable to ask of the social sciences "accurate forecasts of people's actions": rather, "the virtue of the social sciences is that they *sometimes* help us understand just why, and under what special conditions, our expectations of people's behavior – either as individuals or as institutions – can reasonably be relied on" (pp. 208–209, emphasis added). As Toulmin suggested, one result of recognizing the inevitable limitations of their ability to forecast is that the "claims of contemporary sciences, both natural and human, are a good deal more modest [than in the past], seeking neither to deny nor to explain away the contingency of things" (pp. 209–210). Unfortunately, a similar appreciation and modesty are generally lacking among education policy-makers and politicians who have happily embraced and generously funded the quest for best practice, including value-added research efforts designed to support the ranking, rewarding, or punishing of individual teachers and their schools (Ballou, Sanders, & Wright, 2004). Conceptual and philosophical issues aside, such efforts face virtually impossible technical impediments to realizing accurate, let alone fair and equitable, judgments of teacher quality or value (Berliner, 2014, 2018; Ford, Van Sickle, Clark, Fazio-Brunson, & Schween, 2017; Martineau, 2006; Papay, 2011). Think again of the Xerox machines. Moreover, questions of teacher quality or value are themselves highly contentious, as they should be.

Given the human condition, Toulmin suggested that the appropriate course of action is to "map the range of possible futures open to us — either as individuals or as political and social collaborators — and do our best to create conditions that will help us move in *better instead of worse directions*" (2001, p. 211 emphasis added). Like Dewey, he pleaded for better (not best) practices: actions framed by reflection, driven by dreams and emerging ideals, but disciplined by conflicting interests, differing life conditions, and prevailing stubbornness of human and institutional histories. On this view, what counts as effective practice is a type of intelligent, forward-looking, well-informed and opportunistic tinkering, and a sensitive and responsive feeling of one's way along with others toward evolving but worthy and maturing goals.

It is here where robust attention to outliers, not just to central tendencies, finds a place, for attending carefully to outliers can be helpful in anticipating what is coming and in envisioning and planning for different and possible futures. Extending the point, Toulmin (2001) drew on an insight from Eudora Welty to argue that often "the eccentric can be used to explain the central, rather than the other way around!" (p. 30). Indeed, outliers reveal and problematize what counts as normal. Writing about normality in medicine, Stigler (1999) made a parallel point: that knowledge may be best advanced by "looking at the more extreme variations" (p. 424). Everyone, Stigler suggested, is in some sense sick, as illness is, in fact, normal. In medicine, the connection between noting the extremes in illness and anticipating what is coming is a connection relatively easily made. In education, such links may prove more elusive, yet they are abundant: whether signaling, say, the first signs of change following a large demographic shift or the technological and cultural developments that manifest themselves in differing forms and levels of feeling for school among students. They reveal variations in interest, ability, and life condition from rising levels of diagnosed autism to increasing familial instability following a severe economic downturn like the Great Recession. Thus, yesterday's outliers frequently become tomorrow's norm.

Of even greater consequence for educators, however, is an insight offered by Paul Feyerabend (1994) in his provocative book *Against Method*. Suggesting the importance of dialectical thinking, Feyerabend wrote,

> The first step in our criticism of commonly-used concepts is to create a measure of criticism, something with which these concepts can be compared. Of course, we shall later want to know a little more about the measuring-stick itself; for example, we shall want to know whether it is better than, or perhaps not as good as, the material examined. But in order for this examination to start there must be a measuring-stick in the first place. (p. 52)

Broadening Feyerabend's point: for educators, rather than concepts, the most powerful measuring stick of any and all educational practices, including those well grounded in research and sold as best practices, is found in the effects of those practices on an individual child's total experience of school and on the quality of the teacher and student relationship. Here is where a teacher's critical sensibilities come alive and resistance may follow. At such times, a best practice approach may conflict with other higher educational values, as when a system-wide emphasis on drill and practice eliminated the play of recess or the joy of artistic performance; here, best practices become bad practices (Kane, 2010). Generally speaking, for educators the well-being of the individual child in all his or her complexity, in school and in class, not a general pattern, tempers and consistently trumps other concerns and raises insistent questions about the purposes of both teaching and schooling.

Here too the careful and consistent attentiveness to outliers in practice and in research is important. Outliers challenge not only methods of education (with children who do not respond as anticipated to one or another preferred method or intervention, what might be termed *methodological outliers*), but also the aims of education (with those for whom the established purposes of schooling need to be questioned). It is in part because of this second category of outliers for whom the favored and now sharply narrowing purposes of schooling prove troubling that we are witnessing, for example, the rapid growth in both charter schools and home schooling in the US. Since commonly in education the ends and means are thought of as separate and separable, it might appear that there is no issue here. The domain of means is widely assumed to be the teacher's purview, while others set the ends of education. However, as suggested previously, such views deny what should be obvious: Whosoever sets the aims of education also determines the means; in turn, available means, including the relative generosity or scarcity of resources, set boundaries around achievement.

LOCAL STUDIES AND VALIDITY

"Educational practices provide the data, the subject-matter, which form the problems of inquiry [...] These educational practices are also the final test of the value of the conclusion of all researches" (Dewey, 1929b, p. 33).

By local studies, I mean formal inquiries into questions that arise directly out of specific communities of practice (Wenger, 1998). Such studies usually do not seek generalizable results; rather, they represent, as Gallimore, Ermeling, Saunders, and Goldenberg (2009, p. 550) suggested, "setting-focused interventions" that aim at improving, enriching, and sometimes redirecting a specific practice or set of practices. Thus, local studies are deeply interested studies, drawing on insiders and depending on insider knowledge when framing questions and interpreting, not just implementing, results.

This characteristic of local studies cuts two ways. On the one hand, heavy reliance on insiders makes certain that the questions addressed speak to genuine issues and concerns, makes available a broad range of data, including and especially related to outliers, and enables sensitive and deeply informed interpretations of those data to possess potentially high *validity*. On the other hand, depending on insiders may lead to avoiding some issues for fear of disrupting relationships or offending a friend, also to insularity and cultural blindness, when data interpretations are bounded by the range of understandings and insights readily available within a given context. Depth of desire, as Jensen (2007) suggested, is crucial to overcoming the first issue. The second requires reaching beyond the common sense of a community of practice to consider alternative interpretative possibilities, ways of thinking, making sense, and acting. Perspective may be gained, as noted previously, by engaging in systematic comparison (Feyerabend, 1994); by reading and discussing published research, the stuff of public theory, related to the current question; and by involving selected outsiders, persons who can knowledgeably speak with the insider from the outside. Lacking outside perspectives, the danger is that what is seen is what is already believed (Rabinow, 2008).

While local studies do not seek generalization of results (i.e., reliability), they do seek high validity; when published, such studies should invite readers into acts of experiential comparison. Readers should be able to understand clearly where their experiences as teachers, as parents, or even as students parallel or divert from what is being described and advanced. As a means for widening and enriching the conversation about teaching and learning and for recognizing work well done, sharing results is critically important, whether by providing newsletters to school patrons and educators working within a school or district or by publishing and distributing an article printed in an international journal for teacher educators. Effective communication of results requires inclusion of sufficient contextual information and detail to allow readers to enter the story and make connections across experiences or locate tensions without undue difficulty. Transparent methods, rich contextual descriptions, clear writing (including consistent use of terms), generous use of data, and some recognition of blind spots or weaknesses are required to establish study relevance, value, and validity. For educators, matters of validity are of paramount importance.

In its various forms, local research, like some forms of action research and of self-study (Loughran, Hamilton, LaBoskey, & Russell, 2004; Pinnegar & Hamilton, 2009), seeks to sharpen practice–theory links in context, where theory is practiced and practice is theorized (Bullough, 1997). The aim is both better theory and better practice within specific programs and settings, for specific purposes and for specific participants. To this end, local research requires attentive observation and careful listening to those being taught or studied and to one's own experience, or else the noise of external critics will distract and confuse. Sadly, researchers often both serve these critics and invite distraction by requiring even the most able of teachers to deny the authority of their own teaching experience. In addition, local studies respect the rhythm of research, a rhythm imposed by contexts and of work and patterns of learning while working. External researchers are always in a hurry, and in the rush to judgment teacher learning is likely short-changed.

In addition to their promise as powerful forms of professional development, there are abundant reasons for investing in local studies of one kind or another. Perhaps the most obvious is that all change is local; curiosity about the effects and educational possibilities of a new practice is another. Then, there is excitement about a new understanding of a topic or increased interest in a colleague's program. Despite the generally depressing effects of high-stakes testing on teacher morale (Pearson, 2009), another reason is the need to raise student test scores. It is tempting to dismiss raising test scores as a legitimate reason for inquiry, but to do so would be foolish in the present political climate — a climate that adds a layer or two of complexity to the work of educators. To this end, as Vescio, Ross, and Adams (2008) suggested, work done within professional learning communities that involves groups of teachers sharply focused on studying their practice in relation to student work produces gains in tested learning. Regardless of the driving concern, what is important is that local studies directly address problems of genuine moment to teachers and students in their full living particularity and peculiarity and in full response to their life context and culture. When they do, local studies prove empowering, opening the possibility for educators to become their own "best theorists" (Hunt, 1987).

Local studies that involve what Jensen (2007) described as a "'back and forth' looping between theory and practice" (p. 495) open the possibility of revealing and testing implicit or personal theories against public theory and, conversely, of testing public theory, even "best practice," against personal experience and theory. Rather than cutting them off from their experience, local studies invite teachers deeper into the context of their work and into the lives and experiences of their colleagues and of those they teach. The same is true for teacher educators. That local studies take place in a specific context and with colleagues brings contextual peculiarities and cultural idiosyncrasies to view, potentially leading to identification of unrecognized resources, specific and unique points for action, and opportunities for improvement. No institutional cultures are wholly congruent; every culture both enables and limits meaning, preferring or discouraging some ways of thinking, acting, and being, and also promoting some forms of role enactment over others. When values clash, local studies provide opportunities to confront the limiting functions of culture and to reconsider values and commitments. The focus on outliers holds similar promise. Moreover, such studies offer opportunities to locate strengths that may be extended and built upon. Undoubtedly, some studies may seek to avoid such tensions or minimize their importance, but the tensions are always present to some degree, even if suppressed.

> Local studies have revelatory and disciplinary functions; comparing results reveals where central tendencies collapse and where prejudices lie hidden [...] They "account for the particular" and encourage (drawing on Garrison, 1997) "outlaw thinking", normative discourse that enables the raising of questions that reside outside of established methodological parameters and taken-for-granted system imperatives. (Bullough, 2008, p. 11)

In contrast, researchers mostly concerned with fidelity to best practice seek to shape, control, and direct teachers' classroom actions. For teachers, research can be seen as distant, something someone else does and experienced as disempowering, as a form of colonialization of the classroom and of the curriculum. There is no doubt that in the pursuit of best practice the control of teachers often becomes a dominating concern manifested through prescribed curricula, tightly monitored and set practices, and aggressive and often punitive evaluation and accountability systems. Clearly, belief in the need for controlling teachers permeates the language of school change, where *reforming, reculturing,* and *restucturing* rather than *renewing* (Goodlad, 1994) dominate discourse. Local studies seek renewal. The difference in intention is evident and large: a difference between seeking to replace or fix something broken, or presumed to be broken, and building to teacher strength and to invigorate imagination. Underpinning these views of school change is a fundamental distrust of teachers and an implicit doubt about their ability to grow on the job and into teaching excellence (Brill, 2011). What is lacking is the kind of trust evident in Dewey's argument for including teachers in research and teaching as thoughtful practice, always involving some form of research. Excluding teachers from participating in setting the aims of education is a strong manifestation of distrust; in contrast, including them builds trust and confidence.

Remarkably, the dominance of means over ends, of rules over principles, and the acceptance of teaching as primarily concerned with tasks of transmission and content delivery (means narrowly construed) linger even in some of the most sophisticated of current conceptualizations of teaching. For example, Hammerness, Darling-Hammond, and Bransford (2005) offered the metaphor of "teachers as adaptive experts" as a way for thinking about teacher education and teacher development. The argument centers on the importance of teachers being able to teach efficiently and to develop innovative strategies for responding to situations where established routines fail: that is, methodological outliers. Thus, the emphasis on "adaptive" expertise and on being able to "innovate within constraints" (p. 364) is primarily a matter of teachers getting their instructional house in order; ends are set.

In Dewey's view, research begins and ends with practice. By virtue of the great variability among communities, schools, classrooms, teachers, and students, inevitably the relationships between theory and practice and between ends and means are dynamic; always the proof of the value of any action is found in the resulting consequences, some of which are unanticipated. In this view, the value of even the most robust of rules is only "indirect," as more or less useful "intellectual instrumentalities" (Dewey, 1929b, p. 28). It is this "more or less" quality of the value of rules to which the concept of "adaptive expertise" speaks, as does Schön's (1984) concept of reflection in action. There is no doubt that rules offer beginning teachers' points of departure or of orientation, a place to begin, but only a place to begin framing, making sense of, and initially responding to the problems and dilemmas of teaching and learning. However, over time rules that are externally imposed yet strongly held inevitably limit imagination and cripple innovation.

CONCLUSION

A few years before the passage of No Child Left Behind in the US, with its aggressive program of accountability, and as Ofsted in the UK was gaining power, John Goodlad (1994) identified what motivates teachers in their daily work:

> Good teachers are driven neither by the goals of improving the nation's economic competitiveness nor that of enhancing the school's test scores. Instead, they are driven by a desire to teach satisfyingly, to have all their students excited about learning, to have their daily work square with their conception of what this work should be and do. (p. 203)

Motivations may have changed somewhat since Goodlad wrote, but his assessment is arguably still largely correct. What is evident is that when facing the current challenges of teaching, educators need a good deal of help from one another and from the wider research community to realize the "desire to [work] satisfyingly." In this effort systematic, institutionally well-supported, sharply focused, and publicly recognized local studies hold genuine promise. Such work will seldom if ever meet current "gold standards" for research and most assuredly will never lead to the sort of system-wide permanent changes sought by policy-makers and believers in best practice. It will, however, enrich and enliven the conversation about teaching, produce better, more intelligent, and contextually fitting practices, and, as suggested, probably raise test scores, to boot.

There is no doubt that Sprat was right to warn members of the Royal Society of the twin dangers of enthusiasm and skepticism. Enthusiasm leads to advocating aggressively, to taking strong ideological positions, and to over-promising — outcomes associated with the quest for best practice. As Toulmin suggested, the best that can be hoped for from the social sciences is a "sometimes" and, undoubtedly, temporary better practice. So it is with an art like education. Blind advocacy and indiscriminate skepticism like Brill's (2011) undermine any and all efforts at improving practice while encouraging teacher disengagement and assuring displacement of responsibility to others willing and able, even eager, to take charge and dictate directions for change.

Modesty is called for on the part of those of us who see ourselves primarily as researchers, as well as a deep respect of the sort Dewey possessed for the difficulty of teaching and of teaching well. Such respect is prerequisite to producing research worth its salt. A tempering of the ambition to fix things is also needed, replaced by a lively desire to increase understanding and build more far-reaching, inclusive, and generous research communities that do not deny the challenges of uncertainty, but delight in them, especially in outliers from whom much can be learned. As researchers, teacher educators need to be clear about who or what we serve. While our legacy coming from political arithmetic may be that of state service, like teachers, our first and foremost responsibility is to do our work in ways that nurture the young and those who serve them, as well as strengthen our democratic traditions. Ultimately, this is precisely what local studies should seek to do. The last words of this chapter come from two complexity theorists who argue there is a need to move "away from the Enlightenment dream of universal laws, perfect predictability and rational control [in educational research] to a new recognition that all genuinely complex systems are individual, surprising, and not a little perverse. Just like us" (Lemke & Sabelli, 2008, p. 122).

PART II
THE INNER DRAMA OF TEACHING

CHAPTER 5

GETTING MOTIVATION RIGHT: THE CALL TO TEACH AND TEACHER HOPEFULNESS

INTRODUCTION

Imagine for a moment: what if teachers really did believe their most important work was raising standardized test scores? What if they aggressively competed with colleagues over who could achieve the greatest gain for their class on the annual state assessments required nationwide? What if there really was a trick to jumping ahead in first-grade reading scores and only one teacher knew it and she kept it secret? What if teachers refused to work on their lessons at home and instead taught directly out of the test guides? What if a child fell off the monkey bars, got hurt, and started to cry and the teacher turned and walked away without helping? What would we think of teachers who acted in these ways? Would we want our children to spend their days with them?

Much has been written about the influence of federal education policies bringing the new managerialism that dominates public schooling, "in which trust, partnership, collegiality and discretion have increasingly been replaced by performance review [and] assessment" (Hall & McGinity, 2015, pp. 3–4). Grounded in a punishing rather than a positive psychology (Ball, 2003), two robust assumptions are much in evidence: (1) threats of punishment – from teacher termination to school closure – motivate teachers to work harder and more efficiently, and (2) student scores on standardized tests accurately (or more or less satisfactorily) capture both school and individual teacher performance (Nichols & Berliner, 2007). As previously noted, it is widely believed that comparisons of student scores can and should be used to judge teacher quality, the value teachers add to student learning (Schmidt, Houang, & McKnight, 2005). In response to tightening accountability measures coupled with ever-rising expectations, teachers increasingly find themselves needing to engage in "defensive teaching" (Bracey, 2009, p. 531); being threatened and feeling vulnerable, some teachers may teach out of their fears.

For good and ill, the culture of schooling has changed. As Olsen and Sexton (2009) argued, an organization under siege "responds in identifiable ways: structures tighten; centralized control increases; conformity is stressed; accountability and efficiency measures are emphasized; and alternative or innovative thinking is discouraged" (p. 15). Under such conditions, one wonders what sort of individuals are likely to be attracted to teaching. Is it possible that the future of teaching will be in the hands of quietly conforming individuals – the sort of folks the romantic critics of the 1960s worried about, institutional functionaries who, out of deepening fears and insecurity, uncritically embrace the free-floating rules of best practice and do not expect to have any say over what they teach? Or, alternatively, perhaps the future will be in the hands of teachers who skillfully find spaces within their workday for personal expression even as they keep a watchful eye fixed on student standardized test performance. Either one or both approaches would appear to offer unsatisfying prospects for the future.

The purpose of this chapter is to explore aspects of teacher motivation: what is it about teaching that inspires commitment and encourages teacher well-being? Without an intimate understanding of who teachers are as people and what they most value and find motivating about the work of teaching, even the most well-intentioned of school reforms are likely to come up short. Alternative approaches are needed to improve education, approaches that honor the deepest values of teachers and speak to their greatest strengths as people responsible for caring for, educating, and nurturing the young. The discussion focuses on two critical concepts: the notions of a *calling to teach* and of *hopefulness in teaching*, a topic that will return in Chapter 11. These constructs have received surprisingly little attention in the wider professional literature, but they are of genuine consequence to the work of teaching.

TEACHING AS A CALLING

In North America, teaching has long been associated with individuals sensing that they have been called, sometimes described as having found one's "vocation" (Hansen, 1995; Mattingly, 1975). To be "called" means responding to a summons by sources variously experienced as inner or outer – perceived by some as from God, a "divine summons" (Mayes, 2005b, p. 16; Mayes, Mayes, & Sagmiller, 2005). Parker Palmer (1998) described the call as coming from "the voice of the teacher within, the voice that invites me to honor the nature of my true self" (p. 29) which, when answered, brings a sense of profound well-being. The experience of finding one's calling is expressed confidently: "It seemed natural to go into teaching. It just feels right" (Serow, 1994, p. 70). Bellah, Madsen, Sullivan, Swidler, and Tipton (1985) concluded that having a strong "sense of a 'calling' [...] constitutes a practical ideal of activity and character that makes a person's work morally inseparable from his or her life" (p. 66). Hence, when an individual with a strong sense of calling identifies herself as a teacher, she is saying more than that she does the work of teaching; literally, she *is* a teacher – to teach is a way of coming at life, of finding and expressing oneself, which is often experienced as deeply spiritual and life-affirming, a matter of living a life that is authentic, a life that matters. Answering the call offers a means of being and of being whole, gives purpose and direction along with a moral grounding. Thus, teaching as a calling represents a distinctive and deep service ethic (Serow,

Eaker, & Forrest, 1994). For called teachers, teaching truly is "something that [they] love to do" (Buskist, Benson, & Sikorski, 2005, p. 118).

Serow (1994) examined responses by preservice teachers to a single survey question: "I feel that teaching is my calling in life"; a simple positive or negative indication revealed profound differences in "basic orientations to teaching" (p. 70).

> Those who view teaching as their calling in life display significantly greater enthusiasm and commitment to the idea of a teaching career, are more mindful of its potential impact on other people, are less concerned about the sacrifices that such a career might entail, and are more willing to accept the extra duties that often accompany the teacher's role. (p. 70)

Manuel and Brindley (2005) concluded, "Despite differences in time, place and external conditions, research has demonstrated, decade after decade, that those entering the teaching profession do so primarily because of [...] intrinsic reasons" (p. 42). Serow (1995) reached the same conclusion as more recently have Blömeke, Houang, Hsieh, and Wang (2018) and Richardson and Watt (2006): "[P]articipants seek out those rewards that come from the experience of teaching, and the opportunity structure which teaching affords to provide for the realization of their personal and social values" (p. 51). According to The National Teacher Survey (Rentner, Kober, Ferguson, & Frizzell, 2016), 82% of teachers reported the most rewarding aspect of being a teacher was "making a difference in students' lives" (Table 1-A).

Although not directly concerned with teaching as a calling, a study by Yee (1990) of teachers who taught or had taught in one of three high schools, inner city, suburban, and working class, further highlighted the nature of called teachers. Yee interviewed 15 former and 44 practicing teachers and administered surveys to 215 teachers. She placed these teachers in one of five categories according to their views of and attitudes toward teaching and their ways of making sense of their teaching career: good-fit stayers, good-fit undecideds, good-fit leavers, weak-fit stayers, and weak-fit leavers. By *good-fit,* Yee meant teachers well suited to teaching, who felt comfortable and at home with young people and enjoyed teaching. In contrast, by w*eak-fit,* she designated teachers who felt miscast in the role and work of teaching. Of the 59 teachers interviewed, 12 were categorized as *good-fit stayers*, and 16 were classified as *good-fit leavers*. The *good-fit* teachers who left, like Glazer's (2018) 25 "invested leavers" (p. 63), had come to teaching for intrinsic reasons, primarily "out of a desire to work with young people or to be of service" (Yee, 1990, p. 109). Yee's descriptions suggest these teachers likely were called to teach:

> Comments such as "my main enjoyment is contact with kids" or "I love to watch the excitement of their learning" capture these teachers' positive attitudes about their work. Good-fit teachers, moreover, typically are uninterested in administrative work because they are unwilling to lose touch with the students. These teachers are also more apt to say such things as "I love my students" or "the kids are great" and to view their students as a source of fun, stimulation, and appreciation. (p. 95)

Yee observed that in contrast to their *weak-fit* peers, the *good-fit* teachers had a strong sense of self-efficacy and commitment to teaching, evidenced in working harder and longer hours than others; were highly involved professionally;

and, of particular importance, kept learning: "Good-fit teachers do not stop learning and acquiring new skills as they gain in seniority" (p. 96). Moreover, as Gu and Day (2007) suggested, generally such teachers are resilient, possessing resources that can be drawn upon during difficult times that facilitate successful coping. When *good-fit leavers* exit teaching, they do so for reasons quite different from their *weak-fit* colleagues, an issue that will be addressed shortly. One common thread of *good-fit leavers* was an increasing dissatisfaction with their achievements with students: for many, this resulted from inappropriate teaching assignments in which otherwise competent teachers were not allowed to teach what they knew or as they knew they could (Ingersoll, 2007).

Based on his data for preservice teachers, Serow (1994) concluded that "the calling is a useful concept for understanding the career motives of some preservice teachers" (p. 71). Yee's (1990) and Gu and Day's (2007) studies would seem to indicate a similar conclusion is warranted for inservice teachers, at least for the *good-fit* teachers. Serow wondered how or if being called to teach might influence how preservice teachers respond to the "various practical obstacles to entry and retention within the field" (p. 71). Yee and Gu and Day appear to offer a partial answer to Serow's question, which has only increased in importance in recent years of increasing teacher shortages.

HOPE AND THE HOPE SCALE

Surprisingly, little research has been done on the hopefulness of teachers, although a massive amount has examined the related concept of teacher efficacy, including the contribution of teacher "academic optimism" to student performance (Hoy, Hoy, & Tarter, 2006). Optimism and hope are often connected in the wider literature (Peterson, 2006) although the concepts have important differences (Bullough, 2011a, 2011b). As Lazarus (1999) observed,

> The difference between hope and optimism is logically substantial. In hope, the belief that circumstances could get better goes hand-in-hand with anxiety about the potential for a negative outcome. In optimism as it is usually defined, however, there is little or no room for doubt. One is confident that everything will work out well. (p. 672)

Lazarus cautioned that although often things do not work out well, hopefulness may endure and may inspire actions that result in altered conditions. He wrote, "Hope is a galvanizer of action" (1999, p. 666), in contrast to the inactivity of despair.

As a trait and state, hope was extensively studied by researchers at the University of Kansas, developers of the Hope Scale (Snyder, Rand, & Sigmon, 2005; Snyder et al., 1991, 1996), but not in relationship to teachers. Judged reliable and valid, comprised of two subscales, Trait and State, the Hope Scale has been shown by Snyder and his colleagues (1991) to contribute "some unique predictive variance in relation to other cognitive- and emotion-based dispositional measures" (p. 582) even when compared to measures of optimism and efficacy. Grounded in the assumption that humans are goal-directed, the Hope Scale combines self-reports of *agency* and of *pathways*; when taken together, these two components are assumed to capture the essence of hope, an assumption that is not wholly justified as Lazarus (1999; see Chapter 11) suggested. Nevertheless, the definition proves useful. *Agency* is a "sense of successful determination in meeting goals in the past, present and future"; *pathways* represent "sense of being able to generate successful plans to meet goals" (Snyder et al., 1991, p. 570).

Studies using the Hope Scale reveal a wide range of differences between individuals with higher and lower hope scores – differences of potential importance to educators and policy-makers concerned with school improvement. Among these differences, individuals with higher scores reported higher self-esteem, greater optimism, less depression, more positive, and less negative affectivity; they tended to present themselves in a more favorable light. These qualities are parallel to those in the literature on teacher retention (see Blömeke et al., 2018). Additionally, the high-hope individuals engaged in better problem-focused coping, exercised greater agency in the face of negative feedback, and sought more pathways to solving problems when blocked, experience a higher sense of well-being and, of particular importance, sought more challenging goals.

THE STUDY

Research Context

Findings of previous studies validated the conclusion that wise educational policy should encourage teachers to develop and sustain hopefulness, not only because teacher hopefulness likely supports student learning. This conclusion finds additional support from studies of academic optimism, noted previously, and of happiness (Noddings, 2003). Reviewing the studies by Serow and his colleagues, including Yee and others, suggests a connection between teachers' sense of calling and their hopefulness. While a sense of calling may draw an individual to teaching, bringing with it a deep determination to succeed and to persist even in the presence of what Margolis (2008) described as the "ugly stuff" (p. 179), it is also apparent that maintaining a sense of calling over time likely depends on the ability to maintain hopefulness – to achieve desired aims and to find ways of resolving or moving past the problems of teaching (see Hartwick & Kang, 2013). *Good-fit stayer* "Steven Philips," described by Yee (1990), was an example of such a person, one who despite hostile work conditions, including lack of administrative support, persisted because "teaching allow[ed] him to live out his personal and social values" (p. 24). Could there be a connection between a teacher's hopefulness and sense of calling?

Participants

In his 1994 study, Serow gathered surveys from 525 students being prepared as preservice teachers, most of them enrolled in foundations courses. Of these, 236 (45%) responded positively to the statement that "I feel that teaching is my calling in life," and 289 (55%) responded negatively. The samples in all of his studies were heavily skewed toward preservice secondary teachers (53% secondary to

22% elementary in the 1994 study). This has presented a problem, for, as Manuel and Brindley (2005) suggested, many secondary teachers may be called by the disciplines rather than to the work of teaching. Based on previous research, we considered it likely that much higher percentages of elementary than secondary teachers would report themselves as called to teach (Bullough, Young, & Draper, 2004). Considering these differences in orientation toward teaching (Decker & Rimm-Kaufman, 2008) and the greater impact on elementary schools of mounting accountability pressures, we decided to gather data only from elementary preservice and inservice teachers.

We (Bullough and Hall-Kenyon) surveyed a convenience sample of preservice teachers enrolled in elementary education methods courses at three very different institutions: (1) a large public urban doctoral degree-granting institution in the Southeastern USA; (2) a large private, religiously affiliated university emphasizing teaching over research and scholarship, with a large teacher education program in a Western state; and (3) a small four-year teaching institution with a small teacher education program in a Western state. In addition, we revised the survey slightly to reflect inservice rather than preservice teachers' experience and distributed it, with school building administrator approval, to faculties of three urban elementary schools in Salt Lake City, Utah. We chose urban schools with the expectation they would offer insight into teacher values and beliefs in challenging teaching situations. In total, 175 preservice and 44 inservice surveys were completed; 14 of the teachers (8 preservice and 6 inservice) did not complete the entire survey and were eliminated from the study. Due to the proportions of women and men who go into elementary school, the sample included very few men.

Teaching Instruments

A brief survey instrument was developed (for details, see Bullough & Hall-Kenyon, 2011). Noting, with Serow, that definitions of calling given by preservice teachers reveal considerable differences in understanding, the question about "calling" was replaced with three statements representing a strong sense of being called to teach. Respondents were asked to rate on a one (*definitely false*) to eight (*definitely true*) scale the degree to which these statements captured how they felt about teaching: "I know that teaching is what I am supposed to do in life"; "I was destined to become a teacher"; and " It was meant to be." Measures of preservice and inservice teacher hope were obtained by using the items of the Trait and State Hope Scales which seek to measure respondents' sense of agency and perceived ability to generate pathways to achieve desired goals. The Trait Scale focuses on hope as a disposition or personal characteristic, while the State Scale indicates current feelings about agency and pathways, how the respondent thinks about self *right now*. Even with the two parts and the calling questions, the entire instrument took less than five minutes to complete and actually stimulated considerable interest among those who completed it.

Analyses

Analyses were conducted on 167 preservice and 38 inservice teacher surveys. Descriptive data (means and SDS) were calculated to examine the teachers' sense of calling and levels of hope. Analyses (ANOVA and MANOVAs) were then conducted to determine differences between the preservice and inservice teachers based on their sense of calling and their scores on the two subscales of the Hope Scale, Trait and State (pathways, agency, and total scale score). Correlations between teachers' sense of calling and their level of hope were also examined (see Bullough & Hall-Kenyon, 2011 for details).

Results

Before presenting our specific findings, two surprising conclusions should be noted. First, nearly every surveyed teacher reported being called to teach and being very hopeful. Second, we found no significant relationship between the teachers' sense of calling and measures of their hopefulness.

Overwhelmingly, both preservice and inservice teachers in the sample reported that they felt "called" to teach. The mean rating (from a max of 8) was 7.00 for preservice teachers and 6.68 for inservice teachers – there were no significant differences between the two groups ($F(1,203) = 2.25$; $p = 0.135$).

Teacher responses to both the Trait and State Hope Subscales indicated high levels of hope. For the preservice teachers, the mean total score on the Trait Scale (with a max of 64) was 54.56; for inservice, the mean was 56.50. Similarly, agency and pathway scores on the Trait Scale were overwhelmingly high for both groups. Results were similar for the State Scale. The mean total score (with a max of 48) was 40.98 for preservice teachers and 41.45 for inservice teachers. Mean scores for agency and pathway on the State Scale were also high for both groups. There was a main effect for group differences (inservice and preservice). Follow-up univariate analyses revealed statistically significant differences between the two groups on the pathway subscale, but no differences on the agency subscale.

Calling and Hope Relationship

To determine the relationship between calling and hope for the preservice and inservice teachers, correlations (Pearson's r) between the teachers' sense of calling and their scores on the subtests of the two Hope Scales were established. Overall, there does not appear to be a relationship between calling and hope for either category of teachers. However, a small positive correlation was noted between the preservice teachers' sense of calling and their agency and trait scores and the total score on the State Scale. This lack of relationship proved somewhat surprising and will be considered shortly.

Years of Teaching Experience

The inservice teachers who participated in this study had a wide range of experience (0.5 years to 39 years). A post hoc analysis was conducted to determine whether or not years of experience had any effect on inservice teachers' sense of calling and levels of hope. Accordingly, the 38 inservice teachers who completed the surveys were grouped into four categories by years of experience: (1) those reported having taught 0–5 years ($n = 10$), (2) 6–10 years ($n = 4$), (3) 11–20 years ($n = 9$), and 20 or more years ($n = 14$). One teacher out of the 38 did not report years of experience. Hence, for analysis, data from inservice teacher surveys were placed in five groups: (1) 0–5 years, (2) 6–10 years, (3) 11–20 years, (4) 21+ years, and (5) not reported. One ANOVA and two MANOVAs were conducted to determine if there were any differences in the inservice teachers' survey responses based on years of experience.

Results of the ANOVA suggested that these teachers' years of experience did slightly impact their sense of calling: examining the pairwise comparisons indicated that teachers who had 6–10 years of experience reported having a lower sense of calling than any of the other groups (0–5 years $p = 0.006$; 11–20 years $p = 0.019$; 21+ years $p = 0.035$), with the exception of the one teacher who did not report years of experience ($p = 0.884$). There were no significant differences between the other groups. Teachers' years of experience did not appear to have any effect on their levels of hope. Results of the two MANOVAs revealed no main effect for the Trait Scale and/or the State Scale.

DISCUSSION

Reviewing the data, several striking findings emerge. These will be discussed under three headings: teacher calling, teacher hopefulness, and the relation between teacher calling and hopefulness.

Teacher Calling

As noted, the high percentage of teachers, both preservice and inservice, who reported sensing a strong call to teach was surprising—nearly universally shared within this population – underscoring how teaching and identity are often tightly linked, especially among elementary school teachers. One implication of this finding was clearly apparent: when teachers identify so completely with their work, as these teachers seemed to do, successful school improvement efforts must seek not merely to alter teacher behavior but also to engage teacher conceptions of self-as-teacher. Teachers with a strong sense of calling may resist efforts at school change that downplay or deny their intrinsic reasons for teaching and for staying in teaching (Glazer, 2018). While a sense of calling may weaken over time, as evident in Yee's (1990) conclusion about good-fit leavers, consistent with the positive movement in psychology (Peterson, 2006), we suspect that the more productive approach to improving schools is to build on and seek to extend teacher strengths – in effect build on teachers' lively sense of calling and develop their deep hopefulness. This view is consistent with the most promising work underway currently to form in schools' professional learning communities (Hord, 2003, 2009; Hord & Sommers, 2008; Mullen, 2009). Finally, these teachers discovered their calling at times varying from early life to later in college. Hence, a strong sense of calling does not necessarily mean a teacher has always wanted to teach: A calling may come at virtually any time.

Teacher Hopefulness

We entered the study believing that teachers are inherently hopeful people. If they were not hopeful one wonders, why would teachers choose to work with children and generally be so willing to sacrifice for their benefit? We had not anticipated, however, the strength of both inservice and preservice teachers' hopefulness. Years ago, Weinstein (1989) described what she characterized as the "unrealistic optimism" (p. 53) of preservice teachers, on the whole assuming they would be well above average as teachers. This conclusion was judged negatively, and some teacher educators felt challenged to provide a "more realistic" teacher education. Another view of this finding is more positive that teachers are a hopeful lot and that this ought to be celebrated. We have already noted benefits of being hopeful, which can have extraordinary significance for school improvement and for student learning: better problem-focused coping, more determination, more pathways to solving problems, and increased inclination to stretch and grow. Yet, we also recognize, as Kelchtermans (1999) observed, the need for teachers to achieve a "realistic balance between [...] commitments and task perceptions and the demands of school and classroom" (p. 187).

This conclusion, however, is incomplete. As mentioned, no significant differences were found between the preservice and inservice teachers' agency. Certainly, those who lack or fail to maintain a strong sense of agency leave teaching, but the strong sense shared by the groups that they can accomplish their goals is noteworthy. This belief keeps teachers pushing to achieve their goals even through considerable opposition from children, other teachers, parents, and administrators. Also this belief, as previously noted, is likely a source of teacher resilience (Gu & Day, 2007). One might wonder if beginning teachers who lack a strong sense of agency survive the classroom. On the pathway subscale items, the inservice teachers scored slightly higher than the preservice teachers. Perhaps this finding should be expected; certainly, it would be hoped for. It implies that with increased experience and maturity, these teachers have gained in their ability to resolve problems including, we think, problems of teaching. More experience alone, however, may not be the most important explanation of this finding. As Dewey (1938) argued, not all experience is educative; often experience is miseducative. These resilient teachers have apparently invested in their own learning and growth and have become increasingly effective in the classroom.

The Teacher Calling and Hopefulness Relationship

As suggested in the introduction to this chapter, a working assumption preceded this study: that for both the preservice and inservice teachers a relationship was likely between a sense of calling to teach and teacher hopefulness. But, except for a very small positive correlation for the preservice teachers, the results suggested that no relationship exists. Several explanations are possible for these findings, some of which have to do with the nature of teaching in urban schools. While all of the three participating elementary schools were described as urban, they varied in numerous ways. Each had large percentages of children designated as economically disadvantaged for federal reporting purposes (from 41 to 76%). One school was a majority-minority school (66%) with a high percentage of English language learners (40%). While the student populations were quite transient in the three schools, in this school student turnover was dramatic.

Admittedly speculative, we suspect that teachers working in challenging schools like these experience a particularly dynamic and shifting relationship between sense of calling and hope. This conclusion is supported indirectly by studies of human well-being and happiness, which also raise questions about our use of the Hope Scales. Writing of the research on happiness, Nettle (2005) observed,

> Judgments about happiness are fickle and sensitive to context. We may think in general that we are happy, but it would suffice to point out a few bad things about recent life, and suddenly the question looks a little different. (p. 61)

The frame of reference from which life judgments are made alters responses, at least when the questions asked relate to happiness, well-being, or optimism and perhaps also to hope. To answer the questions asked in the Hope Scale, a context is necessarily inferred. The degree to which the respondents in this study framed their judgments about hope by their experience as teachers or preservice teachers is unclear. Thus, it is possible that the very strong sense of hope expressed by these teachers may have more to do with a general disposition, a feeling about themselves as human beings, than with the more specific assessment of how they experience and feel about the work of teaching. A teacher may be very hopeful about his life and problem-solving abilities generally, and perhaps also about his ability to be an effective teacher, but not as hopeful about work done within a specific school for a specific principal or with an individual child or group of children and their parents – a point partially supported by Yee (1990) with her good-fit leavers. Such individuals may have a very strong sense of calling to teach and be very hopeful but be less than satisfied with their current work situation. In effect, perhaps the Hope Scale as used did not get at teachers' hope in a fully meaningful way. As Yee (1990) suggested, hostile work conditions can and do weaken a teacher's sense of calling and perception of hope. Clearly, the relationship between teacher calling and teacher hope is much more complex than the data reveal.

Years of teaching experience had no effect on Hope Scale scores. But, as noted, in one instance, years of experience did affect the sense of calling. The few teachers having between six and 10 years of experience had a weaker sense of calling than other age groups. While this finding should be interpreted carefully because the sample is very small (n = 4), it may be important. Huberman (1992) observed that somewhere in the early years of teaching, a period of stabilization is generally achieved:

> One has worked up a rudimentary instructional repertoire that fits most situations encountered in the initial three to four years of teaching, and one is now adding to it, refining it, molding it to fit one's own, more congenial style of instruction. There is also an attendant sense of relief at having reached this stage. (p. 124)

Stabilization is followed by multiple patterns including a growing sense of being stale that leads to experimentation and for some a desire to alter work conditions that interfere with effectiveness. Stock-taking followed by self-doubts may emerge, and these patterns may be indicated by a weakened sense of calling indicated by the data (responses of "slightly true" to the feeling of being called to teach). The fit between Huberman's model and these teachers' self-assessment is striking. That so few teachers fell into the category reminds us that there are many reasons teachers exit teaching—to marry, to raise a family, to accept a new job, to follow a spouse who changes jobs — as well as dissatisfaction. Indeed, reasons like these may disproportionately impact this category of teachers.

CONCLUSION

Most of the preservice and inservice teachers in this study felt a strong calling to teach and viewed themselves as rather hopeful people. Although data from this study are only suggestive, a few conclusions seem warranted. First, that teachers are hopeful people and large numbers of them are likely called to teaching highlights the nature of teachers' resilience with investment in and commitment to teaching. These qualities help teachers cope with or get over the problems of teaching and endure even when work conditions deteriorate. Maintaining and deepening teachers' investment in and commitment to teaching are crucially important to improved practice and, therefore, of central importance to any successful effort at school improvement (Park, 2005). Expressed differently, policies that strengthen teachers' hopefulness are likely good for children.

Second, there is good reason to believe that recent reform efforts that produce "threat rigidity" (Olsen & Sexton, 2009, p. 15) and encourage defensive teaching may undermine teacher's sense of professionalism (Darling-Hammond, Burns, Campbell, Goodwin, & Low, 2018) and commitment over time (Glazer, 2018). For many teachers, these changes that flow from neoliberalism have made teaching much more difficult. Because teachers who were no longer teaching were not included in the study, we can say little about conditions that undermine a teacher's sense of calling or hopefulness although spirituality appears to be important to teacher coping (Hartwick & Kang, 2013). The wider literature, however, is suggestive. Peterson (2006), for example, writing of optimism, makes a general point that likely extends to hope as well:

> Constant striving for control over events without the resources to achieve it can take a toll on the individual who faces an objective limit to what can be attained regardless of how hard she works. If optimism is to survive as a social virtue, then the world must have a causal texture that allows this stance to produce valued rewards. If not, people will channel their efforts into unattainable goals and become exhausted, ill, and demoralized. Or people may rechannel their inherent optimism into attainable but undesirable goals. (p. 127)

As indicated by Yee's category of good-fit leavers and Glazer's invested leavers, teachers who have strongly identified with teaching and would have liked to continue may leave for reasons that have nothing to do with teaching and everything to do with deteriorating work conditions and the loss of satisfaction in teaching. In his study of who controls teaching, Ingersoll (2003) underscored the point, noting that being excluded from the decisions that most affect the quality of their professional lives, especially their relationship with students, leads to dissatisfaction and drives teachers from teaching. Despite having "reached a point in their career when they felt competent and satisfied with the teaching they were doing" (p. 65), the teachers in Glazer's (2018) study left teaching. Their predominate reasons for leaving included "interference of imposed curricula" (p. 65); the negative "influence" of testing "on the school environment" (p. 66); and "job insecurity" (p. 68).

Third, a key to maintaining teachers' hopefulness and sense of calling is creating work conditions that allow them to teach as they know they can: to be supported in doing their best work rather than finding themselves having to work against institutional policies and practices to teach well. Resistance is exhausting, an unpleasant diversion. The past several years of school reform in the US have done nothing to increase teacher compensation, have actually weakened teacher collaboration, and have undermined "professional learning opportunities" (Darling-Hammond et al., 2018, p. 347). Accordingly, Darling-Hammond and her colleagues (2018) made an impassioned plea for doing what the most successful systems in the world do: invest in teacher learning and build and sustain a genuine professionalism.

Finally, this study obviously offers only a modest beginning to understanding the nature, influence, and potential power of teachers' sense of calling and hopefulness as elements of teacher motivation. The concern is not to better understand these teacher strengths so that they might be mined or manipulated, but rather to recognize them for what they are: precious resources needing cultivation. The argument is straightforward: when teachers enjoy their work and are happy as they do it, students benefit. Policies and practices that fail to support teacher growth, development, and well-being —including ongoing high-quality, context-sensitive, and engaged teacher education – promise only that many of our best teachers will take their talents elsewhere, and this is a terrible and expensive loss indeed.

CHAPTER 6

THEORIZING TEACHER IDENTITY: EXPLORING SELF-NARRATIVES AND FINDING PLACE IN AN AUDIT SOCIETY

INTRODUCTION

Over the past several years, interest in teachers' identity and identity formation has grown dramatically. Narrative inquiry has proven crucial to opening up this important arena of research (Clandinin, 2007; Clandinin & Connelly, 2000). The tendency, however, has been to tell stories of teachers' lives without linking those lives to history, to the time and the place within which they have taken shape and found expression (Bullough, 2008a). As noted in the Introduction, my argument is that personal troubles and social issues must be joined for, as McAdams (2004, p. 95) wrote, "Life stories reflect the social and cultural worlds within which lives attain their existential meanings." Some researchers do just this (e.g., Biesta, Field, Hodkinson, Macleod, & Goodson, 2011; Day & Gu, 2007, 2010; Goodson & Sikes, 2001; Kelchtermans, 2005).

One reason for the relative paucity of such studies is that questions of identity and of the place of narrative in identity formation in education and teacher education are only beginning to be adequately theorized (Beijaard, Meijer, & Verloop, 2004). To better understand the problem of forming a working professional identity requires more descriptive languages and increasingly more powerful and potentially critical analytic concepts that link troubles and issues, and biography and history (see Shanahan & Macmillan, 2008). From their work on a "dialogical approach towards identity," Akkerman and Meijer (2011, p. 309) came to a similar conclusion.

This chapter was written in the hope of contributing to this effort by introducing and then exploring concepts drawn from psychosocial constructivism and life course theory and research, two orientations that have received rather little attention in education but that seem promising for illuminating the processes of educator identity formation. The challenge presented was captured by Kenneth Burke (1989) when he observed,

> The nature of our terms affect[s] the nature of our observations, in the sense that the terms direct the attention to one field rather than to another. Also, *many of the "observations" are but implications of the particular terminology in terms of which the observations are made.* In brief, much that we take as observations about "reality" may be but the spinning out of possibilities implicit in our particular choice of terms. (Burke, 1989, p. 116, italics in the original)

Richer experience and greater depth and breadth of understanding are dependent upon the languages, or conceptual systems we possess or that possess us. As noted in Chapter 3, the point was expressed differently by Coles (1989) when he observed that the "critical root" of the word theory is "I behold," that our beholding is a matter of our implicit and explicit theories of the world (p. 20).

ANALYTIC APPROACH AND CHAPTER ORGANIZATION

The analysis that follows draws heavily upon insights from literary studies. Five sections follow. The first begins by situating identity and identity formation in narrative and narrative formation. Elements of the research program of psychosocial constructivism developed by D. P. McAdams as a language for thinking about identity and identity development are presented. Next, McAdams' position is expanded somewhat to fill in what appear to be analytic weaknesses by drawing on select concepts from life course research, a complementary second lens to psychosocial constructivism especially helpful for thinking historically and contextually about human development and identity formation (Biesta, Hodkinson, & Goodson, 2004). This section joins what Burke (1989, p. 114) described as a "terministic screen" (see Chapter 3), in this case from psychology, with a second screen drawn from sociology, the result of which broadens the ways identity narratives may be developed. The third section very briefly reviews the "scene" of an audit society (see Chapter 1), the political and historical context of the time and place within which life narratives are formed and are authorized or dismissed.

The fourth segment presents part of a narrative written by Peter Kent, headteacher of Lawrence Sheriff School in Rugby, England, and published in *Secondary Headship*. Mr Kent's narrative was chosen for analysis not only because he teaches in the United Kingdom (UK), where auditing in education has become a way of life, but because his is an educator-written narrative that passionately and eloquently describes an educator's struggle when his identity is under attack, also offering provocative hints about re-authoring himself. The last section of this chapter offers a "close reading" of Mr Kent's narrative using the concepts presented. Close reading, a practice introduced in Chapter 3, involves a "dynamic process in which texts and knowledges are thrown together, with the reader opening themselves up 'to receiving numerous significations, a complex web of possible meanings, a skein of traces and inscriptions within the single- and singular-word'" (McCaw, 2011, p. 31). A practice common in literary studies, "To read closely is to investigate the specific strength of a literary work in as many details as possible. It also means understanding how a text works, how it creates its effects" (Mikics, 2007, p. 61).

THEORIZING IDENTITY: ELEMENTS OF PSYCHOSOCIAL CONSTRUCTIVISM

A good deal of research has been conducted outside of the field of education on identity formation, on the place of narrative in human experience, and on the ways identity takes narrative form and evolves over time. One of the more promising research programs is "psychosocial constructivism" (McAdams, Diamon, de St. Aubin, & Mansfield, 1997, p. 690), a framework that represents a "middle position" that recognizes identity as both "complex and dynamic [but also] stable and coherent" (Akkerman & Meijer, 2011, p. 311). Contrary to many claims, identity is not wholly fluid, as Erikson (1968) asserted: Persons and contexts evolve together; so identity formation is a "process 'located' *in the core of the individual* and yet also *in the core of his communal culture*, a process which establishes, in fact, the identity of those two identities" (p. 22).

Supporting a now widely shared view, some years ago McAdams (1990) argued that, much like a dramatist, "a person defines him- or herself by constructing an autobiographical story of the self, complete with setting, scene, character, plot, and theme" (p. 151). The narrative produced is the person's identity, a story that provides a sense of coherence (McAdams, 2006) and of purpose for living. Clandinin and Connelly (2000) characterized these as "stories to live by" (p. 129). The importance of such stories to human growth and development is hard to underestimate, as Baskin (2008) wrote, "We don't experience life [...] We experience the stories we tell to explain what happens to us" (p. 1). Convery (1999) offered a similar conclusion: "Identity is created rather than revealed through narrative" (p. 139).

Developing throughout childhood, identity formation reaches its critical period in late adolescence and young adulthood (to the middle-20s); McAdams (2001, p. 101) described the process,

> People living in modern societies begin to reconstruct the personal past, perceive the present, and anticipate the future in terms of an internalized and evolving self-story, an integrative narrative of self that provides modern life with some modicum of psychosocial unity and purpose. (McAdams, 2001, p. 101)

For McAdams, as for Erikson (1975), prior to adolescence it would be inaccurate to speak about the possession of identity, as formerly all that could be said was about a self: children have a sense of self but not an identity. Often these two concepts are used interchangeably among educators, yet there are significant differences. In late adolescence when the ideological and occupational options available in society are explored and the social roles opened to scrutiny, beliefs and values begin to consolidate into a "personal ideology" (McAdams, 2001, p. 102). The challenge is to find place, a meaningful niche for self in society, and in finding place, as McAdams stated, a "*modicum* of psychosocial unity and purpose" is gained (italics added). This process, as Baskin (2005) noted, involves experimenting with identity, being part of a "feedback loop," of telling and testing self-stories; as one acts on a story, the narrative and the external world are tested, and if new experiences confirm expectations, the story is reinforced and deepened.

Thus, for McAdams (2001, p. 102), identity "is an integrative configuration of self-in-the-adult world." As such, the development of identity is crucially important for educators, including teacher educators, for it is this developmental crisis that preoccupies many, perhaps most, of our students, young people intending to become teachers (Rodgers & Scott, 2008). Biology and culture interact and conspire to create the crisis of identity, so that "both society and the emerging adult are ready for the individual's identity experiments by the time he or she has in fact become an emerging adult" (McAdams, 2001, p. 103). Much is at stake in these experiments, as John Dewey (1922) long ago suggested:

> There is no ready-made self behind activities. These are complex, unstable, opposing attitudes, habits, impulses which gradually come to terms with one another, and assume a certain consistency of configuration, even though [often] only by means of a distribution of inconsistencies. (p. 138)

Through narrative, the results of these experiments are made to cohere, more or less, and that one comes to think of the self as an agent, an actor with purpose and intentionality, and a person with identity.

The Story Form

Children come early to understanding the canonical components of stories they need to form a self and forge identity, so that by adolescence the story form of explanation comes easily and naturally. As noted, intentionality — the person as actor — is an important component of these narratives: "The development of intentionality in humans is of prime importance in establishing the mental conditions necessary for storytelling and story comprehension" (McAdams, 2001, p. 103). Successfully addressing the crisis of identity involves putting a life together into stories that advance goal achievement and include explanatory power: why I do what I do; why others do what they do; how I got to where I am today; and where I am headed. Having achieved a level of story coherence, as McAdams (1990, p. 165) suggested, a "more personalized and complex ideological position" may follow, a system or network of beliefs and values, a moral stance that, when coherent, can support and sustain agency (Beauchamp & Thomas, 2009) and allows others to anticipate one's actions and to act accordingly. Eventually, as Dewey (1922) suggested, this stance becomes a habit, a way of being that others recognize and depend on, including students.

Humans call on multiple strategies for attaining narrative coherence. Drawing on the work of Habermas and Bluck (2000), McAdams (2001) suggested these strategies involve biography (events belonging to a life lived within cultural conventions), temporality (the flow of time which frames one's sense of development), causality (causes and connections of events, real or imagined — learning to read time backward), and strong themes (values and principles that cut across life events). At different times in life, different strategies may be more prominent. Thus to make sense of identity and identity formation, researchers face the daunting challenge of understanding how these strategies find narrative expression and, in particular, how they support coherence and inform action. Here, Watson's (2009) analysis of Roddy's story as a story of redemption, a "triumph over adversity," is nicely illustrative (p. 480).

Evolving Stories: Evolving Identities and Imagoes

Contrary to a number of theorists, McAdams (2001) argued that while life stories reveal themselves in adolescence and early adulthood, "identity construction does not end when this developmental epoch is over" (p. 106). Life stories evolve and change: individuals seek coherence, but the identity stories evolve, sometimes changing dramatically as, for instance, in religious conversion when one life narrative is replaced by another. This conclusion is of profound importance for teachers and for the children they teach, who rely on and desperately need adult predictability, for it is against or in relationship to teacher identities that children learn to be students. When teachers waffle, uncertain of just where they stand or who they are as teachers, problems follow for students as well as for the teachers (Bullough, 1992).

While the first stages of identity formation for teachers likely reach back to when they were students undergoing their "apprenticeship of observation" (Lottie, 1975, p. 61), which may be connected to a range of events that took place in school and college, later developments also may prove powerful. Work experiences, perhaps marriage and the birth of a first child, a change in school or teaching assignment, transition to principalship, or from a broader perspective, divorce, or the onset of serious illness, may or even require new narratives. As one identifies, articulates, and refines new main characters who represent different mixes or constellations of values, beliefs, and purposes, creating what McAdams described as Imagoes is central to identity formation. Personal teaching metaphors (Bullough, 1991; Bullough & Stokes, 1994; Pinnegar, Mangelson, Reed, & Groves, 2011), the multiple *I positions* discussed by Akkerman and Meijer (2011, p. 312), and *possible selves* (Hamman, Gosselin, Romano, & Bunuan, 2010) each speak directly to McAdams' (2001) notion of imagoes:

> The construction of imagoes helps to integrate a life by bringing into the same narrative format different personifications of the me: the self-as-loving-wife, the self-as-ardent-feminist. (p. 106)

Such changes may represent a shifting balance between a desire for connection and intimacy and for autonomy and independence (see Kegan, 1982). Significant changes within one of the many cultural contexts surrounding life may signal changing roles and relationships, including ways of being with and working for young people.

Narrative Tone

McAdams (1990) observed that the stories people tell of themselves have a "narrative tone" (p. 152). Tone supports continuity (McAdams et al., 2006), underscoring the centrality of emotion in forming identity (Rodgers & Scott, 2008) and in either facilitating or inhibiting adaptability and change.

> A hopeful, optimistic narrative tone or attitude suggests that human beings are capable of attaining their "fervent wishes," that human intentions may be realized over time. It suggests that the world is predictable and understandable, that things can work out in the long run, that stories have happy endings [...] A relatively hopeless, pessimistic narrative tone or attitude suggests that human beings do not get what they wish for, that human intentions are repeatedly foiled over time. (McAdams, 1990, pp. 152–153)

The tonal range of such stories is from hopeful and trusting to hopeless and distrustful, reflecting not merely matters of individual temperament and biography but of cultural well-being or disease – a period like our own, for example, when many teachers feel besieged, nearly overwhelmed by mandated, narrow, and unforgiving accountability systems, increasing expectations and diminishing resources. At such times, seeking self-preservation and doubting self-competence, some educators may respond by engaging in what they know is unethical behavior, perhaps even changing student test scores, with far-reaching implications for how they think of themselves as persons (see *New York Times*, July 18, 2011, A9). Changing tones is very much a part of changing identities.

Memory and Autobiographical Knowledge

For McAdams, as for Freud (1920/1935), memories were considered crucially important to forming identity. Loftus (2003) put the case succinctly: memories "give us identity" (p. 231). But when the choice is between story coherence and truth, coherence wins in recollection, and a kind of personal fiction is created. To a degree, as Baskin (2005) has suggested, such choices are inevitable because stories necessarily involve reductions (the unknown is fitted into the known) and thus simplification of the complexity and contradiction inherent in the world. Choices must be made and where possible these are usually self-serving and self-fulfilling, but not always. Moreover, the "truth" of a story is often flexible, varying with the position of the character, such that the same event or episode may occupy very different narrative spaces and be understood in fundamentally different ways. For example, a traumatic and pivotal event suggesting betrayal by an administrator might be crucially important in the identity of a first-year teacher while that same event might be understood by that administrator as a silly inconvenience soon to be forgotten. W. I. Thomas' remark comes to mind: "If men define situations as real, they are real in their consequences" (Thomas & Thomas, 1928, p. 572).

When exploring how such autobiographical knowledge is organized, McAdams drew insight from the work of Conway and Pleydell-Pearce (2000). These authors argued that memories are organized into three different emotion-laden levels: lifetime periods (described by McAdams as "chapters"), general events, and event-specific knowledge. The first level marks off large sections of time and includes "evaluative attitudes toward the period" (McAdams, 2001): adolescence, for example, recalled as a generally happy or profoundly sad time. The second level represents clusterings of similar events that often "highlight memories of events relating to the attainment of or failure to attain goals." The third level, described by McAdams as involving "nuclear episodes," represents "event-specific knowledge as particular details of specific scenes from the past" (p. 108).

According to Conway and Pleydell-Pearce (2000), autobiographical knowledge is "encoded through the goal structure of the working self, which also takes a major role in the construction of specific memories during remembering" (p. 266). Thus, goals and memories — from all of the three levels — intertwine and are more or less mutually reinforcing, establishing tone as well as influencing how and what memories can be and are accessed and how they are organized for telling. Autobiographical knowledge and cultural expectations in turn delimit what goals, what "possible futures" (Shanahan & Macmillan, 2008, p. 41), are thought plausible and reasonable. In this way, discrepancy is reduced and the stories individuals tell of themselves are generally confirmed and strengthened, thereby supporting continuity even if based on distortions. This is facilitated, in part, by seeking others who give feedback verifying the self-assessment; people who tend to see the individual as he sees himself. Conversely, generally, storytellers flee contexts that prove too sharply disconfirming (see Swann, 1996). A conclusion of this kind, of course, presents serious social, educational, and therapeutic challenges, since change of identity and growth generally arise from sustained and sometimes shocking discrepancy.

As McAdams noted, in some cultural contexts — no doubt including schools — some narratives simply cannot be told and lies are lived as a result. Under such conditions, the emotional cost of achieving and then maintaining coherence may be very high where institutionally preferred narratives and supportive roles prove a poor fit. This insight has special importance for educators, a point for later consideration. Within the third level of autobiographical knowledge — nuclear episodes — sometimes singular events prove overpowering and changes are forced which reverberate upward through the other two levels, transforming them and consequently the individual's identity.

These are moments of great importance in the formation of identity or in the story that is identity. Well-being may depend on how successful one is in turning significant painful events into challenges, with resulting emergence of stories showing redemption and growth (Bauer, McAdams, & Pals, 2008; McAdams, 2005). Identity altering events might range from falling in love or sustaining and recovering from traumatic brain injury (Bullough, 2011a, 2011b). As previously noted, positive or negative work-related events may also influence identity: for instance, when a beginning teacher's car tires were slashed in the school parking lot, she became disoriented and started questioning the nature of her relationships with students and lost confidence in herself as a teacher (Bullough & Knowles, 1991). Despite the power of such events, as McAdams (2001) argued, it is important when thinking about growth and development to recognize that they ultimately enjoy their status and power because they are chosen, embraced as self-determining, even as their emotional loading seems to make them insistent.

Stories that Can and Cannot be Told

Reviewing the range of stories that can and cannot be told within a culture, McAdams (2001) observed,

> Life stories mirror the culture wherein the story is made and told. Stories live in culture [and cultures live through stories]. Stories are born, grow, proliferate, and may eventually die according to the norms, rules and traditions that prevail in a given society, according to a society's implicit understandings of what counts as a tellable story, a tellable life. (p. 114)

As commonly recognized, cultures tell lives in different ways. In cultures most influenced by globalism and postmodernism, for example, telling a coherent tale of self is likely becoming ever more difficult. Yet even if a single story of self cannot be told and multiple stories are required, these generally will be nested in one another and thematically interwoven, thus reflecting how identity is simultaneously both stable and dynamic. By living within small groups and within specific contexts – families, neighborhoods, churches, schools – relatively stable roles and relatively predictable relationships form, even as the wider cultural context may be rather fluid.

Within the process of working out our individual identities – sharing contexts, institutional placements, traditions, forms of discourse, and mythic cultural stories – common themes emerge and find support. Together, as Greeley (1972) argued, these form personal and cultural "paradigms" (p. 93) for sensemaking that set proper role definitions and mark the range of the stories of self that are formed and may be told, including what counts as a counter-narrative (Watson, 2009). Once set, myths ground cultures – setting boundaries for social participation and, of particular importance, rules for group membership, and they normalize and justify both thought and action. Powerful, cultural myths may conflict with aspects of one's identity and in various ways give rise to forms of social and organizational maladaption, including overt countercultural resistance that may open avenues for individual and institutional change.

A COMPLEMENTARY SECOND LENS: THE LIFE COURSE

For educators, McAdams' framework of identity formation and narrative development is rich and provocative, but incomplete in part because it does not fully attend to time and historical context; it is undersocialized. Concepts drawn from life course theory and research prove helpfully complementary in their attention to these issues. In part reflecting disappointment in the common usage of the concept of "career" as a way of linking roles across time in human lives, the development of life course theory provided "mechanisms [for] connecting lives with biographical and historical time, and the changes in social life that spanned this time" (Elder, Johnson, & Crosnoe, 2004, p. 7). Of particular importance was the development of the concept of social pathways, "normal" routes to and through adulthood. "*Social pathways* are trajectories of education and work, family and residences that are followed by individuals and groups through society. These pathways are shaped by historical forces and are structured by social institutions" (Elder et al., 2004, p. 8, italics in the original). Trajectories involve sequences of roles and experiences; they are composed of *transitions* or changes in role or position that, importantly, may signal changes in status and in identity. Transitions signaling a dramatic change in life trajectory are termed *turning points*, likely recalled as a crucial event or nuclear episode, as McAdams described.

Given life course researchers' interest in linking biography and historical time, the concepts of *generations* and *cohorts* have proven fruitful. In this context, the concept of the cohort is of more consequence.

> Locating people in cohorts by birth year provides more precise historical placement. Cohorts, in effect, link age and historical time. Historical changes often have different implications for people of different ages–that is, for people who differ in life stage. (Elder et al., 2004, p. 9)

A *period effect* results when the impact of historical change is relatively consistent across time and across cohorts (see, e.g., Terkel, 1970). When cohorts are differentially affected by social and historical events, a cohort effect results. Both effects have profound implications for identity formation, favoring some types of self-stories over others.

Viewing identity formation through life course concepts calls attention to the ways in which lives move and are embedded in multiple and shared institutional roles and relationships which, themselves, are embedded in cultural traditions (myths) and social organizations and practices. Family, work, and social networks, including churches and, as Leisering (2004) suggested, "the state," impinge on the course of life giving it direction, pattern, and shaping purpose. Gender, religion, social class, race, special abilities, and health each play a part in shaping the trajectory of a life, each representing yet another formative part of what is the narrative space within which identity is forged and evolves. Cohler and Hostetler (2004) made the point nicely: "While cohort or generation represents the more general level at which culturally and historically embedded 'plots' of the life course are enacted, intra-cohort variation and idiosyncratic life-events give shape to [developmental trajectories] that make each life story unique" (p. 556).

AUDITING: LIVING AND WRITING IN HIGHER EDUCATION AND IN THE SCHOOLS

To preface a section using several concepts from McAdams' framework and from life course theory to illuminate aspects of the processes involved in educator identity formation and change, a brief description of the historical context within which educators now live and work is provided, suggesting the emergence of a strong period effect (see Chapter 1).

David Hartley (2003) has aptly described the past two decades in the field of education as involving a "search for certainty and standards" (p. 8). In a brilliant special issue on capacity building in teacher education research, authors writing for *The Journal of Education for Teaching* (November, 2009) described how this search has and is affecting teacher education in the four nations comprising the UK. Their evidence suggested that the pattern of consistent and persistent government inspection they described has had and will continue to have significant effects on how educators and teacher educators think about and experience their work and compose themselves as educators. One reported result, for example, was that many teacher educators and some entire institutions no longer consider involvement in research on teaching as being of particular importance to quality teacher education and they no longer aspire to be or become researchers, an issue noted in Chapter 3. Other identities capture them. The evidence presented in this issue suggested that this or a similar pattern of inspection and aggressive external control of teachers' work is spreading as many nations have embraced the goals of audit societies. For this reason, among others, the following sample narrative from the UK was selected for analysis.

Developments in the US and the UK run along parallel lines. In the US, Baez and Boyles (2009) described how the quest for accountability and for a standardized test-driven science of education (as discussed in Chapter 3) is redefining the nature of educational research and the roles of teacher educators and of teachers, narrowing definitions of quality, and conceptions of who is a researcher. Strongly supported by accreditation requirements in the US (see Johnson, Johnson, Farenga, & Ness, 2005), the implications of these developments for identity formation are deeply disturbing (see Bullough, 2008b).

By law, auditing is now a way of life in the schools of England. Following guidelines presented in a 79 page School Inspection Handbook (Ofsted, 2018), schools conduct self-evaluations in preparation for a two-day assessment visit by a team of inspectors from the Office for Standards in Education. Usually inspections take place every five years, unless a school is judged to be "causing concern" (p. 34). During their visit, "Inspectors will spend most of their time gathering first-hand evidence to inform judgements" (p. 24). In preparation for the inspection, in addition to the self-evaluation, students and parents are invited to complete on-line questionnaires. Inspectors gather, evidence about the quality of teaching, learning and assessment and in lessons and other learning activities, to collect a range of evidence about the typicality of teaching, learning and assessment in the schools. Inspectors will scrutinize pupils' work, talk to pupils about their work, gauging both their understanding and their engagement in learning, and obtain pupils' perceptions of the typical quality of teaching in a range of subjects. (p. 25).

Additional evidence is gathered in meetings with staff and parents, school leadership, classroom observations, reviews of student work, and schools records and documentation. Judgements of overall "effectiveness" and of specific program elements are made based on a four-point scale with descriptors: outstanding, good, requires improvement, and inadequate.

Inspectors sign the Office Secrets Act (which prohibits them from publishing anything about the process). The headteacher is invited to attend the final team meeting "to listen to the scrutiny of evidence and corporate judgements made by the inspection team" (p. 30). The lead inspector writes the final report. Results are made widely available. Additionally, "league tables" provide rankings of schools based on student performance on standardized tests, which are published in local and national newspapers and read with great interest. It is important to note that standards are rising, so that having one year gained a satisfactory rating on an Ofsted inspection does not mean that the same performance level will be judged satisfactory at the next inspection. Schools judged inadequate receive either a "notice to improve," indicating inspectors' belief that the school could be improved under current management or, in severe cases, "special measures," mandating dramatic changes. Under both categories, intense scrutiny follows.

MR KENT'S STORY: PLOT LINES OF TEACHING IN AN AUDIT SOCIETY

Like all institutions, schools represent narrative spaces for stories to be told, myths encountered, and identities formed and changed. As both McAdams and life course researchers have argued, changes in contexts, particularly dramatic changes, often have profound effects on *social pathways*, affecting what and how life stories unfold and how they are told. The development of audit cultures and inspectorial societies within schools and increasingly in teacher education and higher education certainly constitutes such a change.

The narrative that follows was written by Mr Peter Kent, headteacher at the Lawrence Sheriff School, an old, selective, endowed secondary boys school. Mr Kent wrote of the effects of league tables and school inspections on how he experienced his work and how his experience of work was changing as a result, changes that contributed to what has been described by researchers as a "chronic shortage of talent willing to take on [headships]" (Maddern, 2009).

Mr Kent's story is compelling in part because he had worked in the Lawrence Sheriff School long enough to notice dramatic changes in teaching and in the nature of his teaching life as auditing took hold — changes that did not sit well. He did not write to complain, but to express his solidarity with other heads and his own determination that by publishing his narrative he could let others know they were not alone in their struggle to manage the effects of auditing and to preserve something of the values of education.

Mr Kent's school did well in the league tables and was among a small handful of schools judged by Ofsted inspectors as "outstanding" in every area, so he wrote from a position of strength, of having succeeded. The Ofsted inspection report concluded, "Lawrence Sheriff is an outstandingly successful school that provides students with an excellent standard of education. As a result, they develop academically and personally into well-rounded young men who are prepared extremely well for their future lives. The school's strength lies in its culture of very high achievement, innovation and great sense of community" (Lawrence Sheriff School Inspection Report, 2007, p. 4).

Yet, Mr Kent felt vulnerable and seemed to doubt the future; potentially, he was one negative report away from needing to find different employment. Considering his work, including how his situation had changed, and of how he experienced those changes in relation to how he thought about himself as a person and as an educator, Mr Kent wrote:

> I have been turned into a football. As I complete my ninth summer as a headteacher, I am increasingly convinced that my job has less to do with education and more to do with the realities of running a football club. "Blimey, you must like reading!"—I heard these words regularly in mid-August as I trudged to the newsagent's desk to pay for my armful of newspapers. I had to check the different league tables produced by every newspaper after [the school test results were published]. You might well ask: Why bother? Wouldn't it be best to show a lofty disapproval for the tables by ignoring them? Having tried this approach, I know that it is fraught with difficulties (the less you know about what is written about your school, the more vulnerable you are to ambush from a variety of groups) [...] Unsupportive governing bodies have been known to use one poor set of results plus a less than positive Ofsted inspection to ease school leaders out of their jobs. We seem to be creating a culture within education where headteachers are only as good as their last set of results. Sounds familiar? At least when the pundits at the end of Match of the Day tell us that, "At the end of the day the league tables do not lie," they are broadly correct [...] Most [...] groups in society, including politicians, seem to be heading towards the premier league approach of basing all judgements around a plethora of statistics and floor targets. If you think that league tables don't lie, you have not spent much time in schools recently [...] Leaving aside last year's results, it would seem not unreasonable to ask why, if the standard of marking was so good, the test-marking agency have been dismissed and the National Assessment Agency have battened down the hatches in readiness for a record number of re-marks. Despite widespread derision about dodgy marking and rushed jobs, ministers have allowed results to be published [...] We are seeing an emerging consensus that headteachers are almost identical to football managers, but without the salaries or job security. And like them, we are judged on results and often carry an impossible weight of expectation. While we both have loyal groups of supporters, in each case the people with real power expect us to work miracles and to work them quickly. (Kent, 2008, pp. 1–2)

IDENTITY REVEALED IN MR KENT'S NARRATIVE: A CLOSE READING

Viewing Mr Kent's statement through the lenses provided by McAdams' framework and life course theory reveals aspects of the drama of identity within a specific work and life space.

In this section, the foundational concepts from these two frameworks serve as overlays for study of Mr Kent's identity story. The concepts include: (1) *Story elements* including *plot*; (2) strategies for attaining narrative coherence (biographical, causal, and strong themes); (3) *personal ideology*; (4) the challenge of coherence and place of change in self-narratives evident in the generation of new *imagoes*, imagined new ways of being; (5) *narrative tone, memories,* and *periodicity* (life "chapters," general events, event-specific knowledge); (6) *goal structures*; (7) *myths* and, in the conclusion, the question of what stories can and cannot be told. From life course theory, the concepts of *social pathways, turning points,* and *cohorts* find place.

Story Plot

Analysis begins with a general orienting question: "What is the story, what is the *plot line*?" Mr Kent has been a headteacher for nine years at an elite and highly successful school. Following a well-understood *pathway*, he liked his work, but the job was changing, moving in unsettling directions. He had worked long and hard to maintain the standing of the school but was under increasing, and seemingly endless, pressure to increase what were already high standards of performance. He felt like a misplaced football, wondering if his administrative work actually connected with his *goal structure*. Educating the young had seemed to center his identity, a goal that gave his life meaning and purpose. His journey from teacher had been long and rewarding, certainly filled with identity-sustaining and narrative-embedded *memories* of the boys he had taught and of his and his colleagues' accomplishments at school. Reviewing the past, Mr Kent realized he had made a positive difference in the lives of those with whom and for whom he had worked. He seems to have been proud of what he accomplished and proud of the school. In his *personal ideology*, the work of teaching and of being a teacher was life-affirming and purposeful.

Mr Kent was an experienced educator, one who had been headteacher long enough to have witnessed the evolution and expansion of Ofsted's power and influence. Work was changing, he wrote, and increasingly, he found himself needing to respond to outside agencies and critics in ways that seemed somewhat demeaning — certainly off-putting. His values, the *strong themes* that characterized his professional life and around which his identity had formed, were increasingly in tension with those of the inspectors who audited his work. Given his position within the school, he did what seemed necessary to protect his staff and maintain the school's reputation, but he also cared deeply about the quality of the education offered to the young men attending the Lawrence Sheriff School. The narrative expresses his anxiety that in the quest to maintain the high standing in the league tables that Lawrence Sheriff attained, he might have to compromise some of his most cherished values.

This is the story, generally. A closer reading through the language and concepts of the two lenses follows. Other interpretations of the narrative are possible; the point of the close reading is to demonstrate the fruitfulness of the lenses for opening up and making sense of identity formation. A second goal: to establish the reasonableness of the interpretation offered even as interpretations always reach beyond texts to the place where the "cultural background of both reader and text [meet]" (McCaw, 2011, p. 31).

Personal Ideology

Through his many years of teaching, Mr Kent developed a clear sense of himself, who he was, what he valued, why he did, and what he did. He thought *of himself as* a teacher. Teaching was not a role he assumed, a mask he wore at work and then discarded at home, but a biographically embedded and tested way of being in the world complete with a *personal ideology* of service and sacrifice with a strong commitment to student academic performance. In the narrative, clear *causal* links can be recognized between what he has done as teacher and then as headteacher and student learning and school quality, a conclusion shared by the inspectors.

Challenge of Coherence and Change

But Mr Kent was feeling conflicted. The *narrative coherence* he had achieved and enjoyed was under assault, and the self-story he told to his fellow headteachers seemed of necessity to be changing not in directions he found affirming. He had been accustomed to *assuming responsibility for his actions*, taking charge, standing for something, but increasingly he found himself responding to forces beyond his influence, those "unsupportive governing bodies" who did not seem to share his commitment to or his vision for educating the young. Feeling vulnerable, and concerned for the students' educational success and his staff's well-being, Mr Kent continued to work very hard and very long hours, but apparently less toward the *goals* he most valued – those anchoring his educator identity.

The narrative suggested Mr Kent was emotionally on edge. A great deal of responsibility for the school's success rested on his shoulders, as the Ofsted report indicated: "The head teacher's outstanding leadership, together with the very strong support of his deputy and the senior leadership team, underpins much of the school's success. There is a *relentless focus* on raising standards, improving teaching and learning, and sharpening the quality of leadership and management" (Lawrence Sheriff School Inspector Report, 2007, p. 6, italics added). Any slippage in school standing would be shattering, reflecting directly and negatively on Mr Kent and on his management team. Failure was unthinkable.

Tone

Yet clearly, Mr Kent doubted the validity of much that goes on when schools are ranked in league tables and assessed by Ofsted. Even following the good news of yet another highly successful inspection for his school and the continued improvement in standardized student test scores, Mr Kent prepared himself for attack. The *emotional tone* of his story is defensive, a bit fearful. Mr Kent seems out of sorts, not quite himself. In mid-August, feeling a good deal of angst, Mr Kent checked the "different league tables" to make certain his labor had paid off and, perhaps, to see how the competition fared. He found himself looking outside of himself and his school, to others he likely did not know nor respect, for confirmation of himself as a headteacher not because he wanted to, but because he felt he had to – even as he doubted the legitimacy of the assessment. Under such conditions, more and more looking to others outside of the school for self-confirmation (by Mr Kent and other headteachers) seems almost normal, expected. We see signs of performativity (Ball, 2003).

Memory/Periodicity: Event-specific Knowledge

Mr Kent suggested he was increasingly dissatisfied with his work, and this is not only a result of disappointment with the salaries headteachers were paid for what was and is often recognized as nearly an impossible job. What seemed to trouble him most was that expectations were rising, and, he knew, many expectations are impossible to meet even if worthy. He knew improvement in any complex human activity such as teaching takes time and often seems grindingly slow because it involves working with and through people, but an abundance of time was something he did not have; patience was not a virtue. He had to be relentless! Others looked for miracles; Mr Kent seemed to know better: at some point, failure was certain if only because league tables do not lie.

Social Pathways, Turning Points, and Anchoring Myths

Mr Kent's narrative was a story of a forced shift in *pathways*, the institutionally recognized role of headteacher had changed and was continuing to change rapidly. He had no apparent influence on these changes; he could only respond to them. Accordingly, for Mr Kent, the period of this narrative was a time of reduced agency and of growing instability, of unraveling *anchoring myths* that had long normalized school relations, stabilized practice, and supported and sustained teacher and headteacher relationships and identity.

Strategies for Attaining Narrative Coherence

There are hints within the story of Mr Kent approaching a *turning point*, a moment of losing self-story coherence even as he seemed to be composing a new story with a different *plot line* — *choosing* to portray himself in some sense as one of many victims, a theme that contains elements of an assumed moral superiority with hints of a fallen hero's tale. After nine highly successful years, successful according to the auditors, as headteacher, Mr Kent could not help but *remember* what life used to be like, perhaps recalling a happier *chapter* in his professional life, a time of strong congruence between his wider sense of himself as educator — and the stories he told — and his work as teacher and then headteacher, a time of deep and energizing authenticity and of growing confidence. Passing inspection likely produced feelings of relief mixed with pleasure. There is more than a little hint of defensiveness in Mr Kent's story, and a lot of frustration born of doing well something that was not particularly valued yet was all consuming. As noted previously, challenges to identity are experienced as highly emotionally charged.

New Imagoes

Writing of headteachers as football coaches presented a fresh yet troubling set of identity images, *imagoes*, as McAdams described them. Mr Kent was feeling compelled to try on a new identity, a new character, and set of metaphors, but he found the fit with football coach not just uncomfortable but morally dubious. This image ill suited him, and he was pushing back in small ways even as he seemed to be adjusting. Publishing his story in *The Secondary Headship* and going public may have proven cathartic.

Perhaps over time Mr Kent generated and experimented with imagoes that would better enable him to continue to find pleasure in his work but also satisfactorily meet state expectations. If so, he would create a new professional identity and perhaps broaden his personal narrative. It is also possible, however, that like many headteachers, he would be unable to overcome increasing discrepancies. Many who are worn down by participating in a duplicitous role play between who they are as educators and what they are required to do when working choose to retire: to close this chapter of life to open another as soon as possible. Remaking himself into a more institutionally fitting educator might not be possible. As noted previously, humans tend to flee consistently disconfirming contexts (first psychologically) where and when they can, and so Mr Kent may flee.

Cohorts and Generations

The life course concept of a *cohort effect*, rather than a *generational effect*, is analytically appropriate here. Brand new headteachers begin their work under school conditions very different than veterans like Mr Kent. For these newcomers, the dominating *themes* of an audit society may be less troubling, perhaps offering what is thought to be a new *social pathway* to the headship. In contrast, Mr Kent, and others of his age cohort, know there are other ways of being in schools and other ways of making life and work meaningful. They have lived these less-audit-driven ways, the experience of which grounds their *biographies* and shapes their identity narratives. Having such *memories* inevitably embedded in the *goal structure* underpinning the early career ambitions that defined their success results in the disillusionment evident in Mr Kent's story.

More Story Elements

The main theme underpinning the plot and giving coherence to Mr Kent's story is loss of control as responsibilities increase. His is potentially a victim's narrative increasingly common among teachers. Yet, the narrative seems to offer more a warning than whining, and perhaps a growth theme will emerge. On every front, teachers feeling beleaguered are hunkering down, doing what they must to satisfy the auditors, and coping, as Gu and Day (2007) have argued, doing the best they can under increasingly trying circumstances. Despite feeling somewhat gloomy about the future of education in the hands of auditors and nitpicking politicians, one would guess that Mr Kent probably persisted even as his disgust with league tables and disdain for those who produced them increased. No single *episode* seems to have moved him to the place in his thinking expressed in this narrative; rather, it appears to have emerged from a persistent flow of insistent events. Like most educators, Mr Kent was at base a hopeful person — to teach is to be hopeful (see Chapter 11); he basically still believed in what he was doing and delighted in having a hand in the growth and development of young people despite all the distractions. Yet, as Mr Kent wrote, making a way of life in school that was deeply satisfying, experienced as authentic and life-affirming, was becoming ever more difficult.

CONCLUSION

My intention in this chapter has been to describe and then demonstrate the usefulness of an orientation and concepts for thinking about the drama of teacher identity and in connection both to the person and to the historical and cultural context of identity formation. As noted, some self-stories simply cannot be told in some places and at some times, or if they are told, they are told on the sly. Looking ahead, one wonders which self-stories and which educator identities will be excluded in an audit society. Which will be favored, judged normal, and ultimately honored? And what will be the costs if valued institutional identities conflict with wider cultural and individual aspirations and teacher motives (see Chapter 5)? The importance of these questions may not be self-evident.

Who teachers are as people and how they understand the work of teaching clearly influences, positively and negatively, what young people experience in school, shaping what and how they learn. The cost of intensive auditing and its quest for certainty may well be educational quality, but it likely also presents a serious cost to teacher growth and well-being. Here, the findings of research grounded in self-determination theory (SDT) are on point. SDT focuses on "people's inherent growth tendencies and innate psychological needs that are the basis for their self-motivation and personality integration, as well as for the conditions that foster those positive processes" (Ryan & Deci, 2000, p. 68). Three fundamental needs for human flourishing have been identified: (1) *autonomy*, understood as a feeling of volition rather than an assertion of individuality, (2) *competence*, and (3) *relatedness*, experienced as being connected in meaningful ways to others. Robust evidence affirms that together these three factors anticipate performance and well-being at work. The contrary is also true: "Excessive control, nonoptimal challenges, and lack of connectedness," all factors that were very much a part of Mr Kent's work life, "disrupt inherent actualizing and organizational tendencies endowed by nature, and thus such factors result not only in the lack of initiative and responsibility but also in distress and psychopathology" (p. 76).

Aggressive external auditing of schools undermines conditions that support autonomy, competence, and relatedness, as Mr Kent's story suggests. While the drama of identity formation and change generally takes place internally, the importance of this drama requires that it be brought forward and considered in relation to how it is shaped by history, culture, and context. In addition, the drama of identity formation must be linked to our highest aspirations for children and concern for their well-being. Clearly, teachers' and student lives are intertwined and their well-being is ineluctably linked; within schools, student well-being cannot flourish without teacher well-being.

Hopefully, the frameworks and concepts discussed in this chapter will prove useful in the efforts to better understand processes involved in educator identity formation: how the work of teaching shapes teachers and how educators might be more effective in shaping their own work to better support their highest aspirations. Those of us who care about young people, including their education, and about teacher education need to know more about the sort of people our institutions most value and to understand how the focus on identity and identity formation opens avenues for such inquiries. Studies of teacher satisfaction and burnout are inadequate to the challenge. A broader question must be considered: what sort of people do we want teaching our children? To answer this question requires a consideration of a prior question: what sort of people do we want our children to become?

CHAPTER 7

TEACHING AND LEARNING WITH PARABLES: REIMAGINING THE SELF AND THE WORLD

INTRODUCTION

Recently, while observing a colleague teach, I was struck by his use of narratives to illustrate points and answer questions. Over the past 20 years, narratives have garnered considerable research attention among teacher educators (Carter, 1993; Clandinin, 2007; Pinnegar, 1996). Egan (1988), among many, has asserted the value of narratives as a powerful instructional strategy. Great teachers, from Zeno and Lao Tzu to Jesus of Nazareth, were storytellers (Common, 1991).

Sitting in my colleague's classroom, I could not help but notice his ways of telling stories and think about his intent in using these narratives when teaching. Drawing heavily on his experiences as a teacher and school administrator, he primarily used stories to illustrate promising teaching practices. He told fables, a few I suspected were fairy tales, and a story or two that seemed to aspire to legendary status. Implicitly, recollections of his teaching were offered as models of good teaching. This is not surprising. Teacher educators often ground their claims to authority in their prior experience, even though they may feel uneasy as they recognize that such experience is becoming more remote and so increasingly suspect to students. Nevertheless, the implicit promise to the novice teacher is straightforward: do as I do (or as I recall I did) and good results will follow.

Using narratives in this way is commonplace in teacher education, especially, I suspect, among the large numbers of clinical teacher education faculty hired in part because they have an abundance of fresh stories to tell of their presumably exemplary teaching. Such approaches to teacher education find support in widely shared and highly valued teacher lore: the wisdom of the craft (Schubert & Ayers, 1992). As Scott and Dinham (2008) have argued, "Teachers who are looking for ways to solve problems or make decisions in their classrooms are highly likely to prefer the example or advice of a colleague to the disembodied wisdom of a theory or set of empirical findings" (p. 116). It is doubtful, of course, that my friend would be recognized as a colleague by schoolteachers, even as he presented himself as experienced in a classroom. In any event, generally the beginning teacher's goal is to find out "what works" when teaching, not why, and often teacher educators play into and support this expectation by the stories we tell, even as these stories may undermine our students' perceptions of the value of education theory and research.

Similarly, cases and case analysis occupy a significant place in the curriculum of teacher education. Although case analysis may potentially only confirm teacher prejudices, usually the argument is that analysis provides vicarious experience and offers a means for novices to think systematically about the practical implications of teaching and learning theories. A case may be viewed from multiple theoretical perspectives as students are seeking the most promising approaches to managing the problems of teaching. Accordingly, it is argued, theories are given life and made useful, and novices begin to learn *about* the rules of good practice.

In addition, participating in case analysis is thought to help beginning teachers learn to think like teachers and to frame and resolve problems in ways that enhance the education of the young and nudge along the development of teaching expertise. This aim may be reinforced when results of the novice teachers' case analyses are compared and contrasted with those of experienced and expert teachers. Teacher educators hope that novices will be encouraged to think more like experts, to recognize an instructional event as an instance of a known category of problems, and have opportunities to tap into a range of preferred responses.

Teacher educators have taken inspiration from both law and business schools in case analysis as an instructional practice (see Sykes & Bird, 1992). Ironically, as teacher educators' interest in case analysis methods increased, just across campus a few critics in law schools were questioning established instructional practices. Lawyers associated with the law and literature movement argued that legal study had "become too 'scientific,' too bound by the casebook method" (Ward, 1993, p. 325). As with Coles' (1989) efforts to broaden medical education and similarly to criticize a narrow, rule-bound professionalism, the solution offered was to broaden the law school curriculum to include literature as a means for introducing students to and enlivening professional problems and dilemmas. Hoping to elevate education over training these critics harkened to "alternative jurisprudential traditions [where] law was taught through the use of stories, metaphors and parables to encourage the creative interpretation of the student" (Ward, 1994, p. 398). Kafka's parables from *The Trial*, among other works, were suggested as content.

Considering the intent of my colleague's teaching, I wondered: if teacher educator stories and case analyses are used primarily to support learning the patterns, characteristics, or even the rules of good practice (certainly a legitimate concern of professional education but not the only important goal), could there be a place in teacher education for other types of stories — narratives that encourage the sort of sensitive and creative interpretations of teaching and learning originally sought by the law and literature critics (Peters, 2005)? Learning to teach and to think like a teacher ought to go beyond the hard work associated with internalizing rules of good practice to also inspire and deepen understanding, invite self-transcendence, and be good fun (see Ward, 1994, on fun and learning the law). If, as Abrahamson (1998) asserted, "Storytelling is the foundation of the teaching profession" (p. 446), that profession must have room for forms of storytelling that speak to something beyond conformity and congruence, forms that have proven themselves provocative, broadening, engaging, and delightfully irritating — forms requiring a stretch. Of proven story forms, the parable certainly meets these standards, yet parables have found virtually no place in professional discourse.

This chapter (1) offers a definition of parables and a few rather speculative reasons why, in contrast to other story forms (fable, fairy tale, legend), generally they have not found a place in professional studies; (2) explores a small cluster of three parables that puzzle, offering especially rich insights into the problems and possibilities of teaching that should hold interest for novice teachers and teacher educators; and (3) considers a few reasons why parables have potential for enhancing teacher education, including as a means for exploring moral commitments and beliefs, for self, and for generating theories about teaching and learning.

ON PARABLES

The Greek origins of the word *parable* are found in *parabole*, to compare. To qualify as a parable, "a story must have aesthetic balance, some trenchant elements of metaphorical imagination, brevity and economy, limited development of characterization, and a concentrated plot with a powerful 'twist' or verbal insight" (Oden, 1978, p. xvi). Parables are, as McCollough (2008) stated, "word pictures," extended metaphors that have "immediate efficacy in communication [as they] instantly communicate meaning from one person to another, as opposed to abstract, discursive, propositional language, which must reference an external, agreed-upon meaning code" (p. 11). Moreover, such images are memorable — they "stay in the mind" (p. 12). Unlike other story forms, parables are meant to puzzle, to "challenge one to a different level of being" (p. 23) and self-understanding. As a form of indirect communication, parables do not flow to an expected conclusion but reveal contrary or unexpected aspects of a dilemma that invite comparison, complicate and deepen experience, and enrich imagination. Moving from concrete and commonplace events and experiences, parables quickly bring readers to the edge of their understanding only to drop them as something unexpected is revealed, requiring that a troubling "imaginative choice" be made that reveals who and what they are, what they value, and where they stand morally (Oden, 1978, p. xiii).

Parables have enjoyed a prominent place not only among the great religious traditions but also in the writings of Plato, Nietzsche, and Kierkegaard, among others. In the more than 2,000-year history of parable writing and speaking, some parables have become almost universally known — the parable of the Good Samaritan, for example. That many parables are so well known says something significant about their power to stir imagination and to settle securely in memory.

A MISSING STORY FORM: PARABLES AND PROFESSIONAL EDUCATION

For several reasons, parables are rare in professional education. Perhaps the most obvious is that few educators are aware of their power or their range of concern, of how parables provocatively open up topics of deep and abiding importance to teachers and teacher educators. When the intent of teaching is student surrender, most educators assume one type of story is probably as good as another. When professional education is narrowly instrumental (see Johnson et al., 2005), it is not surprising that parables receive no attention. Developing trends in accreditation and increasing emphasis on narrow conceptions of educational research and standardized test-driven forms of accountability (see Baez & Boyles, 2009) have fundamentally altered and narrowed the curriculum of teacher education and of schooling particularly at the elementary school level (Berliner, 2011). It is evident that focusing both the novice teacher's and teacher educator's attention on practices promising higher student test scores has dramatically constricted learning opportunities for the young — but for teacher education students opportunities are constricted as well.

As these trends work against the inclusion of parables in the curriculum, they powerfully attest to why their inclusion is worthwhile. Speaking of legal studies, distinguished scholar Julius Getman described a schism "engineered in law school between the 'professional' and the 'human' voice, which is deliberately geared to the dissociation of the lawyer from the human being" (Ward, 1994 p. 395). A similar schism can be recognized in teacher education. The human voice is certainly still heard in teacher education, but that voice needs strengthening. Parables speak directly to and seek to reveal the values and commitments that underlie and sustain human action and to define what counts as a worthy life and honorable practice.

That parables are often associated with religious traditions may also help explain why they are so seldom included in professional education, even when individuals know of them and have experienced their revelatory power. Law schools and medical schools require courses in professional ethics, but in an act of strained reasoning, ethics is separated from morality, a separation that allows avoidance of all things sectarian. In teacher education, ethics has only a visiting appointment. Nevertheless, the great questions that animate ethical debate within the professions, education included, and the positions taken on those questions cannot be so easily insulated. Inevitably, religious values creep into the debate in one form or another, even if they tag onto some safer, more comfortably dressed, language traditions and thereafter remain at the margins. Despite the presumed danger of brushing up against religious values, parables that speak to professional dilemmas hold the potential for both believer and nonbeliever to be surprised: to discover through the encounter something unanticipated about their understanding of themselves and of professional practice that can be liberating, energizing, and simultaneously somewhat troubling, perhaps revealing traces of intellectual narrowness or moral blindness.

It is remarkable that storytelling, thought of as a subject to be studied and a skill to be learned and practiced, is not part of the teacher education curriculum, even in early childhood education. Given the prominence of stories in teaching and learning, it should be. At one time, storytelling had a place in the teacher education curriculum, being, as Horne (1916) stated, one of three "main school arts" (p. 9) of the craft of teaching, joining questioning, and studying.

Another reason parables have not found a place in professional education is the difficulty of skilled storytelling; speaking in and writing parables can be very challenging. Teaching through parables is not like other kinds of storytelling or teaching. Metaphors and similes make conversation possible, but speaking and writing in parables require unique skill and understanding. This point is nicely made by Oden (1978) when writing of Kierkegaard's special gifts as a parablist:

> Like Socrates, Kierkegaard's philosophical quest was full of strife. So it is not surprising that he, like Socrates, so frequently elects to disarm his opponents with a seemingly innocuous story. "In its most characteristic use," wrote A.T. Cadoux, "the parable is a weapon of controversy, not shaped like a sonnet in undisturbed concentration, but improvised in conflict to meet an unpremeditated situation. And with this handicap it has at its best a delicacy and complexity of aptitudes showing a range of mind and genius of association beyond that required for the similes and metaphors of other poetic compositions." It is with such aptitude and genius that Kierkegaard enlists the parable so effectively as a weapon of philosophical conflict. (p. xi)

Certainly, it would be delightful to encounter teachers and teacher educators who speak in parables and use them to further their educational aims. But one does not have to produce parables to enjoy them and to find in them educational value; it is, however, necessary to be able to provide an instructional space conducive to exploring them — a "holding environment" that is safe, open, respectful, and accepting of ambiguity, difference, and perhaps conflict (see Mayes, 2007, pp. 55–56). There is no doubt that already there are parables enough for engaging beginning teachers in a process of reconsidering many of their takenfor-granted notions of teaching and learning — views that if unacknowledged may undermine valued educational aims. However, there may not be educational spaces sufficient for the need. These must be created.

THREE PARABLES

To illustrate the educative power of parables for rethinking the givenness of the world, this section presents three examples: the first from Kierkegaard, "The Storm"; the second from Jesus of Nazareth, "The Sower"; and the third, a Buddhist parable "The Fish and the Turtle." Before exploring these parables, it should be noted that those presenting a parable often finish telling the story with an overwhelming urge to explain it and to fix its meaning, to claim rhetorical authority by being didactic rather than dialogic. Temptation of this sort haunts teachers and teacher educators, giving rise to the monologist residing within. For many educators, this temptation is simply too powerful to resist. The interpretations offered here are merely suggestive, meant to stir thought and not to set ends. The tendency to monologue is no more evident than with several of the parables of Jesus: for example, in the scriptural presentation of "The Sower" (see McCollough, 2008). *The New Testament* books of Mark, Matthew, and

Luke each offer an explanation of why Jesus spoke in parables and give an interpretation of the parable through allegory. (In general, it is thought that these interpretations were added to Jesus' words by the Gospel writers — the parable is present without explanation only in the Gospel of Thomas.) The problem is that once set and having become authoritative, an interpretation closes off fresh insights, weakening the educational value of parables — to provoke thought, challenge understanding, and stretch imagination.

As the stories told by my colleague pointed toward implicit teaching rules, the stuff of "best practice," interpretations of parables may become catechismal so that conclusions — principles of best practice or more broadly of right living — become the focus and point of reference rather than the story and the diffuse light shed by it on the nature and complexity of human experience. Interpretive openness is an essential condition for effective teaching with parables and perhaps all teaching that has education rather than training as an aim; there must always be a genuine possibility for surprise: like all metaphors, parables are never really about what at first they seem to be. Lacking such openness, stories that are taken as having value are those offering a clear conclusion thus confirming the teacher's positional claim to power and authority.

THE STORM

Let us imagine a pilot, and assume that he had passed every examination with distinction, but that he had not as yet been at sea. Imagine him in a storm; he knows everything he ought to do, but he has not known before how terror grips the seafarer when the stars are lost in the blackness of night; he has not known the sense of impotence that comes when the pilot sees the wheel in his hand become a plaything for the waves; he has not known how the blood rushes to the head when one tries to make calculations at such a moment; in short, he has had no conception of the change that takes place in the knower when he has to apply his knowledge. (Oden, 1978, p. 38)

The opening line of *The Storm* immediately points toward questions about the purpose and value of formal education: Is schooling a preparation for life or a form of living? To students of progressive education and readers of John Dewey's *Democracy and Education* (1916), this query is immediately recognizable. At a time when principal employment may rest on rising or falling standardized test scores and school closure is held threateningly over teachers' heads by anxious policy-makers hoping to force improved schooling, there is remarkably little discussion about the purpose or value of testing — or of education, for that matter. What is the educational significance of having "passed every examination with distinction"? (Consider here the definition of teacher quality championed by former Education Secretary Rodney Paige.)

Moreover, why is there so often such a sharp separation of learning and doing, of theory and application, of passing a test and piloting a vessel through a storm in the "blackness of night"? What curricular options are available to narrow the gap? Where did the theories taught come from? Who produced these theories and how were they produced? Figuratively, of course, life is always stormy and in some sense we live in perpetual twilight, always vulnerable to forces outside of ourselves, including for teachers the natural forces of the energetic and not-yet-fully domesticated young. That the elements can be controlled is, of course, an illusion, an Enlightenment fantasy, but they can be better understood and more effectively responded to and exploited for educational purposes. And with greater understanding comes recognition of human limitations and, it is hoped, greater appreciation of our own weaknesses as teachers coupled with a measured acceptance of others' inevitable failings. Under such conditions, judgment must be tempered by mercy even when the judgment is about the quality of a piece of student prose, a first pot thrown, or a student who refuses in utter and complete frustration to do an assignment.

Reading "The Storm" from the perspective of the beginning, teacher opens several rich avenues for consideration. Many years ago, Weinstein (1989) observed what seemed like a rather strange phenomenon: virtually, all beginning teachers considered themselves above average as teachers and fully expected to have relatively few problems in the classroom. When difficulties arise in student teaching, novices explain them away as the result of working within someone else's classroom; surely, they firmly believe, things will be different when they have their own classes and are fully in charge. Long ago, Lottie (1975) warned of the dangers of an "apprenticeship of observation" (p. 61), offering insight into the optimism and remarkable confidence of many beginning teachers. Many think they know how to teach before ever stepping in front of a classroom.

I wonder, shouldn't beginning teachers be frightened, at least a little bit, of the uncertainties of the classroom? And if they are not frightened, would it be wise for those responsible for designing teacher education programs to create experiences in schools and with children that prove shattering, that undermine the set of beliefs about self, subject matter, and teaching that lead to overconfidence? Such failure, of course, must be "wisely handled" (Mayes, 2005c, p. 110). We might also ask about the deepest fears of beginning teachers (or teacher educators, for that matter) and ponder whether there is value in making these fears explicit – an outcome to which parables are peculiarly well suited.

Clearly, our fears, perhaps even more than our dreams or ambitions, say more about us as people than possibly anything else. Teacher fears ground and justify prejudice, as offstage they quietly censor the curriculum, closing off without notice student opportunities to learn. As Palmer (1998) observed, there is genuine danger in teaching out of our fear – children are harmed, subject matter distorted, and higher purposes lost. For me, these are but a few of the issues that come to mind as I think about "*The Storm.*" These are lively issues, at least for me, having as a beginning teacher and teacher educator taught at times out of fear and having come to recognize later some of the damage I caused.

THE SOWER

Jesus was teaching a "great multitude."

> Hearken; Behold, there went out a sower to sow: And it came to pass, as he sowed, some [seed] fell by the way side, and the fowls of the air came and devoured it up. And some fell on stony ground, where it had not much earth; and immediately it sprang up, because it had no

> depth of earth: But when the sun was up, it was scorched; and because it had not root, it with-
> ered away. And some fell among thorns, and the thorns grew up, and choked it, and it yielded
> no fruit. And other fell on good ground, and did yield fruit that sprang up and increased; and
> brought forth, some thirty, and some sixty, and some an hundred. And he said unto them, He
> that hath ears to hear, let him hear. (King James Bible, Mark 4:3–9)

The explanation that follows the parable portrays the seeds as the Word of God. To the Hebrews listening to Jesus, planting analogies would have been very familiar, as were images of shallow and dry soil and of a scorching sun. However, for teachers, the parable calls forth additional images, other possibilities for meaning: the seeds might be virtually anything that is to be taught. Turning the lens 180 degrees, concern shifts from seeds to conditions, toward the challenges of preparing for learning — and of making "good ground."

I bring to this parable a long-standing fascination with the concept of human growth, in part informed by years of reading the writings of Dewey, but also underpinned by study of teaching metaphors in which images associated with nurturing and caring for the young are common (Bullough, 1991, 1993). The metaphors used to talk about and make sense of experience profoundly shape which actions we think are right and proper or even possible for teachers and students; accordingly, we open or close learning opportunities (Lakoff & Johnson, 1980/2003). Although growth metaphors — teacher as nurturer, hus-bandman, gardener — place heavy responsibilities on teachers to create the inner and outer environments most conducive to learning (to prepare the soil), they also underscore how learning must include hard and persistent work, sometimes toil, and a measure of serendipity, of plain and often dumb good luck.

These metaphors may suggest as well the lively presence of magic and mystery in teaching, aspects of teaching wholly absent from currently dominant educational discourses. How does a seed sprout and become something incredi-bly beautiful, something perhaps never imagined by even the most dedicated, attentive, and forward-looking of teachers? Recognition of the unanticipated and surprising in teaching and learning is humbling, even as such outcomes are more rather than less likely for some sowers than for others. What are the quali-ties, knowledge, and skills, of such gifted sowers; where and how do they gain and productively share this knowledge with others who are younger and less worldly? Despite the frequent attacks on the value of teacher education, surely knowledge of this kind is not reinvented anew by each generation; it thus deserves preservation and extension within colleges and universities (see Dewey, 1904; Darling-Hammond & colleagues, 2018).

THE FISH AND THE TURTLE

> Once upon a time there was a fish. And just because it was a fish, it had lived all its life in the
> water and knew nothing whatever about anything else but water. And one day as it swam
> about in the lake where all its days had been spent, it happened to meet a turtle of its acquain-
> tance who had just come back from a little excursion on the land. "Good day, Mr. Turtle!"
> said the fish. "I have not seen you for a long time. Where have you been?"

"Oh," said the turtle, "I have just been for a trip on dry land." "On dry land!" exclaimed the fish. "What do you mean by on dry land? There is no dry land. I had never seen such a thing. Dry land is nothing." "Well," said the turtle good-naturedly. "If you want to think so, of course you may; there is no one who can hinder you. But that's where I've been, all the same." "Oh, come," said the fish. "Try to talk sense. Just tell me now what is this land of yours like? Is it all wet?" "No, it is not wet," said the turtle. "Is it nice and fresh and cool?" asked the fish. "No, it is not nice and fresh and cool," the turtle replied.

"Is it clear so that light can come through it?" "No, it is not clear. Light cannot come through it." "Is it soft and yielding, so that I can move my fins about in it and push my nose through it?" "No, it is not soft and yielding. You could not swim in it." "Does it move or flow in streams?" "No, it neither moves nor flows in streams." "Does it ever rise up into waves then, with white foams in them?" asked the fish. "No!" replied the turtle, truthfully. "It never rises up into waves that I have seen." "There now," exclaimed the fish triumphantly. "Didn't I tell you that this land of yours was just nothing? I have just asked, and you have answered me that it is neither wet nor cool, not clear nor soft and that it does not flow in streams nor rise up into waves. And if it isn't a single one of these things what else is it but nothing? Don't tell me." "Well, well," said the turtle, "If you are determined to think that dry land is nothing, I suppose you must just go on thinking so. But anyone who knows what is water and what is land would say you were just a silly fish, for you think that anything you have never known is nothing just because you have never known it." And with that the turtle turned away and leaving the fish behind in its little pond of water, set out on another excursion over the dry land that was nothing. (*Buddhist Parables*, 2002, pp. 33–34)

Whether the teacher or the student is the turtle or the fish, matters of being open or closed to alternative experiences represent a fundamentally important challenge to both teaching and learning. The first line of the parable raises disturbing questions: are we condemned forever to live within the conceptual and moral limitations imposed by the circumstances of birth? How, if at all, is it possible to transcend those circumstances? What does it mean to learn? In what ways are learners responsible for their own learning, especially at a time like our own when some argue that teaching is becoming less and less important (see Natriello, 2007)? Other questions follow: how does someone come to understand something that does not exist and that fails to meet the standards for being real? Change begins in imagination, and imagination is often closed off and cowardly, separated firmly from action and set in its ways, fish-like. Often, the world is taken-for-granted as given, without awareness that legitimate and contrasting worldviews exist, including views represented by the children who sit in every teacher's classroom.

Consistently and persistently seeking self-confirmation, we humans assume that our own experience and sense of the world is normative, even in the face of substantial evidence to the contrary. Representing one kind of orthodoxy or another, disciplinary points of view are maintained even when patently wrong (Hamilton, 1997; Toulmin, 2001). Gould (1983) offered a remarkable example of such blindness when the great naturalist and vigorous opponent of evolution Louis Agassiz, at the behest of his friend Benjamin Peirce, visited the Galapagos Islands in 1872. Retracing part of the famous voyage of The Beagle, apparently Agassiz saw nothing to challenge his views. As Gould wrote,

Scientific discovery is not a one-way transfer of information from unambiguous nature to minds that are always open. It is a reciprocal interaction between a multifarious and confusing nature and minds sufficiently receptive (as many are not) to extract a weak but sensible pattern from the prevailing noise. (p. 118)

A recent and compelling study of the difficulty of seeing outside of taken-for-granted beliefs appears in *Strangers in their Own Land* (Hochschild, 2016). Obviously, like Agassiz, some few teachers maintain academic, social, and cultural views that, in their blindness, undermine student learning. I recall, for instance, a teacher I knew well who early in his career had been dynamic and engaging, turtle-like in his willingness to explore ideas, but who some years later eagerly looked toward retirement, lamenting that "the students have changed." He said he no longer understood them, that they were rude, lazy, and unteachable — there was no "dry land." He did not or could not imagine without help that he also might have changed or that he needed to alter his understanding of the purposes of his work but had failed to do so.

The turtle's response to the fish, his willingness to turn away and leave the fish to her "little pond," opens several provocative interpretive possibilities. Perhaps recognizing that learning cannot be compelled — only enticed, invited, encouraged, and inspired — and sensing a lack of readiness to learn, the turtle concluded that it was best to go elsewhere, perhaps to another pond in search of a more mature and eager fish — a better "class" of students, more open to the possibility of the existence of dry land and more interesting to talk with.

But now bringing this parable into conversation with "The Sower," perhaps the turtle knew that we educate indirectly (Dewey, 1916, p. 22) and so he left the small pond, sat in the sun and contemplated for a time what he could do. What sort of experiences could be provided that would stir the fish's imagination and invite a reconsideration of her belief that the only existing world was the wet, cool, and foamy one she knew? How might a fish experience dryness? Perhaps working from the perspective of schema theory, the turtle began thinking about how the fish's belief system might be gently weakened, made vulnerable and susceptible to change so other ideas and concepts might be planted and grow. Seeing value in dialectical reasoning, of bringing opposites together in an uncomfortable relationship and in the quest for broadened sympathies, perhaps the turtle concluded that he needed to linger for several days and pose questions of the fish. Maybe some questions would lead her to consider the idea that there were other possible ways of being.

A moral dilemma might have presented itself, and parables have morals: the turtle may have wondered if he had the right to shatter the fish's worldview (perhaps the fish was a supporter of creation science and the turtle an evolutionary biologist by training — or the converse). Believing provincialism a greater danger than the emotional turmoil that follows a loss of faith, the turtle's thinking may have led to questions about how to help the fish reconstitute a working worldview after being set "adrift." A teacher's responsibility does not end with deconstruction but only begins there, ever seeking, as Dewey argued, to reconstruct experience and on a higher, richer, more life-affirming, and more deeply social plane. Alternatively, fed up, the turtle might have insisted that the fish pay attention and agree that dry land exists, reminding the fish of its relative weakness and that if the fish continued being so stupid, he could make life miserable in all sorts of ways, from fouling the water to eating her young. Wanting to please the turtle but feeling a bit defensive, like so many good students, the fish might have spoken as though she accepted the existence of dry land but never really believing it, at least not until the split second before a fisherman dragged her to shore, clubbed her on the head, and tossed her flailing about into his wicker basket to take home for supper – when it was too late.

Each of the three parables presents a wide range of interpretive possibilities for fresh thinking about teaching and learning and learning to teach, even though not one mentions a teacher. That connections come so easily is not surprising. Between the moments of birth and death, the human experience is essentially about teaching and learning – about how generations interact across time and about how earnestly the old, out of both fear and professed love, seek to protect and then shape the young into their own image, of how each person in his or her dependency is ultimately condemned to make sense of life, even when unaware of or in denial of having inherited the product of centuries of meaning-making – usually experienced as water to a fish. Each must confront limitations, and learn, as Dewey (1910) once wrote, how to "get over" (p. 19) problems by reframing and reconstituting the questions that grab us and doing so in ways that keep us open to further growth in the richness and diversity of experience.

REIMAGINING TEACHING: PARABLES AND SELF-UNDERSTANDING

> Just as we seek out metaphors to highlight and make coherent what we have in common with someone else, so we seek out personal metaphors to highlight and make coherent our own pasts, our present activities, and our dreams, hopes, and goals as well. A large part of self-understanding is the search for appropriate personal metaphors that make sense of our lives. Self-understanding requires unending negotiation and renegotiation of the meaning of your experiences to yourself [...]. The process of self-understanding is the continual development of new life stories for yourself. (Lakoff & Johnson, 1980/2003, pp. 232–233)

One of the distinctive features of parables is that they have "some trenchant elements of metaphorical imagination" (Oden, 1978. p. xvi). Expressed more simply, they have a metaphoric edge to them. Within parables, metaphors and the worldviews they support are placed in inescapable tension; comparisons are made and positions revealed. An essential aspect of the apprenticeship of observation is that beginning teachers often come to teacher education embedded in a way of thinking about teaching and learning, complete with a set of metaphors that is as comfortable as it is limiting. For many beginning teachers, teaching is telling, mothering, directing, and guiding, and each of these metaphors brings its own inevitable set of limitations. As Lakoff and Johnson (1980/2003) observed, "Metaphors may create realities for us, especially social realities. A metaphor may thus be a guide for future action. Such actions will, of course, fit the metaphor [which] in turn [reinforces] the power of the metaphor to make experience coherent" (p. 156). By their nature, parables challenge the metaphors that sustain both truth claims and direct action and thereby invite reconsideration of beliefs and commitments, and the potential result is generation of new ways of seeing and understanding – which is to say new theories and ways of beholding. Of course, reaffirmation or silence may also follow. After a brief confrontation, both Plato's and Jesus' parables often left their opponents speechless; with so much at stake in established conceptions of self and world, disengagement and silence followed. In such situations, the teacher's challenge is to keep the conversation going.

If change begins in the imagination, as I believe it does, the essential value of exploring parables in teacher education is their capacity to stretch and enliven ways of thinking even as they reveal rigidities. Comparison is the key, and this is so for reasons suggested by Feyerabend (1975) when he wrote of the work of scientists: "Prejudices are found by contrast, not by analysis" (p. 31). What we must compare are metaphors — foundational concepts — that speak directly and forcefully to the human condition, especially for teachers, to different ways and associated qualities of being for oneself and being for and with one's students. Because teaching is first and foremost a moral relationship, the comparisons of parables point toward teacher duties and responsibilities as much as they do toward opportunities to promote learning. Moreover, the study of parables does more than reveal prejudice and suggest alternate ways of thinking. Although involving serious intellectual work, parabolic inquiry is fun. At the present time, fun is something desperately needed and too often lacking within teacher education.

CHAPTER 8

TEACHABILITY AND VULNERABILITY

INTRODUCTION

Teachers immediately resonate with Parker Palmer's conclusion that teaching is a "daily exercise in vulnerability" (1998, p. 17). Vulnerability is a *"constitutive characteristic of teaching as such* and thus *a structural condition* teachers (or educators in general) find themselves in" (Kelchtermans, 2011, p. 80). Hence to teach is to be vulnerable; it is the way "teachers live in their job situation" (Kelchtermans, 1996, p. 307). No surprise, generally speaking, vulnerability is associated with "weakness and passivity, qualities and states of personhood to be assiduously avoided" (Dale & Frye, 2009, p. 123).

But what is vulnerability? Drawing on Robert Solomon's insight that emotions are judgments that have objects, vulnerability is a mood: "There are passions which need not even begin with a particular incident or object, which need not be about anything in particular; these are moods" (1993, p. 112). Vulnerability is a mood born of a demanding and uncertain environment (Helsing, 2007) within which teachers confront ever present and constant reminders of their limitations, as reflected in the eyes of a disappointed pupil or in the gossip of a grumbling and dissatisfied parent. Vulnerability is an inevitable outcome of living within "an institutional and political context obsessed with [surveillance]" (Bullough, 2009, p. 37). To be vulnerable is to be capable of being hurt, but to be invulnerable, if such a state is possible, is to limit the potential for learning. There is the rub.

While vulnerability is part of teaching, teachers manage the mood differently, and these differences have profound importance for teachers and their development, students and their learning, and teacher educators and their practice. Some teachers seek to make themselves invulnerable and immune to the possibility of failure, perhaps by limiting risk, while others who possess a "desire" to learn (Jensen, 2007) or the "will to learn" (Van Eekelen, Vermunt, & Boshuizen, 2006), seem to enjoy putting themselves at risk; such people push boundaries and "become more teachable" (Bullough, 2009, p. 37). That said, measures of risk and invulnerability are uneven and situational; because they are developmental, they are evolving (for better or for worse).

Learning is revealed in the ways today's threat or frustration becomes tomorrow's interesting problem, as Kegan (1982) suggested in his discussion of the tensions between the twinned human drives of self-preservation and self-transformation (see Chapter 11). Additionally, differences in the work context heighten teachers' sense of vulnerability or diminish it, enabling or limiting the ability to realize aims and to preserve senses of self, an issue that underscores the power of neoliberalism (see Chapter 1). This point is evident in studies of teacher stress: increases in the symptoms of teacher depression are generally independent of preexisting symptoms but directly related to adversity in school environments, including "events that demonstrate to the individual a strong sense of personal disappointment and thwarted goals" (Schonfeld, 1992, p. 137). Under such conditions, generally, the struggle is to shoreup, not re-imagine identity, which may require reinterpreting or even ignoring contrary evidence, thereby revealing the play of self-confirmation bias.

Some schools and some faculties clearly offer better places to work than do others, and impacts are not limited to teachers. Brouwers and Tomic (2000), for example, have argued that emotional exhaustion, which is a "long-term stress reaction" (p. 249) connected to the inability to cope with vulnerability, leads to a decrease in teacher self-efficacy and diminished classroom performance. Children suffer. Such findings may lead to the conclusion that correcting the conditions causing teacher vulnerability is a worthy educational aim: good for teachers, good for students. A compassionate aim – but not all sources of vulnerability are alike in origin or effect; as suggested, vulnerability can be both positive and negative (Bullough, 2006; Meyer, Le Fevre, & Robinson, 2017, p. 223).

Kelchtermans (2011) has identified a handful of vulnerability sources in teacher "career stories": educational administration and policy, professional relationships, and limited efficacy (pp. 67–72). No doubt there are others, including sources external to and constraining of the teacher–student relationship, such as inadequate instructional materials, frequent mandated high stakes testing, and constant and often ill-informed criticism in the press. These sources are of a different order from sources affecting human relationships and the development of competence. External sources suggest the need for different responses than do sources arising from human interaction. Altering the former may require political action, while the latter may require something deeper and more personal, perhaps confronting personal limitations and biases; accepting counseling, coaching, or mentoring; and trusting colleagues and valuing learning communities (Kelly, 2013).

Clearly, such distinctions are not easily made nor maintained. In fact, a teacher might respond similarly to both kinds of sources, seeking certainty and security rather than growth. As Dewey (1929) argued, despite the desire for self-transcendence noted by Kegan, humans' first tendency is to strive for certainty and security:

> The quest for certainty is a quest for a peace which is assured, an object which is unqualified by risk and the shadow of fear which action casts. For it is not uncertainty per se which men dislike, but the fact that uncertainty involves us in peril of evils. (p. 8)

Dewey continued, "The natural man dislikes the disease which accompanies the doubtful and is ready to take almost any means to end it [...]. Long exposure to danger breeds an overpowering love of security" (p. 227). When an individual faces situations with the possibility of harm, Dewey considered two courses of action open:

> [He can] make a change in himself either by running away from trouble or by steeling himself to Stoic endurance; or he can set to work to do something so as to change the conditions of which unsatisfactoriness is a quality. When the later course is impossible, nothing remains but the former. (pp. 232–33)

In either case, certainty is not a genuine possibility, for arrested development, dogmatism, professional incompetence, and "irresponsible dependence and sloth" follow (pp. 227–228). Uncertainty is a condition of freedom and insecurity a fact of life essential to growth and development.

Vulnerability, then, is not merely a part of teaching that must be managed; when not overwhelming, it can be a powerful motivating force behind human development and a determining factor of competence. With the existence of genuine possibilities of failure and connections to unpredictability in relationships, vulnerability can be a source of much that is delightful and inspiring about teaching. Thus, the burden of vulnerability when it is too heavy may crush one's hopes and dreams; in other forms and under other conditions, it may spur a reshaping and then a realization of them. The latter is most likely within a committed professional community and least likely in isolation. As Dewey implied, certainty as the absence of vulnerability is probably a desperate delusion; for teachers, vulnerability comes with the job, it need not be sought, as Palmer observed.

STUDY FOCUS

In lieu of student teaching, teacher candidates are employed in many school districts as interns: full-time placements as teachers with half salary and full benefits. By employing two interns, one experienced teacher is freed to mentor two beginning teachers. The study presented in this chapter is a follow-up to a larger study of the internship year of 23 interns drawn from a sample of 100 (Bullough et al., 2004). In that study, teacher vulnerability was a dominant theme. Sources of vulnerability paralleled those discussed in the wider literature, including (1) the external forms connected to the bureaucratic nature of teachers' work, the busyness of teaching, the stress of administrator evaluation, and the rise in standardized testing and (2) the internal forms linked to student behavior and to the complexity of parent and teacher relationships. Most of these items were present in Fuller and Bown's (1975) ground-breaking study that pointed them toward what they called "survival concerns" of beginning teachers: concerns about "one's adequacy and survival as a teacher" (p. 37). The interns in this study "responded to their feelings of vulnerability by working harder to increase their teaching competency, seeking help especially from their mentors, and striving to improve their curriculum and instruction" (Bullough et al., 2004, p. 381). Only two of the 23 interns ended the year with marked signs of self-doubt. In large measure, this finding was attributed to consistent mentor support, but the dataset did not allow a detailed exploration of this conclusion.

The study reported in this chapter followed the approach taken in the first, but more data were gathered including from mentors and on mentor–intern relationships. Drawing once again from a set of about 100 interns, data from 18 mentors and 36 interns were analyzed. From this second dataset, the single case study reported here was constructed, consisting of a mentor and two interns. This triad was selected for study because it was one of two from the entire dataset where the two interns had radically different and contrasting experiences with mentoring. These differences, which profoundly affected the mentors, in surprising ways opened for exploration of the emotional landscape of beginning teaching.

The specific purpose for presenting this case study is to examine the processes involved for both mentors and interns as development is managed and encouraged. Data from the mentor are included because involved mentors profoundly influence the kind and quality of interns' teaching experience and also because mentors may contribute to beginning teacher vulnerability in a variety of unexpected ways (see Maguire, 2001). Moreover, mentoring itself is often highly stressful (Bullough & Draper, 2004).

Data Collection and Analysis

Interns responded weekly to an email protocol providing information about their experience as beginning teachers, both high and low points, as well as about their relationship with their mentor, including issues faced and frequency of interaction. Twice during the year, the interns were asked to step back and assess their development as beginning teachers.

Mentors were asked to respond to a similar protocol every other week. After providing two adjectives that characterized their relationship with the interns, they were to identify high and low points for the interns, to describe how they as mentors responded to the high and low points, and to state insights they gained about teaching, mentoring, and themselves as mentors. In addition, they were asked how many times they had met with the interns during the two weeks separating their responses, who set the agenda for those meetings, and what was discussed.

The emails for both the interns and mentors were organized chronologically, and each set was analyzed by two researchers to identify central themes (see Young, Bullough, Draper, Smith, & Erickson, 2005). Interpretations were compared to identify differences, which were remarkably few. Two basic questions were asked: "What is going on here?" and "What is the story?" A matrix was created (Miles & Huberman, 1984) to enable comparison along what appeared to be the salient dimensions of the stories, including development over time, dominant mentor and intern concerns, emotionality, mentoring roles, and kind and quality of mentor–intern relationships (based on who set meeting agendas, how often meetings were held, what quality level of feedback was given, and how the intern assessed the relationship – including praiseworthy acts and disappointments).

Patterns in the Dataset

The dominant pattern of mentoring (12 of 18 intern pairs) was for mentors to be *responsive* to the interns, to do whatever they could to facilitate intern development, and to be supportive, especially emotionally, but not pushy. Other studies have reported similar findings, including a hesitancy by mentors to interfere with novices' autonomy (Wang, 2001). In effect, interns set the agendas for meetings and other mentor action either by requesting specific assistance or by demonstrating a need recognized by the mentor, who responded. A variation (4 of 18 intern pairs) was for the mentors to be directive for a short time at the beginning of the year to help the interns settle in, get oriented to the school, and recognize and begin to grapple with established institutional and curricular tasks, but then to back away into a more responsive mode of offering assistance when it was requested or clearly needed. These mentors consciously avoided being pushy, believing that each intern needed to find her own way into teaching and establish her own comfortable style; they were seldom if ever judgmental or critical in their feedback. The belief that beginning teachers should develop in their own way (Beck & Kosnik, 2002) reportedly is common (see Feiman-Nemser, 2001). Except at the beginning of the year, mentors resisted being directive preferring to respond to the interns rather than to guide them in their development. Like the mentors in a study by Strong and Baron (2004), these mentors went to "extreme efforts […] to avoid giving direct advice" (p. 55).

Interns were offered generous opportunities for interaction with their mentors, at least until mid-year when many withdrew from active mentoring believing the interns needed to be wholly responsible for their classrooms (see Hawkey, 1997). Mentors were considered first and foremost as sources of emotional support and also as resources for materials and ideas useful for teaching. As in the first intern study, interns were overall sharply focused on student learning as a dominant concern, which included the importance of building warm and caring relationships with students. Talk of loving students and of being disappointed when something went awry was common. In both datasets, vulnerability was a dominant mood, but tempered by growing confidence and a maturing optimism from almost every intern about her ability to become an effective teacher.

RESULTS: CASE STUDY OF MRS EDDINGTON, ALLIE, AND KATHERINE

After 16 years as an active mentor, Mrs Eddington was well seasoned in mentoring roles as well as teaching experience. In mentoring both Allie and Katherine (pseudonyms), she began with the mentor pattern dominant in the dataset. As one of the 12 mentioned as "responsive" mentors (Young et al., 2005), she began the year trying to meet all the interns' requests as well as anticipate their needs.

Over time Mrs Eddington had established a set of practices that had proven of value for her and for those she mentored. Before the school year began, she met with the interns to help them plan for the upcoming year. Once school began, each Monday she scheduled what she called a "milk and cookies" meeting where in addition to feeding them she shared information the interns might have missed about the upcoming week and chatted with them about their concerns. By setting the agenda for each Monday meeting a week in advance, Mrs Eddington had time to prepare responses to requests: "I try to find the answer if I don't have it or find someone who is better at [what] they want to know, [like] how to use [the computer grading] program."

Early in the year, Mrs Eddington asked questions to help her interns clarify their thinking and worked with them to identify and find solutions to their problems. She assumed a therapist role when that seemed necessary, giving unqualified and much appreciated emotional support. Sometimes she worked as an aide for her interns, and consistently, she served as a resource seeking to meet any and all of their requests. In addition, she observed each intern weekly and set a time to talk about the observation. She actively sought opportunities to praise the interns' work. She did not wish to correct, but to support them. The data revealed virtually no instances when she acted judgmentally. But although she treated her interns much alike, they responded very differently to her efforts as well as to their classes and teaching tasks.

Needs and Differences

Early in the year, Mrs Eddington realized she had to reconsider her approach to mentoring. For Katherine, Mrs Eddington remained a supportive resource all year long, but Allie, Mrs Eddington concluded, had very different needs. As a mentor, she could not follow Allie's lead. Much like "James" in a study conducted by Page, Rudney, and Marxen (2004), Allie seemed to be unteachable and lacked what Mrs Eddington thought were some basic teaching skills. For the sake of the children and, Mrs Eddington concluded, for Allie's development as a teacher, she needed to become directive and critical, a mentor role not natural or desirable to Mrs Eddington. But she felt the need as a mentor to increase Allie's vulnerability by forcing her to confront her limitations.

Three weeks into the school year, Mrs Eddington was worried that Allie was having serious difficulties, especially with taking charge and managing her class and with creating a positive learning climate. Allie expressed frustration and became increasingly angry with student misbehavior. Finally, one day Allie exploded in class: "I found myself yelling [at the children]." She was embarrassed by her behavior, but disgusted with the class. Despite years of experience as a mentor, Mrs Eddington struggled to decide what to do for Allie, noting that her efforts were failing: "I am not good at confrontation and need help when it comes to correcting behavior that is not acceptable," she admitted. Feeling uncomfortable and seeking confirmation, she visited with the principal for advice and to "see if what I am doing [as a mentor) is appropriate."

Mrs Eddington involved herself more with Allie, asking questions, making suggestions, and indirectly pointing out possible directions for change, hoping that Allie would take hold of some suggestions. Allie resisted. Mrs Eddington scheduled more meetings with Allie and made herself more available to answer questions. Like other struggling teachers who suddenly find themselves the object of increased attention (Page et al., 2004), Allie found these actions disturbing, not helpful; revealing signs of increasing vulnerability, she wrote that she wished Mrs Eddington "didn't come in every day to check up on me. I like my freedom." At the same time, Allie reported a weakening commitment to teaching.

More Desperate Measures

Relying on hints, tactfully offered suggestions, and questions aimed at encouraging Allie to evaluate her teaching and reconsider some decisions did not lead to any apparent changes in Allie's attitude or classroom behavior. By the end of October, almost in desperation Mrs Eddington gathered her courage and stepped out of her comfortable mentor role, set aside her mentor identity, shifted strategies, and told Allie directly that "she was not doing an appropriate job and needed to improve." She then gave Allie specific suggestions to improve her classroom learning climate. The meeting was very upsetting for both Allie and Mrs Eddington. It ended with Mrs Eddington telling Allie, sincerely, that she was "here and would really like to help her become the teacher [...] she [could] be."

Stunned by Mrs Eddington's negative assessment, Allie listened and said very little, only that she "wanted time to think about the situation." She did not recognize herself in Mrs Eddington's criticism. Afterward, doubting that Allie had received the message, Mrs Eddington concluded that she had not been "direct enough." "I tried to [help her] make corrections by being positive and modeling what was expected. I tried to treat her as I would expect her to treat her students in a positive way, hoping that the concept [and practice] would transfer, [but it didn't]."

Only after a university supervisor visited and assessed the situation in much the same way as she had did Mrs Eddington begin to think she "was on the right track" with Allie. Up to that time, she had fretted, prayed, and gingerly felt her way along. Like Allie, Mrs Eddington was feeling vulnerable and in need of external confirmation.

Asked to describe the situation with Allie, Mrs Eddington chose two adjectives, "strained" and "tense." As Allie's anger simmered and deepened, Mrs Eddington forced herself to stay involved in Allie's classroom and with Allie, even though she disliked conflict and would have liked to disengage. As Mrs Eddington became more directive, Allie withdrew further and the situation worsened: for Mrs Eddington, who continued to look to Allie for clues about what she should be doing as mentor, and for Allie, who in frustration blamed her disappointment on the students. "I can't be the only one to care if my students do their work. They must care too," she complained. She also complained about Mrs Eddington, who she charged with being unsupportive: "This week I wish my mentor had given me a compliment." Even while being pushed away Mrs Eddington kept trying to engage Allie in conversation to help her to gain perspective on what Mrs Eddington saw as edginess and failing classroom practices.

A Question and a Hug

One day, Allie reported, Mrs Eddington pointedly asked her, "Do you like your class?" The question stung. "I realized," Allie later wrote, "that I don't always come off as liking my class." After considering the situation, she recognized that she did not laugh often with the children, nor act in other ways to let them know she enjoyed their company and cared about their learning. Still, Allie complained: "This week I wish my mentor had not made me feel like she noticed all the bad things I've done so far." Mrs Eddington took no pleasure in being pointedly critical; this was not the kind of relationship she wanted with an intern — not a role she wished to play as a mentor. She remarked that the stress from her relationship with Allie was spilling over into her home life, and that she was affected "greatly" and negatively by school events, even as she chided herself for not being able to set her feelings aside and better manage her emotions and mood.

While Mrs Eddington was comforted that her actions were confirmed by the visit and advice of the university supervisor, Allie broke down in tears. "Everything just came out. [The supervisor] told me that I have a lot to work on. She told me that right now I'm not a marketable teacher." Recognizing that Allie was devastated by her meeting with the supervisor, Mrs Eddington dropped by her classroom, walked up to her, and gave her a hug. This act of kindness profoundly shook Allie, who, feeling conflicted, momentarily reassessed her feelings about Mrs Eddington. "I need to develop a better relationship with her. She's here for me. I just don't know what I want her to do for me." Yet, only a couple of weeks later, Allie wrote: "[Mrs Eddington] is my supervisor. She wants to be my friend too, but it's a little too weird."

A Christmas Break

Mentor—intern relationships can become volatile when development and evaluation responsibilities clash, as they often do. The first week of December Allie wrote:

> I'm not glad about anything [having to do with] my mentor. She picks me apart. She sits in the back of my classroom and finds anything negative about me and my lessons, and then tells me. I don't feel like she's on my side [...]. I think she is out to get me.

Despite the personal costs, Mrs Eddington reported she was doing all she could to assist Allie, but Allie could only see Mrs Eddington as on the attack, an enemy—and her vulnerability grew, found its object, and turned to anger.

Christmas break came and little had changed. But over the break and away from the children and Mrs Eddington, Allie reviewed her situation and began to reconsider, then reaffirm, her desire to teach. She vowed to work harder and to improve. Time away from mentoring also helped Mrs Eddington gain perspective, and she returned to her duties with renewed energy and resolve, with a revised plan for working with Allie. During the first milk and cookies meeting after the break, Mrs Eddington reviewed "expectations for the new year." She was positive, upbeat, and interested. She reassured Allie, letting her know that she expected her to improve and had faith that she could and would become an effective teacher.

Having reviewed her teaching difficulties during over the break, Allie recognized she needed Mrs Eddington's help to succeed, and she decided she would openly seek it. In effect, she determined to become more teachable.

Allie planned more carefully, made her classes more interesting for the children, was more consistent in managing her class, and focused more sharply on the children's learning. All were topics that Mrs Eddington had addressed earlier, but with no discernable effect. As Allie showed her determination to improve and her increased effort, Mrs Eddington stopped looming over her. She continued to drop by Allie's classroom, but with less frequency and less lingering. Also, she actively sought opportunities to compliment Allie. Gradually, Mrs Eddington started to be more like the responsive mentor she desired to be.

KATHERINE

Allie's emotional turmoil was worsened, and Mrs Eddington's sanity was possibly saved by Katherine's success and by her warm and positive relationship with her mentor — a relationship which Allie recognized and envied. In Katherine, Mrs Eddington found a source of constant delight and personal pride. With Katherine, she was the mentor she wished to be. As Allie described a week in October as "difficult" and "trying," Katherine characterized the same week as "great, crazy, fun, dangerous, silly, hard, exhausting." While Allie lamented that the demands of teaching "never end," Katherine worried that she needed to do more. As Allie complained about lack of support from Mrs Eddington, Katherine expressed gratitude for all the help she received from Mrs Eddington and concern that Mrs Eddington was working far too hard as a mentor and teacher.

In contrast to Allie, Katherine began and ended the year wonderfully teachable and sharply focused on student learning. The children enjoyed being in Katherine's classroom, Mrs Eddington reported. Katherine had relatively few management problems because, as she self-reported, she worked hard and was consistent, and the students started to "follow procedures without me reminding them. [Following my rules] is almost becoming natural to them." Katherine's biggest disappointment came when, as she wrote, "I know that my students are capable of accomplishing something or acting a certain way and they choose not to do it." She carefully attended to student assessment and was delighted when she saw evidence that "most of [the students] have improved."

Katherine worked diligently to improve her practice and unlike Allie, was openly self-critical of her work in the classroom as well as of her treatment of students: "If I expect students to act a certain way, then I must act like that also because they are watching." "I need to tighten down on my transitions." Statements like these were wholly absent in Allie's emails. In November, Katherine reviewed her development as a teacher in response to a reflective question: "Are you on course to becoming the kind of teacher you imagined yourself capable of becoming?" She wrote:

> Yes, I am on course, but I am not there yet. There are so many things that I want to do. Every day I teach I discover things about myself and my students. I know every one of my

students pretty well. I try to get to know them and know what they like and what their personalities are like. I think this is very important.

When thinking about Mrs Eddington, Katherine responded:

I know that she cares and is always willing to help me. By the things that she does for me I can tell that she puts a lot of time, effort, and thought into helping me as a teacher. Not only does she help me as a teacher, but she also helps me as a friend.

Despite her growing confidence and overall teaching success, Katherine also had difficult days. Teaching was not easy for Katherine; it isn't easy for any new teacher. For example, she said that because of having to spend a good deal of time preparing for parent–teacher conferences she did not prepare with care for the next day's classes. Upon arriving at school, the next day she realized she had forgotten she would be observed by her university supervisor, who fortunately "was very understanding." But Katherine wrote, "I was just so stressed out and felt unprepared." In this instance, she worried about herself and the negative evaluation she might receive, but did not. Katherine rarely expressed self-concerns and never survival concerns.

SELF-CONFIRMATION, TRANSCENDENCE, AND POSITIONING

To help make sense of the data, three theoretical lenses will be employed.

Self-confirmation

As with all systems, teachers above all else seek to keep themselves in "an ordered state" (Csikszentmihalyi, 1993, p. 20) – a matter of self-preservation (Kegan, 1982). In desiring security but feeling vulnerable, "all too often we notice and add to our memory store only what supports a strongly held belief, ignoring any that does not" (Hunt, 1993, p. 546). We seek self-confirmation; we want to know that we are all right. When a beginning teacher's conception of self-as-teacher – her identity – proves inadequate or unsuitable, teaching may prove shocking, and one tends sometimes to hunker down for self-protection (Bullough, 1992). Struggling with "reality shock," many "neophyte teachers [...] become disillusioned with their own practice. At this time there is a tendency to blame the preservice teacher education programs for not providing an accurate enough picture of what they might expect" (Goddard & Foster, 2001, p. 360).

Expertise and Self-transcendence

How the threat to self is met determines, in large measure, what sort of teacher the neophyte becomes. Mirroring Dewey's comments noted above, Csikszentmihalyi (1993) observed that: "it is easier to develop selves around goals that lead to stagnation rather than to grow[th]" (pp. 245–246). Self-protection comes naturally, but of particular importance is that humans also crave self-transcendence. On this issue, research on the development of expertise conducted some years ago by Bereiter and Scardamalia (1993) is helpful. Why do some people close down when threatened, while others, those of interest to these authors, press on and move toward becoming expert? Working at the edge of their competence, experts get to be expert by pushing boundaries; literally, they engage in a "venture beyond natural abilities" (p. 4). I have addressed this issue elsewhere:

> What a context demands of a teacher, and the structural and personal support that is available along with the teacher's individual traits, matter a great deal [to the outcome]. With respect to the former: "it seems that our skills develop up to the level that is required for the environment" (Bereiter & Scardamalia, 1993, p. 91). With respect to the later: "persistence, industry, and desire for excellence are relevant," as are innate talents (p. 43). (Bullough & Baughman, 1997, p. 104)

Demonstrating the will to learn, teachers push boundaries, and in doing so, they confront their vulnerability. They do so for various reasons: (1) it feels good to be stretched and to gain in competence; (2) it is part of the "flow" (Csikszentmihalyi, 1993) of progressing; (3) they feel joy in seeing students progress almost despite themselves; (4) they need to avoid boredom; and (5) the context and one's colleagues, in this instance especially one's mentor and fellow interns, expect it, even demand it (see Bullough & Baughman, 1997, p. 105). In addition, as Bereiter and Scardamalia noted, there is a "heroic element" to self-transcendence that resists explanation but is quite evident. It is present where we expect to find teachers with a lively sense of "calling" (see Chapter 5).

Positioning

Positioning theory provides an additional source of insight. Positioning theory opens up the ways humans are "continuously generating their local sense of the real and the good" (Gergen, 1999, p. 176). As an act, positioning "refers to the assignment of fluid 'parts' or 'roles' to speakers in the discursive construction of personal stories that make a person's actions intelligible and relatively determinate as social acts" (van Langenhove & Harre, 1999, p. 17). It is a "discursive process whereby people are located in conversations as observably and subjectively coherent participants in jointly produced storylines" (Davis & Harre, 1999, p. 37). Speakers position others and are in turn positioned in a shifting set of relationships and within evolving storylines. How parts are assigned and played out reveals how events are understood as well as conveys a sense of how one understands self and others. The process of positioning takes place within specific contexts of meaning that bring with them sets of rights, duties, and obligations which reflect differences in power and authority. Moreover, positioning within these contexts may be tacit or intentional, unrecognized or strategic, and forced.

The quest for self-protection in the face of vulnerability, boundary-pushing, and positioning are all important thematic elements of the case study. Allie began the year resisting Mrs Eddington's efforts to assist her. Desiring above all else to confirm her sense of herself as teacher, she was not teachable. Feeling threatened on many fronts — by what she considered to be student misbehavior, by her inability (or resistance to learning) to effectively manage a classroom, and by Mrs Eddington's looming presence – Allie hunkered down seeking self-protection. To do so, she first looked outside of herself to place blame: on students, which is not uncommon among beginning teachers (McDiarmid, 1990); on the busyness of teaching and the impossibility of doing all that teaching requires; on poor parenting of children; and especially on Mrs Eddington who she saw as unfair and deeply biased against her.

In this mood of vulnerability, Allie was unresponsive to Mrs Eddington's initially rather gentle suggestions and remained closed to change. While Allie's teaching methods may have proven less than effective with the students, they were, nonetheless, still her methods, and as such inextricably intertwined with how she thought of herself as a person and as teacher. The two are not separable (Tirri, Husu, & Kansanen, 1999); thus, criticism was personalized. As Sprinthall, Reiman, and Thies-Sprinthall (1996) have shown, "Restructuring means giving up one's current system and often entails strong feelings of fear and sometimes (even) antagonism" (p. 693).

Sharply focused on self-concerns, as Fuller and Bown (1975) describe them, Allie blocked as best as she could the evidence challenging her views of herself and desperately sought self-confirming evidence, even when there seemed to be precious little of it. Positioning herself as "victim," she complained bitterly, and in disbelief, when Mrs Eddington offered few if any compliments. Ironically, Mrs Eddington badly wanted to be complimentary. When Mrs Eddington's negative assessment of Allie's teaching was confirmed by the university supervisor, Allie could only sob in despair. Feeling alone and without allies, Allie was fully exposed and had no place of refuge, no place to hide herself even as she was unwilling or unable to reach out and ask for help.

When Mrs Eddington's gentle suggestions and careful questioning did not have the desired effect, she forced herself to become more direct and more critical, despite her reluctance; perhaps as a by-product of her inner struggle, she became less forgiving. Emphatically, she did not want to engage in such a role. In turn, Allie became more defensive, distant, and depressed – even less teachable. A cycle spiraled both Allie and Mrs Eddington into deepening self-concerns, positioning and being positioned in ways that closed off opportunities for growth and development. Mrs Eddington worried that she could not help Allie and had taken the wrong tact as a mentor, concluding that she was failing; Allie doubted she should teach and worried she lacked the potential to succeed. Mrs Eddington could at least find self-confirmation in Katherine's classroom success and frequent expressions of appreciation. Katherine embraced her internship as an opportunity to grow and with gratitude and grace became increasingly skilled and effective in her teaching. Allie found some solace in classroom moments when the students behaved as she had hoped and enjoyed an activity. Neither she nor Mrs Eddington took pleasure in their relationship. Both had trouble productively managing their increasing sense of vulnerability and Allie's anger. Both resented being positioned as failures.

Facing similarly difficult situations, many mentors disengage to avoid conflict (Slick, 1997) and hurt. But Mrs Eddington could not back off, both because she cared deeply about Allie's development as a teacher and because she was morally committed to the students who badly needed for Allie to succeed. While Allie sought to pull back from confronting her limitations, Mrs Eddington was determined to push her to face and overcome them. But how? Sprinthall et al. (1996) and his colleagues have written that "of all the developmental conditions, the ability to balance support and challenge is probably the most difficult and the most necessary" (p. 693). Determining and then establishing an appropriate balance is a matter of the mentor's knowledge of the person being mentored, along with skill and artistry. It is also a matter of the mentee's teachability.

Supporting conclusions reached by Bereiter and Scardamalia about the development of expertise, Alfi, Assor, and Katz (2004) wrote about the place of failure in learning, commenting that optimal challenge "entails the possibility of temporary failure and frustration" (p. 32). If growth is to occur, then failure, they argued, must be understood to be only temporary; pupils (like beginning teachers) "benefit from temporary failure only if teachers [read mentors] use educational practices that enable pupils to cope well with temporary failure and prevent it from deteriorating into massive failure" (p. 34). On this point, a critical moment took place in Allie's relationship with Mrs Eddington. In pushing Allie to confront her limitations and to test alternatives, Mrs Eddington had difficulty making her believe there was hope that the failure Allie was experiencing was, in fact, likely to be only temporary.

The hug Mrs Eddington gave Allie was intended as a message of encouragement and hope, a statement that Mrs Eddington would help Allie to improve; she could be counted on. While the gesture was important, accounts do not show that Mrs Eddington followed up this gesture with actions to nourish that hope. Prior to the Christmas break, Allie slipped back into anger and finger-pointing blame. Nevertheless, Mrs Eddington, the university supervisor, and of particular importance, the students had pressed Allie to the edge of her abilities; confidence shaken, she had a choice — self-protection and stagnation or growth. Over the holidays, deciding she would not quit teaching, Allie finally chose growth and entered into a "venture beyond [her] natural abilities" in which she badly needed Mrs Eddington.

The pattern of positioning of the triad members is in some respects remarkable. Prior to the beginning of the school year and during the first few weeks of teaching, Mrs Eddington positioned both Allie and Katherine as promising beginning teachers but in need of experience and coaching. The three shared hope and enthusiasm, a time of optimism and excitement. Mrs Eddington had not imagined that her role would go beyond that of a supporting mentor for both Katherine and Allie. She anticipated praising, not criticizing, both interns, celebrating their accomplishments. Katherine confirmed Mrs Eddington's identification of her as competent, allowing Mrs Eddington to express her mentor identity just as she defined it. Implicitly, she and Katherine agreed on each other's place and position in the story of mentor and beginning teacher.

At the first sign of serious difficulty for Allie, Mrs Eddington seemed stunned. For a time, she waited for Allie to request help and to right herself, but she did not. At first, Mrs Eddington held tightly to her preferred mentoring role and resisted redefining herself which a change in her view of Allie and of Allie's abilities and needs would have required. Mrs Eddington was heavily and personally invested in her responsive mentoring role and resistant to change despite disconfirming evidence of the effectiveness of that role with Allie. When Mrs Eddington shifted positions, simultaneously she repositioned Allie as deficit, which was crushing for Allie and the relationship shattered.

Although unspoken, the original agreement between Mrs Eddington and both Katherine and Allie was that Mrs Eddington would be positive, supportive, and generous in sharing her resources. On their part, Katherine and Allie would work hard, love and care for the children, and succeed in the classroom. Presumably, they each knew their parts: their positions in the story of becoming a teacher and of mentoring. Moreover, the interns knew as a matter of duty and obligation that Mrs Eddington would assess them, but they believed this responsibility was secondary to providing assistance and support. When Mrs Eddington assumed the position of assessor and was direct and critical, Allie felt betrayed for a time and responded with muted anger and a new storyline, that of victim. In turn, Mrs Eddington was positioned by Allie as oppressor and enemy, positions foreign to Mrs Eddington's sense of self and her mentor identity. It is important to note that all of this relational movement took place outside of the relationship Mrs Eddington and Katherine enjoyed; to be understood, these interpersonal shifts must be seen against Katherine's and Mrs Eddington's developing (for Allie threatening) friendship. After the Christmas break, another repositioning took place. Neither Mrs Eddington nor Allie was happy with their relationship prior to the break. Both wanted the relationship to change. Despite Allie's withdrawal and apparent unwillingness to take direction, Mrs Eddington had continued to seek engagement. Obviously, she cared deeply about Allie.

After the break, Mrs Eddington intentionally lightened up. She made milk and cookies Mondays more informal, more playful, and less tense. Allie admitted she had serious problems with classroom management and with relating to some of the students, and she reached out for assistance. Rather than resisting, she tested the ideas offered, some of which proved helpful, and was more willing to welcome Mrs Eddington to her classroom. As Mrs Eddington witnessed positive changes in the classroom climate, she found more and more to praise, which encouraged Allie to make additional adjustments and take new risks, as the pressure of a negative assessment was no longer a source of stress. Mrs Eddington found fewer and fewer reasons to be forceful and direct with Allie, and as Allie sought assistance, Mrs Eddington settled into a role more like her relationship with Katherine, a supportive resource but not quite a friend. And the mood changed. At year's end, Mrs Eddington felt comfortable giving Allie a positive evaluation, indicating increased teachability, when she wrote, "Allie continues to listen to feedback about her teaching and incorporate new ideas into her classroom." She had, Mrs Eddington concluded, made significant progress. Despite the difficulties of the first part of the year, she was pleased with what Allie accomplished.

CONCLUSION

Being a teacher and in particular being a "beginning" teacher implies far more than a merely technical set of tasks that can be reduced to effectively applying curriculum knowledge and didactical skills. The person of the teacher is inevitably also at stake in these professional actions [...]. When one's identity as a teacher, one's professional self-esteem or one's task perception are threatened by the professional context, then self-interests emerge. They always concern the protection of one's professional integrity and identity as a teacher. (Kelchtermans & Ballet, 2002, p. 110)

Standing back from the story an observer might wonder, "Was there an alternative available to Mrs Eddington? Did she need to push Allie so hard in the hope she would become more teachable?" Despite the risks involved, the data suggest there was no other viable alternative. Unlike Katherine, who welcomed Mrs Eddington's feedback and involvement in her class, Allie rejected Mrs Eddington's overtures of help time and time again; she seemed determined to meet her challenges alone. Whether or not the appropriate balance between challenge and support needed to move beyond self-concerns was achieved is not certain, but Mrs Eddington, a highly respected mentor, must be given the benefit of the doubt.

Mrs Eddington desperately did not want to be critical and directive, but she was committed to Allie's professional growth and to doing all she could to assure a good educational experience for Allie's students. If this meant repositioning herself, and becoming hard and demanding, Mrs Eddington would do it, albeit reluctantly and with great difficulty. A mentee's interests and children's interests may sometimes clash, and if Mrs Eddington had been forced to make a choice, she would have chosen the children over Allie and terminated Allie's internship. It is clear that such an action would have been devastating for both Allie and for Mrs Eddington, whose conception of herself as a mentor might not have recovered.

To teach is to be vulnerable and so it is with mentoring. Managing vulnerability is a large part of learning to teach and being effective as a teacher, and of being a mentor as well. For a mentor, managing one's own vulnerability is essential to creating the conditions and providing the kind of support and challenge needed to assist a beginning teacher to learn to manage her own vulnerabilities, to get beyond self-concerns, to become or remain teachable, and to maximize growth. At times, despite hesitancy, it is probably necessary, as Page et al. (2004) suggested, for a mentor to position a beginning teacher where limited confrontation cannot be avoided, especially given the urgency of the mentor's responsibility to protect children. Beginning teachers must be helped to understand and to confront their weaknesses in order to realize their potential, even when they are hesitant to do so and even when mentors, who badly want to be supportive and not directive, would rather disengage than face the stress and conflict that may come with confrontation. While the personal cost to mentors of forcing a beginning teacher to face herself can be high, as it was for Mrs Eddington who worried constantly about Allie and Allie's students, the moral and professional costs of not doing so are far greater and much more lasting.

CHAPTER 9

AN INQUIRY INTO EMPATHY AND TEACHING: IS EMPATHY ALL IT IS CRACKED UP TO BE?

INTRODUCTION

Over the past few decades, empathy has attracted significant research interest in a variety of fields including psychology and philosophy (Coplan & Goldie, 2011; Lipari, 2014; Maibom, 2014a), medicine (Jamison, 2014), nursing (Penprase, Oakley, Ternes, & Driscoll, 2015), and teacher education. In psychology and in the popular literature (de Waal, 2009), which has flowed into education, there has been a great deal of speculation about the role of empathy in learning and development (Iacoboni, 2008; for a critical assessment see Hickok, 2014). In education and teacher education, an additional and very important influence has been the persistent moral and educational challenge presented by the increasing student diversity amplifying the need for teachers to connect across differences: "Researchers agree that empathy is a professional disposition of effective teachers in urban settings and that its application likely improves their teaching effectiveness with students of color" (Warren, 2014, p. 396). Empathy is widely celebrated as a valued quality of successful teachers, credited with healing powers. Yet, there is rather little agreement about just what empathy is or how it works.

Drawing on a variety of studies, this chapter explores empathy and teaching. The intent is to expose a slice of the inner drama of teaching by illuminating and complicating the commonly held and seemingly common sense conclusion that teachers ought to become more empathetic.

To provide some context for the discussion, the first section of this chapter introduces a preschool assistant teacher, Emma, who was thought by her teammates and supervisors to have a serious empathy deficit. Conceptual and definitional problems with empathy are then addressed, followed by discussion of the place of cognition in empathy. If empathy is a valued teacher disposition, some effort is likely needed to determine both its presence and growth, and so, the next section considers measurement issues, including difficulties that arise with heavy reliance on self-reports. The following section addresses a question: "Can there be too much empathy?" Research on empathic inference and accuracy is then discussed. The chapter is brought to closure with a suggestion to turn away from empathy as a teaching disposition in favor of a kind of listening designed to help bridge the experiential, cultural, and knowledge gaps that separate teachers from their students.

AN EMPATHY DEFICIT: "EMMA IS JUST NOT A GOOD FIT"

For a study of an early childhood Head Start program housed in a chronic homeless facility (Bullough & Hall-Kenyon, 2018), I spent a spring term observing in a classroom and interviewing various participants (with IRB, Head Start administrative and participant approval), among them the family advocate, the lead teacher, and the two assistant teachers, including Emma (name and select details changed). Ethnically Chinese, Emma was one of three adopted children. She grew up near Washington D.C. Both of her adoptive parents were highly educated; her father worked for the US federal government in a high-profile position. In contrast to her two colleagues at Head Start, Emma's childhood had been highly privileged. As a child development major in college, Emma felt confident in her knowledge of children and, at the time of the interviews, was planning to pursue a graduate degree in special education in a "year or two."

Before coming to Head Start (where she was in her fourth month when interviewed), Emma had worked in a variety of early childhood settings, where, she said, she was not given "enough [of a] challenge." "I've always served the population where the parents are paying thousands of dollars for their children to go to preschool. I haven't served children whose parents neglect them, who don't have to pay for it [like Head Start]." She enjoyed teaching children, she said, particularly special needs children, those with autism spectrum disorders or Down syndrome. "I love [teaching]," she said.

Observing in the classroom prior to interviewing Emma, it was apparent she was disengaged: disconnected from the children and their parents. Generally, she stayed busy during class time but mostly kept to herself. There appeared to be a disjunction between what Emma said about herself as a teacher and what I witnessed as an observer. In an interview, I asked her indirectly about the children and their families: "I've learned [...] [to not] get my hopes too high for [the parents] just like [the] kids. I have to put my expectations pretty low because they don't know any better. They don't know how to be parents." Parents frustrated Emma: "Okay, look. I've been trying to teach your child every single day not to yell at his friends [...] and you're not teaching him that." She said,

> "[I'm] frightened [...] for the children [...] I fear for the children when I leave for home [...]. In training, [my instructors] always said, 'You can't take work home with you.' And I'm like, 'Ok, fine.' But I fear for them."

When upset, she said she had difficulty coping, but running helped, and "I'll just go home and walk. I will walk it all off."

Emma commented that when she began working in Head Start she was surprised by much of the children's behavior, which was new to her.

> When I was first here, I was confused about what to do [...]. [I thought], "I know how this all works, but being slapped and being hit by these children? What's going on?" [Eventually] I realized, they're being taught this at home. They're watching all this stuff happen at home. It's not because of me. It's because they're so angry at someone else.

When asked if she had any "favorites" among the children, Emma mentioned a girl who, she said, she had become "really good friends" with: "[The girl] always says my name first" (of the three teachers) at the start of the day. Emma could not think of a single boy she felt connected to. After a pause, she mentioned one boy who, she said, "compliments me when I feel ugly; he's like, 'Miss Emma, you're cute.'" Emma was clearly struggling and was increasingly concerned about her own well-being, perhaps more so than the children's.

As the term progressed, Emma's colleagues said they were having difficulty working with her. Early in their time together they were disappointed with the quality of Emma's lesson plans, but more importantly they were concerned about the quality of her relationships with both the parents and the children, which, they said, did not improve. Gradually, Emma became more of an aide than a teacher – someone responsible for the more custodial matters than the relational and instructional responsibilities of teaching young children. During 15 classroom observations, for example, she set up for meals and snacks and cleaned up. Not once did I observe her teach or see her contribute to the required documentation of children's behavior.

In May, feeling very unhappy and disappointed, the lead teacher and the other assistant teacher both mentioned that Emma would not be back next year. The assistant teacher commented that Emma "talks down to the parents," and then quickly added that she would "probably be fine" in a less challenging setting. The family advocate commented,

> Emma has a lot of theoretical background, but [this is] not the site for Emma. I've had numerous parents come up [to me] saying they don't even want her to talk to them [...]. [She] is just not a good fit.

As those who worked closely with Emma characterized the issue, the "fit" problem was not that Emma lacked knowledge of child development or teaching skill per se. In fact, the facilitator commented that Emma possessed considerable knowledge of special education "behavior techniques." But, the facilitator added, Emma tended to rely on those techniques regardless of whether or not a child responded positively to them. Where Emma believed she was coming to know the students and their families well, what her colleagues saw was someone who failed to connect, who failed not merely to understand the challenges of the children or their families, but to experience empathy.

DEFINITIONS AND EXPECTATIONS

The origins of empathy are generally located in the evolutionary need of humans to "promote in-group cooperation" (de Waal, 2009, p. 221). Thus, whatever empathy is, it "builds on proximity, similarity, and familiarity" contributing to human "solidarity" (de Waal, 2009, p. 223). Moreover, individual variations in the ability to be empathetic have been widely explored, notably in studies of psychopathology and of autism (Maibom, 2014b). There is agreement that empathy involves the arousal of emotions caused by recognition of another person's suffering and concern for that person's well-being.

Empathy has inspired considerable enthusiasm. Baron-Cohen (2011), for example, asserted empathy is *"one of the most valuable resources in the world* (italics in original) [...]. With empathy, we have a resource to resolve conflict, increase community cohesion, and dissolve another person's pain."* Unfortunately, as Baron-Cohen claimed, empathy has been "taken for granted" (p. 183) and, given the state of the world we live in, needs somehow to be "turned on" (p. 182). Assumed to have both genetic and environmental groundings, thus suggesting potential for development, empathy is commonly assumed *to be* an emotion. It is not. As Maibom (2014b) suggested, empathy is, rather, "a *way* of feeling emotions" (p. 9). Echoing a widely held view, Baron-Cohen's definition makes the point clearly: empathy is the *"ability to identify what someone else is thinking or feeling and to respond to their thoughts and feelings with an appropriate emotion"* (italics in original; 2011, p. 16). From general agreement on empathy's origins, its genetic and environmental influences, its emotional loading, and its common inaccurate classification as an emotion, definitions diverge.

In the introduction to the edited collection *Empathy*, Coplan and Goldie (2011) portrayed the range of empathy definitions in such broad strokes that readers are left wondering about the sense that can be made of such a complex concept. Differences run deep across fields depending on research interest and content: whether that content involves responses to literature and art; study of supporting brain structures; application to morality, ethics, and prosocial behavior; or conceptions of human nature and development. A fundamental source of difference is found in the relative emphasis placed on the affective and cognitive elements of empathy.

Coplan (2011) emphasized cognition with the following definition: "Empathy is a complex imaginative process in which an observer simulates another person's situated psychological states while maintaining clear self-other differentiation" (p. 5). By *complex* she indicated that empathy has both cognitive and affective dimensions; by *imaginative*, she acknowledged that empathy "involves the representation of a target's states that are activated by, but not directly accessible through, the observer's perception" (pp. 5–6). Finally, her use of the term *simulates* suggested "that the observer replicates or reconstructs the target's experiences, while maintaining a clear sense of self-other differentiation" (p. 6). Hence, for Coplan, empathy involves "affective matching, other-oriented perspective-taking, and self-other differentiation" (p. 6).

Theorists and researchers express considerable disagreement, particularly about the second and third elements of Coplan's definition. For example, respecting replication, Hoffman (2000), among others (Maibom, 2014b), set a more generous standard: that what is felt (or thought) need only be similar to rather than identical with what is felt by a target, along with attentiveness to the other's welfare. The greater the difference between individuals, the greater the difficulty of even approximating what another person is thinking or feeling. Given the work of teaching and the increasing diversity of student populations, this criticism is well taken.

The third element, self-other differentiation, appears to be of special importance for teaching. Certainly, a teacher must not forget she is a responsible adult but not a student's parent or, for that matter, an older friend. When confronting an emotionally charged situation involving children, teachers must respond ethically to a wide range of sometimes conflicting interests and needs that may not be adequately understood. If, for example, at such times, a teacher fully enters into one child's hurt or needs forgetting momentarily that she is the teacher, as her concern dilates on satisfying that particular child – as she understands his needs – she may neglect less conspicuous needs of other children. As Bloom (2016; see also Hoffman, 2014) observed, when a target's needs come to dominate, empathy may be easily manipulated and the results be unjust.

The idea that empathy requires imagination underscores the cognitive demands of perspective taking and suggests that empathy is concerned with beliefs – what is believed is being felt or thought by a target – and beliefs may be biased and false (see Kauppinen, 2014, p. 101). Focusing on the cognitive elements of empathy helps distinguish empathy from "emotional contagion" (Coplin, 2014, p. 7). Emotional contagion involves automatically mimicking others' feelings and behavior, as witnessed in crowds and spectator sports, for example. "Spirit week" at a high school is not designed to evoke empathy, but involuntary arousal which encourages in-group affiliation with emotions meant to be "caught" and shared.

Contagion is sometimes thought of as a low form of empathy: "It seems that what transforms emotional contagion into other-related emotions is cognition" (Maibom, 2014, p. 5). The relative importance placed on affect and cognition has led to distinctions between lower and higher levels or forms of empathy. Representing a folk theory of empathy, the former is thought to be more affective, immediate, and preverbal, the later more cognitive and regulated, and more mature. As Kauppinen (2014) argued, "There are different mechanisms whereby the feelings of others are transmitted to us. Some are cognitively undemanding (low-level empathy) and can be found in other species [...] and others involve inference or association" (p. 100).

In high-level (mature) empathy, processes of self-regulation (SR) generally hold a central and important place. Following an extensive review of the relevant literature, Nigg (2017) described two families of SR processes: one "top-down" and the other "bottom-up." He concluded top-down processes (or competencies) are "deliberate," involving "voluntary or limited-capacity regulation of the self by the self," which includes "both simple processes like response inhibition, and complex processes like preparatory planning to regulate future behavior" (p. 375). Involving complex cognition, some forms of effortful control (EC) or cognitive control are understood to support reasoning and planning essential to successful adaptation. Eisenberg, Smith, and Spinrad (2004), referring to EC, argued that "awareness of one's planned behavior and subjective feelings of voluntary control of thoughts and feelings [...] come into play when resolving conflict (e.g., in regard to discrepant information), correcting errors, and planning new actions" (p. 264).

In contrast, bottom-up processes are "reactive," when behavior or cognition is interrupted and the interruptions become regulating (p. 276). "Reactive control pertains to aspects of control (or the lack thereof) that are relatively nonvolitional and usually automatic, and difficult to modulate effortfully; reactive control is viewed as less flexible and often less adaptive than volitional self-regulation" (Spinrad & Eisenberg, 2015, p. 3). While it appears that SR is heritable, it is also influenced by culture and experience and can be improved through a variety of interventions (see Veronneau, Hiatt, Fosco, & Dishion, 2014 on EC). Teachers, for example, often practice regulating their emotions (Sutton, Mudrey-Camno, & Knight, 2009). As Decety and Jackson (2004) argued, true "empathy [is] an intentional capacity" and is "not a simple resonance of affect between the self and other. It involves an explicit representation of the subjectivity of the other. It is a consciously experienced phenomenon" (p. 93).

MEASUREMENT PROBLEMS

Measures of empathy generally test for either the low affective or high cognitive level of empathy, as described above. Most measures rely on self-reports. Seeking to get at "situational" rather than "dispositional" empathy (Maibom, 2014b, p. 20), vignettes are sometimes used to set the context (see Dedousis-Wallace, Shute, Varlow, Murrihy, & Kidman, 2014). Responses to music, literature, artwork, and facial expressions, along with a variety of physiological measures have been used. Physiological measures, as Maibom (2014b) concluded, "are good indicators of emotional reactions, mostly aversive, to others in distress. On their own, however, they are not very precise indicators of *what* emotions are experienced" (p. 22).

Perhaps, the most widely used self-report instrument is the 28-item Interpersonal Reactivity Index (IRI), which consists of four correlated subscales, each thought to represent a "distinctive pattern of [empathetic] relationships" (Davis, 1983, p. 123). The IRI gives a measure of what Davis argues is a "global concept of empathy" (p. 113). The first subscale, Perspective Taking, includes an assessment of the "tendency to spontaneously adopt the psychological point of view of others" (p. 114), here described as low-level reactive, affective empathy. The second, Fantasy, measures "respondents' tendencies to transpose themselves imaginatively into the feelings and actions of fictitious characters in books, movies, and plays." The third, Empathic Concern, seeks to assess feelings of sympathy and concern for "unfortunate others," and, the fourth, Personal Distress, "measures 'self-oriented' feelings of personal anxiety and unease in tense interpersonal settings" (p. 114).

Maibom (2014b), among others (Bloom, 2016; Decety & Lamm, 2009, p. 208), has criticized reliance on self-report instruments in empathy studies:

> There are [...] good reasons to take self-reports with a grain of salt [...]. [People] often have relatively little access to their mental processes, but are likely to confabulate if pressured. Empathy self-reporting has been found to be influenced by social desirability, desire for

positive self-evaluation, and stereotyping [...]. [Many reported] sex differences [are] due to people attempting to live up to stereotypes, [and] there are other curious results, such as the fact that violent sex offenders have been found to score high on sympathy (empathic concern) on the Interpersonal Reactivity Index. (p. 21)

Bloom (2016) stated the issue boldly: "Some people who aren't actually empathic might believe they are or want others to believe they are and answer accordingly" (p. 78). He continued by calling attention to many of the scales which "include questions that are related to empathy in the sense of mirroring others' feelings, but they also have questions that tap other capacities [which correlate], such as kindness or compassion or interest in others," concluding that it is unclear just what is being measured, a criticism he directed specifically toward the IRI (pp. 78–82).

Some of the challenges of measurement are exemplified by a study that sought to measure "multicultural dispositions" of teacher education students, especially conceptual difficulties. Drawing on responses of 372 preservice teachers, the authors set out to develop a self-report instrument that would measure "five multicultural dispositions of teachers" (Jensen, Whiting, & Chapman, 2018, p. 121) drawn from a literature review of "relevant [disposition] measures" (p. 124): empathy, meekness, social awareness, inclusion, and advocacy. Setting aside the insistent difficulty of determining just what a disposition is (see Meidl & Bauman, 2015), across three phases of analysis two of the dispositions, empathy and inclusion, were merged with the other three. Of 37 original items, eight were intended to capture empathy. Of these, two were reassigned to meekness ("I care what others have to say and listen well to others" and "I feel intimidated by students who come from different backgrounds than me"); four were shifted to advocacy (including "I am able to understand others' perspectives even without the same experiences" and "It hurts my feelings when students are mean to each other"); and two were moved to social awareness ("I like learning about beliefs that differ from mine" and "Student performance is primarily due to their beliefs and effort"). The final survey instrument included 22 items and excluded both empathy and inclusion. Of the three remaining scales, two had only moderately acceptable statistical properties.

When assumed to be a disposition essential to effective teaching, empathy clearly presents a serious if not unresolvable measurement problem. Yet, as will be suggested shortly, there may be other avenues for getting at those aspects of empathy that are widely taken to be of educational importance: specifically coming to greater understanding of and appreciation for another's otherness.

EMPATHY AND DISTRESS

Personal distress, the fourth subscale of the IRI, has less to do with empathy per se than with what happens when there is an empathy surfeit. "The experience of empathy can lead to [...] personal distress[,] an aversive, self-focused emotional reaction to the apprehension or comprehension of another's emotional state or condition [that produces] confusion between self and other"

(Decety & Lamm, 2009, p. 199). A result of putting oneself into another's situation and being unable to "escape from the other's distress cues" (Spinrad & Eisenberg, 2014, p. 61), resulting in one's own distress, is "empathic over-arousal," a sort of "vicarious traumatization" that produces a "turning away from victims" (Hoffman, 2014, p. 77). Expressing a concern for the well-being of caregivers, Figley (2002) characterized this state as "compassion fatigue" (p. 1433), which can lead to exhaustion and burnout (see Vandenberghe & Huberman, 1999).

Empathy, then, is thought to be somewhat fragile although it may be more sturdy than is often thought (see Platsidou & Agaliotis, 2017, p. 68), underscoring the importance of self-regulation, notably emotional regulation and balance. Distress may also arise when an individual, a teacher or school principal, for example, is as a matter of policy made accountable or assumes responsibility for issues that are well beyond her power or ability to manage or resolve and then is blamed for disappointing results (see De Jong, Grundmeyer, & Yankey, 2017; Santoro, 2011). Policy-makers have long-shifted responsibility for a wide range of social ills, from deepening social and economic inequality to bad driving, onto public education while dismissing their own responsibility.

Considerable research exists on emotional regulation. Jiang, Vauras, Volet, and Wang (2016), for example, described several teacher strategies of importance to achieving some sort of personally productive balance: situation selection ("approaching or avoiding certain people or situations to modify their emotional impact," p. 27); situation modification; attention deployment ("focusing attention on or moving attention away from a situation to change the impact," p. 28); cognitive change ("modifying one's evaluations of a situation or one's ability to manipulate a situation," p. 28); and suppression.

Hoffman (2014) discussed another self-regulation strategy that, given the nature of teaching, may be difficult to employ but nevertheless is noteworthy: "ideal-regulated empathy," a "broadly affective response to another's perceived situation that is regulated by reference to an ideal perspective" (p. 105). In this strategy, one steps back and outside of oneself, pauses, however briefly, and assuming what would be or perhaps is the view another person holds of the situation — Jesus, one's mother, a respected teacher or friend — reappraises in light of consequences of the various possible actions and acts (rather than reacts). Ideal-regulated empathy may not involve recalling another person: one might simply recall one's better or best self or reflect on a central moral commitment or animating belief that may serve habitually as a standard of judgment. Mature emotional self-regulation requires (and assumes) considerable self-knowledge, including a sense (or openness to the discovery) of where one's blind spots lie. Such ambitions underscore the claim that teacher education ought to begin with explorations of the self (Bullough & Gitlin, 1995; Bullough et al., 1991), what more recently has been thought of as involving teacher identity (see Chapter 6).

EMPATHIC INFERENCE AND ACCURACY

As noted earlier, empathy is ordinarily assumed to involve making inferences, which Ickes (2009) described as "everyday mind reading that people do whenever they attempt to infer other people's thoughts and feelings" (p. 57). Ickes' interest has been to determine how accurate such inferences are — whether humans are as good at reading other people as we think we are (see Ickes, 2003). Empathic accuracy "is the extent to which such everyday mind reading attempts are successful" (Ickes, 2009, p. 57). It should be noted that "empathic accuracy does not guarantee a compassionate response from the perceiver" (Hodges, Lewis, & Ickes, 2015, p. 322).

Seeking to avoid the weaknesses of self-report data and to get at inference and accuracy, Ickes and his colleagues developed a research program relying on videotaping and analyzing structured and unstructured interactions. Ickes (2009) described the general approach this way:

> Perceivers infer the thoughts or feelings of one or more target persons from a videotaped record of a social interaction in which the target(s) have participated. Immediately following these interactions, the target persons report the actual thoughts and feelings they remember having had at specific points on the videotape. The perceivers in our studies are later asked to view the videotape and, at each of the previously identified "tape stops," infer the specific thought or feeling that the target person(s) reported at that point. When all of the data for a given study are complete, trained raters then compare the content of each actual thought or feeling with the content of the corresponding inference and assign "accuracy points" that are aggregated to create an overall index of empathic accuracy. (p. 58)

Ickes and his colleagues studied a wide variety of persons and kinds of interactions including between strangers, peers, couples in abusive relationships, and dating partners and found their measures to be both valid and reliable.

Several factors have been identified that positively influence a *perceiver*'s empathic accuracy, some of which speak directly to the challenge of teaching (or speaking) across differences. For example, generally mistrusted, "stereotypes may be a very valuable tool(s) for achieving empathic accuracy" (Hodges et al., 2015, p. 325). Perhaps after a second or third year of successfully teaching second graders without having changed buildings, teachers come to planning over the summer with helpful assumptions about where to begin. Hodges explained that having shared past experiences and perhaps overlapping friendships, "acquaintanceship has been shown to give friends an advantage over strangers in guessing each other's thoughts [...] and established dating partners may be even more advantaged" (p. 325). Sharing backgrounds allows perceivers to "start to develop a person-specific schema quite quickly that can be used in making empathic inferences" (p. 326).

Measured intelligence has been found to influence empathic accuracy "but only when the targets were strangers to the perceivers" (p. 328). Given these findings, Hodges et al. concluded that a shift to target variables makes sense. Some targets, they argued, are simply better at revealing their thoughts and feelings than are others: "Although perceivers and targets are equal players in [interaction], when it comes to empathic accuracy research, perceivers have hogged the limelight" (p. 330).

Giving greater attention to targets leads to a conclusion of particular importance to this chapter that "verbal cues, or what a target said, have mattered much more than visual and vocal nonverbal cues [...]. [O]ne obvious target characteristic is the extent to which a target openly expresses information that is diagnostic of his or her current private, subjective mental experience" (p. 330). Expressed differently, some targets are more transparent and more easily (and willing to be) read than others, and this is a quality and skill that can be taught and learned (Ickes, 2003, p. 106). Yet, for a variety of reasons, such as a desire to maintain a relationship or a sense of being threatened, some people, young and old, may be intentionally opaque, self-protective: they do not want to be accurately read. Comparably, and suggesting the strong impact of confirmation bias, when a target is feeling threatened "empathic accuracy may be affected by motivation to maintain a particular view of the world and how people within it behave" (Hodges et al., 2015, p. 337).

Moreover, it is apparent that relying on targets to set the standard of empathic accuracy has problems; many people may not be consciously aware of what they are or were thinking and feeling during an interaction, but still they will say something that then sets the accuracy standard for the perceiver. Hodges and her colleagues (2015) concluded the "other-minds problem pretty much guarantees that people will be making up quite a bit when they try to read other people's minds" (p. 343). Additionally, as teachers, especially those who teach young children, well know, young people often do not know what they are feeling.

Overall, the evidence suggests that despite the claims made for the power of empathy "people are rarely very good at guessing another person's thoughts" (p. 343). Mostly, they are wrong, especially on first guess. Humans are at their best when they know one another well, are friends, and share a framework of beliefs (Ickes, 2003). No surprise, intimate knowledge appears to be most valuable for achieving greater accuracy: "the type of knowledge acquired by experiencing the other person's thoughts and feelings as they are expressed in a close, personal relationship" (p. 101), including the sort of relationships that may form between teachers and students. Furthermore, perceivers are generally much more accurate inferring negative than positive emotions (Ickes, 2009, p. 65): anger and disgust, for example. Finally, "instead of attempting mind reading, [the most] highly effective way to find out what another person is thinking [and feeling] is to ask that person" (Hodges et al., 2015, p. 340) which, by inference, requires the existence of shared and safe spaces, hopefully including schools and classrooms.

EMMA AND EMPATHY

Approximately two months after Emma began teaching in Head Start, all of the teachers in the wider city program, 122 of a possible 154 leads and assistant teachers, completed a survey that included items to assess efficacy, well-being, work satisfaction, concerns, and commitment. Each also completed a lifeline. On her lifeline, Emma indicated that obtaining employment in Head Start had been a personal high point but at the time of completing the survey her view had changed. Nonetheless, her efficacy scores were very high, indicating confidence in her teaching ability. For example, she marked the item "How much can you assist families in helping their children do well in school?" as eight on the 1–9 (high) Likert scale. On the scale seven indicated *quite a bit*, while nine represented *a great deal*. Emma reported her greatest worry was that she would not be able to "help [her] students with their current needs." Her greatest stress was when there was an "outbreak of [bad] behavior" in class. She indicated satisfaction with how her team members were working together as well as with work conditions.

Emma reported being somewhat dissatisfied with the quality of the "supervision" she received. This negative assessment was likely because she was given only a very short orientation to Head Start before beginning her assignment, and no specific effort was made to help her prepare for the children she would be teaching or to help her become knowledgeable about their life challenges. Lacking relevant experience, Emma struggled to imaginatively place herself into the children's lives. The assumption appears to have been that given her solid academic background and prior early childhood teaching experience Emma was well prepared to teach, and that she would, with the help of her teammates, quickly learn what she needed to know and be able to do to be successful. In addition, as the program was all day and classes were held five days a week, no formal planning time was scheduled. Outside of informal conversations during nap time and a few minutes prior to the beginning of class in the morning, not a single planning session was observed. In effect, Emma was expected to fit into the team and to learn on the job. Emma's survey responses indicated that initially she felt confident she was up to the challenge.

Reviewing Emma's interview comments and the classroom observation notes (see above) through a lens informed by the studies of empathy described to this point is revealing. Emma began teaching assuming she already knew the children – a common teacher assumption. They would be challenging, she thought, but she wanted to be challenged. Had she been asked to fill out an empathy survey, she would have reported herself to be very empathetic, able, and willing to connect with children and their parents. She projected her prior experience as a teacher in preschools designed for very privileged children onto the children and the parents of Head Start, for the most part assuming she already "knew" and understood them. Operating bottom-up and reactively, she also brought to the experience assumptions (biases) about herself as a person and as a teacher. When Emma's colleagues described her as having a "fit" problem, they were speaking specifically of the apparent inaccuracy of her assumptions.

Emma still seemed to consider herself empathetic, despite increasing evidence she was not able to meaningfully engage with the children or their parents. She was not enjoying her work. She faced a choice: to reconsider her assumptions or to invest energy to bolster them and thus let the bottom-up reactive and affective elements of empathy maintain control. As noted previously, mature empathy involves "top-down" deliberate cognitive processes, including self-regulation, and demands the effort required for response inhibition and planning. Emma chose to locate deficiency in both the children and their parents, not in herself or her worldview: "I have to put my expectations pretty low because they don't know any better." One set of stereotypes about the nature of children and parents that she had brought with her to Head Start from her prior teaching experience was ultimately replaced by another set, neither one of which supported the children's learning or her growth and development as a teacher. Running and walking helped her suppress the troubling feelings.

The parents, Emma assumed, were childlike and incompetent; thus increasingly, despite her high self-efficacy score on the survey, she came to believe there was little she could do to change the situation. Emma "talked down" to parents, believing they undermined the work of the teachers. Rather than seeking to build the sort of intimacy of relationship that mature empathy requires, she modified the situation and gradually withdrew into the safe and predictable classroom administrative routines of teaching, such as those associated with serving breakfast and lunch. At the same time, Emma said she feared for the children. But the evidence suggests she feared for herself even more, particularly when the children behaved aggressively, as they often did, which proved deeply troubling and so very unlike how children were supposed to behave.

When interviewed, Emma showed signs of distress, expressed as increasing concern with self-preservation. The two children Emma mentioned, the first as a "friend," were valued because they seemed to value Emma: one calling out her name "first" in the morning and the other telling her she was "cute" when she felt "ugly." That she purportedly "talked down to parents" represents another self-protective strategy — dismissing potential critics and putting them in their rightful place. Over time, for Emma pity came to masquerade as empathy.

If Emma were to come to understand the children's behavior that she described as surprising, relational intimacy would be necessary; bottom-up affective and reactive forms of empathy would need to be disciplined or seriously weakened by top-down cognitive processes. In no other way could trust have been established then sustained. For that to happen, Emma needed help, especially from her colleagues who both were recognized by Head Start management as highly effective teachers. The lead teacher, for example, was one of six master teachers program-wide. Echoing past studies of teacher burnout, empathy is generally thought to be an individual capacity and sometimes problem, mostly natural, rather than an expression of cultural or communal commitments. Clearly, Emma needed experience that would have provided her with consistent opportunities to talk with, play with, and learn from the children, and to become part of their lives, an ally. She also needed mentoring and coaching. But for this to happen she would need to have been receptive to the help offered, and in her growing distress, she may not have been open.

CONCLUSION

Among educators, the goodness and value of empathy are taken for granted – one good among the many that teacher education ought to encourage. But as shown in this chapter, there is much debate and lively discussion about just what empathy is, what it does, what it cannot do, and whether or not it has potentially harmful side effects related to distress or even represents a cover for moral blindness. As a form of fellow feeling, empathy expresses a species' concern for one's in-group and its comfort and survival. To stretch a capacity that appears to enable what is believed to be a relatively easy bonding with those who we consider like ourselves to include others who we assume to be in some significant respects quite different requires rethinking empathy, especially as effortful learning: top-down, cognitive, and intentional. Only by such efforts can what goes as unsaid – the biases and prejudices hiding in low-level empathy– be revealed and their moral mischief be exposed. As I have tried to show, not only is empathy a complex and perplexing concept, but in its bottom-up form it is also a source of deeply disturbing beliefs and potentially unjust actions.

For educators who find in empathy a vibrant disposition to be cultivated, clearly more careful and critical thought is necessary to turn the concept into something approaching a point of action that actually leads somewhere promising. But then one must ask challenging questions: what is gained by elevating empathy to the honorific status of a teacher education disposition to be taught and measured? Are the claims made for empathy reasonable, justifiable, and realizable? As debate continues over what a disposition is and what dispositions (if any) should find place within teacher education, it is important to recall what schools are for and what it is teachers are expected to do (and be) within them.

During the past few years, a substantial literature has addressed the value and importance of appreciative and engaged listening – not just speaking – for the health of democratic institutions and of citizenship (see Bullough & Rosenberg, 2018; Dobson, 2014). Although across much of the world discussion of citizenship as an educational aim has been displaced by vocational ambitions, some vision of the most desirable forms of social living is inevitably embedded in all programs. As an educational aim, citizenship raises the fundamental question of how do we and how should we live together? – a central question in the quest for social justice. Within teacher education, this question underpins the desire to strengthen multicultural understandings and commitments. It is here where the literature on listening has importance. Recall the conclusion of Hodges et al. (2015) concerning empathetic accuracy (quoted above) that "instead of attempting mind reading [the most] highly effective way to find out what another person is thinking [and feeling] is to ask that person" (p. 340).

Among the promising and desirable dispositions for teacher education is what Dobson (2014) described as "apophatic listening" (p. 64), a deep compassionate form of listening that indicates a strong desire for "attunement" (see Lipari, 2014) with another. Elbow's (1986) notion of "methodological belief" gets at a similar idea: that to understand another requires not only listening but "actually [trying] to believe any view or hypothesis that a participant seriously wants to advance" (p. 260). In such moments, a "bargain" takes place, with "an exchange of temporary or conditional assent" (p. 259). Hence, to listen *apophatically* requires effort and self-regulation, but can be learned and improved. The point, as Rodriguez, Monreal, and Howard (2018) argue, is that teachers must listen to and understand children's stories in part to develop the "sociopolitical awareness" (p. 11) required to respond helpfully and appropriately to their life situations.

To think of Emma needing to develop greater empathy as the solution to her disengagement with the children and the parents she was supposed to serve — and to assume that such an aim is within the reach of preservice teacher education — seems to be a nonstarter, only a promise of failure. In contrast, to think of Emma's problem as a need to learn to listen, understand, and then thoughtfully act seems both possible and promising.

CHAPTER 10

LIGHT AND DARK HUMOR AND THE INNER DRAMA OF TEACHING

INTRODUCTION

Me thinks I hear the Philosophers opposing it, and saying 'tis a miserable thing for a man to be foolish, to ere, mistake, and know nothing truly." Nay rather, this is to be a man. And why they should call it miserable, I see no reason; forasmuch as we are so born, so bred, so instructed, nay, such is the common condition of us all. (Erasmus, *Praise of Folly*, 1549/1942, pp. 144–145)

Folly is often reduced to foolishness, what one does when playing the fool. A more generous view is that in running counter to prudence, mocking caution, and chiding reason, folly inspires breaking the established rules of good sense and this can be good fun. As such, as Erasmus suggested, humans are born to folly.

Present at all times and in all cultures, humor is among the fields of folly's play and reveals much about the human inner drama. From peak-a-boo to a tickle, infants experience laughter as an overflowing enjoyment. Possessing a quick wit and good sense of humor is a source of adult pride and, psychologists tell us, a much sought after trait in a mate. It is also thought to be essential to teaching effectively and to avoiding the dangers of burnout. The claims made for the value of humor are almost staggering:

Humor can help students understand concepts and lesson content, it can also capture and maintain attention and motivations […]. As a teaching strategy, humor […] can make learning more engaging, enjoyable, and memorable […] [and] it can stimulate brain activity and increase creativity.

It does all of this while reducing "stress and anxiety" (McCabe, Sprute, & Underdown, 2017, p. 5). Humor is basically considered a very good thing.

This chapter explores humor. Rather than offering examples of school humor, I suggest that most humor in education is serious business, even when it is playful.

ON UNDERSTANDING HUMOR

Much of the research on humor related to education involves gathering data from college students enrolled in psychology classes to determine what is found funny or what sort of humor is appropriate or inappropriate when teaching (e.g., Wanzer, Frymier, Wojtaszczyk, & Smith, 2006). One wonders — do psychology undergraduates have some special insight into what is funny that the rest of us lack? Typically, such studies seek to locate the boundaries of what counts as light humor, safe for teaching but still funny. Although results are mixed (Bolkan, Griffen, & Goodboy, 2018), a goal of much of this research has been to determine whether or not the purposeful use of humor increases learning and improves memory, as many authors and many teachers believe it does.

Light humor has many benefits and delights, when it is used with skill and caution. Light humor is often thought to be a motivational tool, useful in classrooms — but then there is the business world. In business, a humor industry for managers has developed (see Morreall, 1997) producing what Collinson (2002) aptly described as "manufactured humor" (p. 279), planned and narrowly instrumental (both Lewis, 2006; Hedges, 2009 have offered biting criticisms of this industry). There are abundant studies of humor of various kinds as a coping mechanism (see Nezleck & Derks, 2001). Seeking a means to reduce teacher burnout, Ho (2016), for example, suggested that "schools may design humor training programs as a theme of professional development for teachers on a regular and on-going basis" (p. 55). Of these studies, one of the more interesting concluded that rather than reducing stress, aggressive and self-deprecating humor actually increases burnout among college instructors (Tumkaya, 2007). Clearly, not all humor is cut out of the same cloth.

"Humor," as Wallinger (1997) stated, "is one of the most promising instruments in the educator's toolbox" (p. 28). But thinking of humor as an instructional "tool" is to simplify and distort a very complex form of human communication and relationship, a form that is not, as Kuiper, Grimshaw, Leite, and Kirsh (2004) argued, "always the best medicine" (p. 135).

Exploring ethical issues related to the uses of humor, Harvey (1995) underscored and extended the point: "Humor is intrinsically a risky business, since it succeeds only if those present respond in the desired way" (p. 20). Sometimes the unspoken intent is to undermine power, other times simply to have a laugh or generate a bit of harm. That humor is risky business is nicely illustrated by an attempt at humor by a school superintendent who, at the opening of each school year, produced a video intended to "welcome everyone back [to school]" and to "inject laughter and humor in the workplace to relieve stress" (Orlando, 2006). Presented to a gathering of about 500 faculty and staff, the video presented a "mock documentary" with teachers' "responses" to dubbed questions.

> "How do you like to unwind," the superintendent asked, and a teacher replied, "I enjoy a lot of leisure activities," the teacher answered. "Such as?" "Killing," the teacher was heard to reply[…]. "What were the results of the last drug test that you took?" another teacher was asked. "It was positive," the teacher said.

"The result [was] a video that makes faculty members out to look like killers, strippers, and drug users." Not funny, many parents and teachers concluded, especially when the video was placed on the web for all the world to see.

THEORIES OF HUMOR

At least four general theories have been developed over the centuries to explain humor and its various human functions (see Martin, 2007; Morreall, 1983, 2009), each theory having its own utility, value, and limitations, yet each getting at some aspect of humor and its relational uses. The first is the "superiority theory," when humor expresses hostility; the second suggests that humor involves the release of pent-up energy, a release that is experienced as pleasurable – having a laugh; the third, characterized by Morreall (2009) as a "minority opinion" (p. 23), considers humor a form of playful relaxation; finally, the "incongruity theory" sees humor as arising out of violations of normal mental patterns, schemas, and scripts – and expectations. Each theory has a place in what follows, although the incongruity theory is of most consequence, for the experience of incongruity proffers an occasion for learning.

Incongruity and Cognitive Shifts

The basic idea behind the incongruity theory is very general and quite simple. We live in [a world] where we have come to expect certain patterns among things, their properties, events, etc. We laugh when we experience something that doesn't fit into these patterns. As Pascal put it, "Nothing produces laughter more than a surprising disproportion between that which one expects and that which one sees." (Morreall, 1983, pp. 16–17)

While recognizing that not all incongruous experience is found humorous, and that humor can be harmful, Morreall (2009) built on and extended the work of other theorists by suggesting that the "basic pattern" of light humor involving incongruity includes four elements:

(1) We experience a cognitive shift – a rapid change in our perceptions or thoughts.
(2) We are in a play mode rather than a serious mode, disengaged from conceptual and practical concerns.
(3) Instead of responding to the cognitive shift with shock, confusion, puzzlement, fear, anger, or other negative emotions, we enjoy it.
(4) Our pleasure at the cognitive shift is expressed in laughter, which signals to others that they can relax and play too (p. 50).

As Moreall explained, in comedy cognitive shift "involves a set-up and a punch" (p. 50). In effect, what is expected – the setup – is not what is delivered – the punch. Humor from this view requires surprise, the unexpected turn. Drawing on the work of Apter (1991), Martin (2007) expanded how one may understand and experience the shift. What is involved is a "reversal" movement from a telic, or goal-directed state "that underlies more serious activities," to a *paratelic* or playful frame of mind. "In the telic state, high arousal is unpleasant (anxiety) and low arousal is preferred (relaxation), whereas in the paratelic state, low arousal is unpleasant (boredom) and high arousal is enjoyable (excitement)" (p. 76). When already in a paratelic state, individuals seek greater arousal, and in this state, they enjoy incongruities rather than seeking to resolve them.

The play mode does not necessarily follow a cognitive shift. In fact, often incongruity is experienced as anything but humorous; rather than being seen as funny, incongruity may be taken as puzzling, threatening, confusing, and irritating. This is what makes humor such a risky business. Indeed, incongruity may actually cause a person to quickly move from a playful to a more serious frame of mind, as when a comment supposedly made in jest proves very disturbing, not funny at all, and the joke falls flat or proves hurtful. Responding to incongruity with puzzlement, for example, invites inquiry, not laughter. An individual who feels puzzled directs energy toward making sense of an event or situation, and disengagement follows. Educationally, such moments are potentially powerful, but after a brief flash of puzzlement, humor may return when the sense sought proves odd or strangely illuminating.

Responses and Strategies

Treating incongruity playfully involves multiple responses or strategies. One of these, among the more important, is *fictionalizing* an event – it is not real or *really* true and can be treated playfully. Being removed or distanced from a problem situation enables humor, making it possible to experience a *real* event as humorous when it may be deeply upsetting to those directly involved. This is the origin of much black humor. The passage of time helps. Another strategy involves interpreting "an action or situation as being less admirable and more trivial (i.e., less serious) than it first seemed" (Martin, 2007, p. 87), putting a funny "spin" on an event or experience.

Storytelling is another strategy: for example, teachers telling teaching stories to other teachers and receiving more stories in return. Such stories are often content laden, and funny, but not always: sometimes teachers simply need to vent. Usually, in moments like these, one story leads to another and another, each opening a window on beliefs, experience, values, and practice. The aim is insider self-confirmation.

> Teacher 1: You won't believe what her mother wrote: "Katie will be checked out early today. We are getting her hair and nails done!"

> Teacher 2: Yesterday I walked into the office. Flynn (name changed) and two other third grade boys were sitting in chairs against the wall waiting to meet with the principal. Flynn, who is a little guy, whose feet didn't touch the floor, sat legs protruding, eyes closed tight, head bowed, his hands clasped in front of his face and his lips were moving rapidly. Not a sound. He was praying, really praying. Scowling, the other two boys looked at him and then at each other, and then back at him again. I thought Flynn must have been in trouble. Nope. Later I found out that the two scowlers had been bullying him. Maybe Flynn's prayers were answered. Boy, *those two* were in trouble.

> Teacher 3: "Well, get this [...]"

As lore, such stories told by veterans to beginning teachers are part of teacher socialization: in community and culture building as well as in coping. Stories like these make a point, sometimes teach a lesson, suggest an alternative, hint at a needed correction or powerful principle, or simply make some sort of sense of an oddly puzzling event.

Enjoying a cognitive shift, which may come at the expense of another, underscores the importance of context in producing the pleasure of humor: knowing Flynn and his tormentors contributes substantially to the humor of the office prayer story. Humor is always social, which is not to say that it is always positive and pleasant for the object of the humor. An eighth-grade math teacher shared this story:

> Last year my school had a fundraiser for the American Red Cross. Students were allowed to duct tape some of their teachers to the gym wall. Each student bought a piece of tape for $1.00 and stuck it across me until I was stuck to the wall. The principal then thought it would be funny to put a piece of tape across my mouth, bringing cheers from all the students. He then asked me how I felt. I said, 'MMMMMMMM!' Everyone laughed.

With the taping of the teacher's mouth, there was a sudden shift that while funny to the principal and students may not have been all that funny to the teacher. For a moment, the teacher may have puzzled over the state of his relationship with the principal, only to dismiss the thought.

We like to laugh with others, finding in laughter a powerful bonding force but also potentially a wicked weapon. Some gatherings lend themselves to laughter much better than do others: we enjoy ourselves most and are disposed to being playful especially with people we like and generally enjoy, people we often identify with. As play, the pleasure of humor, as Morreall (2009) suggested, is found in how it makes us feel mentally and physically, when humor frees the imagination and is arousing and "exhilarating" (p. 55). Then, humor is "liberating. It gets us out of mental ruts [...]. In the humorous frame of mind, we can challenge any standard belief, value, or convention" (pp. 56–57). Finally, laughter is the natural expression of amusement, a play signal sent that communicates a message to one's friends and potential allies: "We are safe. I enjoy this—you enjoy it too" (p. 58).

HUMOR: LIGHT AND DARK

Grounded biologically and culturally, not all humor is light – humor has both a light and a dark side, with shading and mottling possible. Receiving by far the majority of research attention (Attardo, 2010), positive humor, the light kind, is the kind that facilitates cooperation, lowers tension, softens boundaries, and encourages bonding; as mentioned, we experience it as exhilarating, energizing, and fun. Moreover, it regulates and "smooths" interaction (Fine & De Sucey, 2005). In contrast, seeking targets, and often expressing discontent, dark humor, as Lewis (2006) argued, involves, among other characteristics, "butt" warfare (p. 7) and has a conserving function. Primarily, dark humor seeks self-protection and supremacy, but also often expresses compelling human interests.

> Contrary to what many in the positive humor movement in general and the laughter club movement in particular suggest, humor is not a universal experience that necessarily draws humankind together but a *malleable force in communication* (italics added): a source of delight brought by puns, jokes, comic genres, and spontaneous wit, a cue to relax, a way of reaching out to others, and a sign of intelligence, to be sure, but also an effective tool of denigration, misdirection, and attack. (Lewis, 2006, p. 205)

Driven by neediness, especially by feelings of vulnerability and sometimes of superiority, dark humor serves the social function of creating and maintaining within-group status as it strengthens established social boundaries, helping form and then preserve in- and out-groups, even within school faculties. Such humor also shores up personal and professional identity (see Garner, Chandler, & Wallace, 2015). By pinpointing persons and behaviors that are alien and threatening, and by suggesting that others are "not our kind" or not "quite our kind," established social practices are upheld and relationships consistently and sometimes ruthlessly reinforced. Ridiculing one's enemies, say a principal, a veteran team leader, or a group of parents, strengthens social and cultural boundaries among teachers but inhibits boundary crossing and bolsters group insularity.

Speaking to a large gathering of parents, Cathie Black, then chancellor of the New York City Schools, offered a remarkable example of such humor. Speaking to a group of parents deeply concerned about the serious overcrowding in the schools of downtown Manhattan, Chancellor Black quipped, "Could we just have some birth control for a while? It could really help us all out a lot." A few uneasy laughs followed. Commenting on her remarks, Daly (2011) wrote:

> It would really help us if Schools Chancellor Cathie Black would abstain from making insensitive jokes [...] But the parents at that downtown Manhattan meeting were overwhelmingly white and well-off, which may have been why she felt she could make the joke in the first place. She knows that those folks are not going to think she is really telling them to stop breeding [...]. The poor have historically been told by people of Black's station to stop breeding and being such a burden.

The place of humor in forming and maintaining organizational cultures has been the object of several studies, although surprisingly not within schools. Fine and De Sucey (2005), for example, described how "joking cultures" operate to build cohesion, noting that jokes have histories and that how themes circulate through ongoing interaction and support a "social cartography" (p. 6). With Fine and De Sucey (2005) and Holmes and Mara (2002), Garner and his colleagues (2015) noted how work cultures, certainly including schools, support distinctive types and styles of humor.

Holmes and Mara (2002, p. 1687) helpfully distinguished between "broadly supportive humor and broadly contestive humor." Usually dark, broadly contestive humor may facilitate resistant, oppositional culture that seeks to undermine established claims to power and status (see Martin, 2007, p. 5). Along these lines, Attardo (2010) noted that working-class humor "is antagonistic to middle class values" (p. 123). Rodrigues and Collinson (1995) analyzed cartoons published in the Brazilian telecommunications union newspaper, *The Goat*, that displayed especially provocative contestive humor to express worker dissatisfaction. From their analysis, they concluded that playfulness and humor "can be important forms of critique, [means for] questioning the status quo" (Rodrigues & Collinson, 1995, p. 740). This is an important insight to which I will return.

THE PASSIONS OF HUMOR

Speaking generally, dark humor is grounded in two of what Fisher (2002) described as the "vehement passions": fear and anger. No surprise, as Furnham, Richards, and Paulhus (2013) concluded, certain "dark" personalities "prefer aggressive humor styles" (p. 208). Often exploited for political purposes and now nagging, fear in particular grows out of the extreme uncertainty of modern life and encourages and strengthens the need for alliances: something and someone to count on while discouraging the ability to imagine a distant future or a different future at all (see Chapter 1). Undoubtedly, some teachers teach out of fear and anger. These emotions are wrapped up in self-preservation to the point where, at their extreme, "only the self, and, even more, only the self as it is in its current state of panic, or grief, or rage has any reality at all" (Fisher, 2002, p. 60). The self-absorption of fear, whether imminent or extended, and of anger leads to defensiveness and mistrust, two enemies of learning and development, permitting only the most cautious, limited, and short-termed engagement across differences. Fearful or angry, dark humor provides a weapon of self-defense that simultaneously shields those upon whom the self most depends for place, definition, and meaning. Yet, ironically, the object of humorous attack, the oppositional "not self," the "butt," is crucially important for self-definition and identity formation. In fear, the "not self" may become one's enemy, and feeling anger offers justification.

In Carson City, Nevada, thinking their actions funny, a group of five girls used social media to organize an "Attack a Teacher Day." After their arrest, the girls insisted they were only joking, even though they and others had posted online threats against specific teachers. In this instance, anger, fear, and supposed humor produced a frightening effect, one that likely drove a deep wedge of suspicion and distrust between teachers and students. This is not to say, however, that anger and fear are necessarily evil passions, for they are not. Anger may be righteous, focused on injustice, and fear a wise and prudent assessment and response to very real dangers. The issue here, however, is the way in which these passions and the kind of humor they support to narrow the self and limit learning as they discourage engagement across differences and constrict imagination. In fear and anger, there is only a distorted now.

In contrast to fear and anger, other emotions prove expansive: inviting engagement, encouraging self-assessment, and stimulating growth. Mirth, the emotion particularly associated with light humor and amusement is among these, although not always. Mirth involves gaiety, light-heartedness, merriment, and joy, signaling the opening of an experimental attitude. Becoming smug, amusement may accompany dark humor, particularly humor that responds to mild fear or a settled, not hot, anger. It is difficult to conceive of someone being amused yet very angry: when hot, anger overwhelms. A line is crossed when mirth becomes impish, expressive of a need to get even or assert superiority, as in the happiness that may follow the discovery of failure of a despised competitor, a spineless principal, and an arrogant colleague. When expressing good humor, mirth is not self-absorbing, making the person or the object of a joke seem small, not heavy, but expansive – often loud, engaged, and engaging. To be sure, fear and anger are also contagious, and anger is often loud when seething, but mirth is pro-social, implicitly offering an invitation to others to join the fun and to play together. Mirth energizes, sometimes overwhelming the body while producing profound feelings of well-being and connectedness.

HUMOR AND CREATIVITY

Teaching, of course, is filled with moments of incongruity and is embedded in deep and persistent paradox and contradiction – sometimes experienced as overwhelming and threatening, other times as delightfully surprising, wonderfully expansive, very funny, and energizing. The latter experience of humor is important to teachers' motivation to improve and to experience joy in teaching and learning. The puzzlement that sometimes follows an experience of incongruity may have a similar motivating effect. Claims for the worth of humor in teaching go well beyond the coping value of a laugh or the worth of a welcomed diversion, a quick and delightful shift to a paratelic from a somber and serious telic frame of mind, although these are extremely important. As noted, the underlying feature of incongruity theories is a cognitive shift, a switch of schemas such that what seemed to be so proves not to be so or, as in irony or sarcasm, what is meant is not literally what is said. It is this feature of humor that supports the widely held view that good humor, humor mostly of the light kind, and creativity are strongly related. And they are, offering a link of great importance to teaching and to building cultures that support growth and development of both teacher and student.

As Martin (2007) concluded from a review of the relevant literature, there is a relationship between creativity and mirth, but further the exposure to humor increases "fluency, flexibility, and originality, as well as total creativity" (p. 102) – each an essential quality of skilled teaching and of great importance to sustainable and continuous professional growth and program renewal, enabling teachers to grapple with the tough and contentious issues surrounding schooling, teaching, and learning in ways that deepen commitment.

Strong but mostly indirect support for these conclusions comes from a variety of sources. Research conducted by Fredrickson and her colleagues related to the broaden-and-build theory of positive emotions is especially on point. The theory proposes that positive emotions broaden the scope of the individual's focus of attention, allowing for more creative problem-solving and increasing the range of behavioral response options – thus making physical, intellectual, and social resources available to the individual for dealing with challenging situations (Martin, 2007, p. 186)

Fredrickson and Branigan (2005, p. 318) tested two hypotheses arising from the theory: "that, relative to a neutral state, two distinct positive emotions (amusement and contentment) will (a) produce a global bias on a global-local visual processing task, consistent with the broadened scope of attention, and (b) broaden momentary thought-action repertoires." They also tested the corollary hypothesis that "two distinct negative emotions (anger and anxiety) will

(a) produce a local bias on a global-local visual processing task, consistent with a narrowed scope of attention, and (b) narrow momentary thought-action repertoires" (p. 316). The first hypothesis was strongly supported for both amusement and contentment. The second hypothesis received some support, prompting the authors to speculate about problems with study design. Nevertheless, for amusement but not contentment, there was strong evidence supporting increased urges to be playful and socially engaged. A subsequently published review extended this conclusion: "Evidence confirms that positive emotions broaden thought-action repertoires: induced positive emotions produce wider visual search patterns, novel and creative thoughts and actions, more inclusive social groups, and more flexible goals and mindsets" (Cohn, Fredrickson, Brown, Mikels, & Conway, 2009, pp. 361–362).

The first experimental test of the building half of the broaden-and-build theory involved participants in a seven-week program of loving-kindness meditation. The conclusion of this study was that "changes in positive emotions only produced changes in life satisfaction to the extent that they built personal resources" (Fredrickson, Cohn, Coffey, Pek, & Finkel, 2008, p. 1055). The resources built enabled participants to live more successfully, placing "people on trajectories of growth" (Fredrickson et al., 2008, p. 1058). Resources included greater self-acceptance, more positive relations with others, and increased feelings of competence shown in "pathways thinking, environmental mastery, purpose in life, and ego-resilience" (p. 1058) — each resource of obvious value to teachers. Unlike the first, this study only indirectly speaks to the value of humor and well-being, although mirth and amusement are among the positive emotions.

Besides studies related to the cognitive effects of humor on humans, some research has been conducted on the effects of humor creation on wittiness. From this literature, Martin (2007, p. 218) concluded that creating humor involves "divergent thinking, incongruity, surprise, and novelty." Generally, consuming and producing humor require intelligence, an appreciation of the anomalous, and mental elasticity — ultimately the stuff of scientific revolutions (Kuhn, 1970) and a source of the courage that sustains positive deviance (Richards, 2004). Additionally, imagination is important to both good humor and creativity, pointing toward things that are not but might be.

COST/BENEFIT ANALYSIS

At this point, a brief cost/benefit analysis of dark and light humor is in order. But first, a general point: as in dialogue, the "defender of a dominated group does not argue in the same way as the defender of an ideology in power" (Garand, 2009, p. 494); with humor, use is not the same across cultural, ethnic, class, and other groupings (Attardo, 2010; Praag, Stevens, & Houtte, 2017). Thus, without considerable effort and openness, misunderstandings occur and people are hurt. Formed in opposition and concerned with maintaining status and boundaries, dark humor seeks to diminish its butts: The play is one-sided, even when willingly joined. Within established boundaries and seeking self-protection and in-group preservation, aggressors caricature others while mythologizing their own claims of worth. Rooted in neediness, they reject engagement across differences. Emotions of anger and feelings of vulnerability, however, often capture genuine values associated with injustice and unfair treatment. What dark humor has that is potentially of most value is its edge, which, when spoken by a "defender of a dominated group," is often a painful truth, a point forcefully made by Harvey (1995): "The game of humor is not played on an even field – especially when the subject of the humor is present" (p. 21).

Light humor and the emotion of mirth, in particular, are experienced as deeply pleasureful and genuinely fun, worthwhile for their own sake. Light humor is expansive, inviting engagement and inspiring intellectual flexibility, broadened awareness and more effective problem-solving, qualities essential to learning and to quality human performance. Moreover, light humor, in contrast to dark, softens group boundaries and encourages creation of more inclusive groups. Both kinds of humor are experienced as arousing and energizing.

GAUGING TEACHER AND CULTURE WELL-BEING

What educators find funny and how they manifest humor is an important gauge of their health and well-being and of institutional cultures. Most teachers are attracted to teaching for intrinsic reasons, as discussed in Chapter 5. They tend to "seek out those rewards that come from the *experience* of teaching, and the opportunity structure which teaching affords to provide for the realization of their personal and social values" (Richardson & Watt, 2006, p. 44). What teachers value most is working closely with children and adolescents and making a positive difference in their lives and to the world they inhabit. Despite the challenges, they expect to enjoy teaching, and they usually find it personally satisfying and a good deal of fun. The kind and quality of relationships built between teachers and students, including their parents, is critical to realizing these aims, and when these relationships are thwarted, the difficulty in coping may inspire dark humor of the sort expressed by an elementary school teacher of my acquaintance who thought her email address funny: "Ihatestudents." Given current policies and social practices, resisting such tendencies is far from simple or easy for educators.

Recognizing the importance but also the fragility of caring and close relationships to teachers, researchers are increasingly concerned: "In workplace circumstances where these kinds of rewards become swamped by other more immediate and pressing demands, teachers may be less likely to persist in the profession" (Richardson & Watts, 2006, p. 51). Under hostile conditions, teachers find it progressively more difficult to teach as they know they can and should, and also more difficult to find pleasure in their work and in their relationships. Rather than teaching out of their deepest passions that speak to the desire for connectedness and the need to care for and nurture the young, they feel threatened by a loss of intimacy, a flattening and fragmenting of knowledge, a rise in competitiveness, a loss of generosity, and, as noted, a temptation to withdraw. Under such conditions, switching from a telic to a paratelic state, a state of high arousal and good humor, becomes increasingly difficult, and playfulness and optimism wane. (And academic optimism is crucially important to student learning; see Hoy, Hoy, & Kurz, 2008.)

Realization that dark humor has crept into and displaced light humor signals need for a pause and reconsideration. In their study of labor union cartoons, mentioned earlier, Rodrigues and Collinson (1995) noted an edge present in much dark humor. In this edge, Mayo (2010) found part of humor's value to education. His concern was to locate and then exploit the truth spoken in some dark humor.

> Humor's ability to create a way to see differences as generative, even if those differences must also stay different in order to keep the tension necessary for humor to work, mean, I think, that humor is not always or only aggression, it is also a strategy for provisional concord amidst fractured and contentious meaning. (p. 511)

What Mayo recognized is that, on the one hand, humor is play and much sought after for its own sake; laughter feels good. On the other hand, strong incongruities that give rise to dark humor, where significant ideas, perceptions, and viewpoints come into tension, may hint at and potentially reveal deep negative feelings about some widely cherished organizational values or suggest the presence of resentments and disappointments associated with nagging frustrations, displaced professional aspirations, and failed relations that need naming — and thereby troubles are turned into issues.

What often happens in stand-up comedy with an edge hints at what is involved in such moments of recognition when uncomfortable topics are openly spoken in ways that encourage shifts between telic and paratelic states that prove unsettling. Feeling off center and startled, audiences laugh but then the show ends, the audience leaves, and on the way home and surrounded by the safety of friendship people talk seriously as they try to process what was heard and how the hearing felt and what it meant. At such moments, the challenge of humor represents "an invitation to think relations differently" (Mayo, 2010, p. 511).

The presence of safe spaces is crucially important for turning troubles into issues. Dark humor thrives off stage and backstage, where it may fester and grow darker. Healthy school cultures require spaces characterized by trust, places where disagreement is understood as an opportunity and necessary condition for learning (see Edmonson & Roloff, 2009). When thinking about the creation of safe but charged spaces for teachers, recent interest in professional learning communities (PLCs) seems suggestive (see Chapter 11). Bottery (2003), however, gave an important warning: PLCs can easily become arenas for manipulation, where openness to diverse views and the potential for play are displaced by a fearful defensiveness and a narrow instrumentalism tied to raising student standardized test scores. Under intense performance pressures, humor may become primarily strategic, not revelatory, and increasingly darker. Yet, this need not be so. A brief but illustrative historical example of one such space is drawn from the workshops sponsored by the Eight-year Study of the Progressive Education Association (1931–1943; Bullough & Kridel, 2003). Here in the quest to redesign secondary education, teachers, school and district administrators, and social scientists and scholars representing many different fields came together to rethink the place of schooling in a troubled democracy. This example, drawn from the weeks-long summer Rocky Mountain Workshop, nicely illustrates the resistive force as well as the transformative power of humor. In this instance, engagement won out.

> On the second day, one of the [leaders] was "expounding a great idea about personal and social needs, and all of us were doing a great deal of talking, one of us broke out in a witty little tune; before he could be put out, another began shuffling a cowboy dance under the table, and a third pulled out a piece of moist clay from his pocket and began to model." At first the workshop staff was surprised by the mischievousness of the teachers, but they also must have recognized the long and tiring day, working in the heat and humidity and in tight quarters. On this and may other occasions, the teachers needed something more than talk: they needed to play, to celebrate being together, and to take risks that would further both their own development and the work in which they were engaged. Quickly staff members met and adjusted their plans. (Bullough & Kridel, 2007, p. 198)

Leaders of the workshop understood the intent of the humor; although funny, the teachers' actions were contestive, challenging authority and position within the workshop. For a moment, the workshop itself was threatened. However, getting the point, offered indirectly but poignantly, and recognizing its legitimacy, organizers rethought workshop purposes, and as a result, all subsequent association-sponsored workshops were changed, giving teachers much greater power and influence over what was done and how it was done. Moreover, it became clear that workshop success was directly connected to opportunities to play. This was humor with an edge; not dark, but not totally light.

> [Leaders] realized that time would have to be set aside for [workshop] participants to "Sing and dance and write poetry and feel clay under our fingers, throw the shuttle through the opening warp, mass bright colors, and sweep a mural onto a convenient wall." (p. 198)

CONCLUSION

The challenges of education give abundant space for the play of humor, although not so much when dark humor dominates. Dark humor tends toward fixation. Yet, dark humor, ridicule, satire, and irony may encourage resistance, and sometimes all one can do is angrily resist. The kind of truth to which dark humor speaks must be problematized so that specific sources of contention are named and principled points of action identified. This said, as "serious play" humor can help reveal troubles, but then troubles must be turned into issues. Humor can be helpful for gaining understanding of how educational problems are understood and then for reimagining, reframing, and ultimately resolving, living with, or getting over them. Also, good humor can help sustain both the cognitive and the relational conditions needed for getting outside of expected definitions and easy problem solutions as well as for locating and attacking internal and external impediments to improvement. Good humor is also essential for making and sustaining allies for education and for coping with

unfavorable conditions, especially when they seem impermeable to change —
when all one can do is wait, work, and sometimes bitterly laugh.

These are difficult times for educators, but there is no shortage of silliness.
Folly reigns, and there is a lot to laugh about, much that seems serious but is
really silly. There is great strength in human unpredictability and playfulness
and in the ability to laugh, for laughter is both energizing and mostly hopeful.
Clearly, quality education depends on creation of cultures of happiness within
schools, places where good humor (and sometimes humor with a bite) finds a
home, is recognized, cherished, and actively cultivated.

CHAPTER 11

HOPE, HAPPINESS AND SEEKING EUDAIMONIA

INTRODUCTION

The best homes and schools are happy places. The adults in these happy places recognize that one aim of education (and of life itself) is happiness. They also recognize that happiness serves as both means and end. Happy children, growing in their understanding of what happiness is, will seize their educational opportunities with delight, and they will contribute to the happiness of others. Clearly, if children are to be happy in schools, their teachers should also be happy. Too often we forget this obvious connection. Finally, basically happy people who retain an uneasy social conscience will contribute to a happier world. (Noddings, 2003, p. 261)

The straightforward argument presented in this chapter emerges from and draws together insights from the previous chapters:

- Policy-makers have paid far too little attention to educator well-being, a concept that has been sprinkled across the chapters but that was central to the discussion of Chapter 5 on motivation.
- Greater efforts are required within the institutional life of schools to foster conditions that support teacher hope (also discussed in Chapter 5) and happiness as essential conditions for quality teaching and effective student learning.
- Locating these conditions necessitates a much better understanding of the work life and emotions of educators.

The aim for education and educators is *eudaimonia*, a Greek concept often translated as human flourishing, which is of increasing importance to studies of well-being (see Averill & More, 2004). The perspective that underlies this chapter is consistent with positive psychology: that humans are self-directed and adaptive beings who, when they can, "choose behaviors that make them feel fully alive, competent, and creative" (Seligman & Csikszentmihalyi, 2000, p. 9).

ON HOPE

People in Western cultures typically think of hope as a state of mind. When understood as closely related to optimism (Peterson, 2006), they view hope as a personality trait, a matter of temperament; when times are desperate, they speak of it as a coping mechanism most clearly recognized when lost or missing; in its deepest meaning, they acknowledge hope as a virtue — one of three Christian martyrs, daughters of Sophia (Wisdom). As a virtue, hope is to be cultivated and cherished, taught first by parents and later by teachers (Bullough, 2001a), among others. Hope is also an emotion, an "affective blend" (Lazarus, 1999, p. 655) — a mixture of emotions including fear, anxiety, and happiness, each anticipating possible outcomes and all wrapped to some degree in a quiet but determined confidence that supports effort and encourages persistence (see Duckworth, 2016). Thus, hope has a distinctive *feel* about it, distinctive in its emotional blend although its intensity and duration may vary. One knows when one feels hope — and when one loses it.

Teacher–Student Hope

Hope and happiness are essential conditions for living and learning, especially for the well-being of those who, like teachers, live with and for the young (see Elbaz, 1992). Erikson (1964) offered a reminder of just how important hope is for humans:

> Hope is both the earliest and the most indispensable virtue inherent in the state of being alive. Others have called this deepest quality *confidence* [...] If life is to be sustained hope must remain, even where confidence is wounded, trust impaired. (p. 115. Emphasis added)

Hope and happiness, highly complex emotions, are prominent in all things educational. Yet, teachers' hope and happiness are generally taken for granted and dismissed to the sidelines in debates of school of improvement. Everything is about the children. Yet as Noddings noted, teacher and child well-being are inextricably linked. On the topic of teacher well-being, generally there is a deafening silence, but what is needed is a consistent and robust institutional commitment so that saying of a school culture that it is *hopeful* actually means something profound and important. In such a place and within such a culture, citizens feel and act in certain distinctive ways, and these ways are trusting, respectful, invested, and caring.

That hope is too rarely recognized as it should be as central to the work of educators is evident in Fullan's (1997) conclusion following a survey of the impact of several educational reform efforts: most teachers' experience was profoundly negative, leaving behind a "sense of hopelessness, either because they are on the defensive from external attack or because they have been part of small groups of reformers who have burned themselves out" (pp. 229–230). Fullan pleads, teachers must "stay hopeful under negative conditions" (p. 230). We are, he said, "down to our last virtue: hope" (p. 221). Fullan did not plead for optimism but for hope, despite frequent use of the two terms interchangeably (Gillham & Reivich, 2004). Fullan recognized that unlike optimism, which is commonly understood to bring with it an expectation of the best outcome, hope demands something deeper and more precious: in the most dire of circumstances, despite recognition of the limits of one's ability to change a situation, hope supports engagement, not giving up (see Frankl, 1970). For this reason, hope as a virtue to be sought and practiced may be a matter of tenacity, as Bertrand Russell once argued of faith.

Qualities and Characteristics

Given the complexity of hope, some sorting is required and some digging is necessary to identify its educationally important qualities and characteristics. Lazarus (1999) provided a helpful departure point as he described hope as involving and following an appraisal of a situation that concerns "our well-being and the well-being of those about whom we care" (p. 658). In appraising, we realistically assess our situation to guide our action and enable us to cope as we seek "the most favorable spin possible on our plight in order not to undermine hope [and thereby avoid falling into the passivity of despair]" (p. 659). Beginning in infancy, hope develops in maturity to become the "capacity not to panic in tight situations, to find ways and resources to address difficult problems" (Fullan, 1997, p. 221). When facing troubling situations, we desperately seek reasons to sustain hope, even when or especially when doing so seems to others foolish.

We look outside ourselves to others for help and strength, sometimes invoking Providence. In others, we seek signs of hope which are experienced as strengthening — hopeful and confidence building. Giving up or giving in may be the rational, easy, or even the expected thing to do, but to do so is to act without virtue, courage, or integrity: to be found lacking in an essential way as a human being who, perhaps, happens to be employed as an educator — but lacking hope means failing to *be* an educator. To be hopeful, then, is not to expect a perfect outcome, yet because hoping takes us beyond our normal abilities, favorable, though often unexpected, outcomes may follow; receiving an outcome hoped for is in a profound sense to live temporarily in a state of grace. Relief and happiness then follow, and energizing streams of faith and gratitude flow together and confidence grows.

Hope is both taught and learned — or not learned — and is often conditional, dependent for its vitality on who and what is involved in the troubling situation. Who is involved is important for several reasons, among them that hope — like pessimism, fear, and anger — is contagious (McDermott & Hastings, 2000), spread by contact. Remarkably, as Carter (1999) observed, the sight of persons experiencing strong emotions like disgust actually "turns on the observer's brain areas that are associated with [the] feeling" (p. 87). That hope is taught to children or, better expressed, that children absorb it from those around them who possess it, early and usually by example but also through stories, has far-reaching implications for those who lack hope as well as for those who care for and about the well-being of the young. As Lasch (1991) suggested:

> Hope implies a deep-seated trust in life that appears absurd to those who lack it. It rests on confidence not so much in the future as in the past. It derives from early memories—no doubt distorted, overlaid with later memories, and thus not wholly reliable as a guide to any factual construction of past events—in which the experience of order and contentment was so intense that subsequent disillusionments cannot dislodge it. (p. 81)

Thinking of hope as a virtue to be absorbed rather than specifically taught and learned opens the Hope Scale developed by researchers at the University of Kansas (Snyder et al., 1991, 2005) to criticism. As noted in Chapter 5, the Hope

Scale with its trait and state subscales combines self-reports of two elements thought to capture the essential nature of hope: agency, a "sense of successful determination in meeting goals in the past, present and future," and pathways, a "sense of being able to generate successful plans to meet goals" (1991, p. 570). The model emphasizes cognition:

> [Emotions are] the sequelae of cognitive appraisals of goal-related activities. The quality of emotion for a particular goal-related setting depends on the person's perceived hope in that setting. More specifically, the high-hope person's analysis of sufficient agency and pathways in a given goal setting should lead to the perception of relatively high probability of goal attainment, a focus on success rather than failure, a sense of challenge, and a relatively positive emotional state as goal-related activities are conceptualized and undertaken. (p. 571)

Among the critics of Snyder's model, Lazarus (1999) argued that hope cannot be equated to successful agency nor to positive expectations.

> I consider this erroneous because we can hope even when we are helpless to affect the outcome. Self-efficacy, or a sense of competence and control, facilitates hope, and it certainly aids in mobilizing problem-focused coping actions, but it is not essential to hope. (p. 674)

Implicitly to hope is to acknowledge one's own limitations and dependency even while longing for outcomes beyond one's own understanding, influence, or ability. In effect, the Scale appears to undervalue the noncognitive aspects of hope.

Perceived as an emotion, hope has some unusual features. Generally, among the distinguishing characteristics of an emotion is brief duration. Emotions come on quickly with a distinctive physiology – generally including a high state of system arousal. On this view, hope may be more of a mood or an emotional attitude than an emotion. By emotional attitude, Ekman (1992) meant emotions like love and hatred that are sustained and "typically involve more than one emotion" (p. 194). As a positive emotion or emotional attitude, hope, like happiness and many other emotions, is more difficult to distinguish than negative emotions like anger, fear, and disgust. In contrast to such emotions, which Fisher (2002) aptly characterized as the "vehement passions," hope often brings an acute awareness of others. The Hope Scale, however, has been criticized for reflecting "more egotistical than collective concerns" (Snyder, Cheavens, & Sympson, 1997, p. 107). Generally, the vehement passions tend to "extinguish the reality and claims of others while creating, as illness does, an almost painfully pressing awareness of self – to the point that only the self, and, even more, only the self as it is in its current state of panic, or grief, or rage has any reality at all" (Fisher, 2002, p. 60). By implication, hopelessness is selfish, and selfish teachers are highly unlikely to be effective educators.

ON HAPPINESS

On the surface, the connection between hope and happiness seems obvious: "In the context of hope theory, barriers [to achievement of goals] produce negative emotions, especially when a child encounters profound blockages. However, the successful pursuit of goals tends to produce positive emotions, especially when barriers are overcome" (Snyder et al., 1997, p. 108).

Connections of Hope to Happiness

For Snyder and his colleagues, both hope and happiness have a great deal to do with stress, with the persistent and daily challenges of living, and with the ways those challenges are met such that happiness or sadness follow and hope is strengthened or diminished. Arendt (1958) made the point this way:

> There is no lasting happiness outside the prescribed cycle of painful exhaustion and pleasurable regeneration, and whatever throws this cycle out of balance—poverty and misery where exhaustion is followed by wretchedness instead of regeneration, or great riches and entirely effortless life where boredom takes the place of exhaustion and where the mills of necessity, of consumption and digestion, grind an impotent body mercilessly and barrenly to death—ruins the elemental happiness that comes from being alive. (p. 108)

Happiness is an odd emotion. Often lacking an object, it is more like a mood than an emotion. Other times, it has a clear object, perhaps experiencing a breakthrough with a child who has struggled with reading or noticing students respond to an engaging science lesson in ways that confirm one's identity as an inquiry teacher (Bullough & Knowles, 1990). As Day, Kington, Stobart, and Sammons (2006) concluded from a study of 300 English educators, at moments when teachers are able to teach in ways that are congruent with their deepest values and when they recognize themselves as teachers, they feel confirmed, happy, and hopeful – and they flourish. Conversely, being compelled to teach in ways that are experienced as disconfirming, as reflecting being other than one-self, is experienced as frustrating, a source of anger. Generally, happiness is "the emotional state associated with full engagement or optimal performance in meaningful activity" (Averill & More, 2004, p. 664); as such, like hope, happiness spills outward and is infectious (McDermott & Hastings, 2000). The result builds confidence.

Peterson (2006) argued that hope leads to happiness: the "strengths 'of the heart,'" among them gratitude, hope, and love, make humans happy because they "orient us toward others" (pp. 154–155). Peterson's point, in part, is that greater happiness follows a life of engagement, of being deeply connected to and invested in others and in their well-being, and so hope is inevitably and ineluctably tied to happiness. From another angle, Fullan (1997) suggested that hope and emotions share an "intimate two-way link" (p. 221): hope disciplines the passions, offering means for avoiding despair and containing fear and anger. As a means for coping, hope keeps open the door to the positive possibility of being, as C. S. Lewis expressed it, "surprised by joy." On this view, the hopeful is prepared for the worst yet remain open to the best of possible outcomes, and proof of openness comes as they act in ways that reflect this possibility as not fanciful, but genuine.

Kinds of Happiness

As an emotion, happiness is understood in multiple ways: "brief events, extended moods, and stable predispositions to particular emotional states" (Bates, 2000, p. 382). Such multiplicity adds to the difficulty of saying something meaningful about the relationship between hope and happiness. Nettle (2005) helped sort out the confusion by positing "three increasingly inclusive senses [of happiness]" (pp. 16–17). The first level represents the most immediate and direct sense of happiness as a feeling "brought on by a desired state being (perhaps unexpectedly) attained, and there is not much cognition involved, beyond the recognition that the desired thing has happened" (p. 17). Level 1 is all about feeling good. The second sense, Level 2, centers on general or overall well-being:

> When people say that they are happy with their lives [...]. [t]hey mean that, upon reflection on the balance sheet of pleasures and pains, they feel the balance to be reasonably positive over the long term [...]. It concerns not so much feelings, as judgements about the balance of feelings. Thus it is a hybrid of emotion, and judgement about emotion. Its synonyms are things like contentment and life satisfaction. (p. 19)

Level 3 happiness, Nettle suggested, is represented by Aristotle's ideal of the good life, *eudaimonia* – fulfilling one's full potential:

> Contemporary psychologists and philosophers have sometimes talked of happiness when they really mean the good life or *eudaimonia* [...]. Note that 'level three happiness' has no characteristic phenomenology since it is not an emotional state. There is no single thing that it feels like to achieve *eudaimonia*, since everyone's potential is different. (Nettle, 2005, p. 20)

This conclusion, however, does not seem to be fully justified, as studies of the development of expertise suggest (Bereiter & Scardamalia, 1993). There are moments, sometimes extended, when humans flourish, and these are well-remembered and immediately recognized as possessing commonly experienced qualities. Such happiness, a kind of deep satisfaction, is evident during the experience of "flow" (Csikszentmihalyi, 1990): times when one is working at the very edge of one's ability and is fully and deeply invested in a valued activity – studying physics, playing a musical instrument, watching children at play, or possibly teaching.

Speaking about Level 2 happiness, frequently described by researchers as "subjective well-being" (SWB; Diener & Lucas, 2000), Nettle raised serious questions about the widely recognized conclusion that most people report themselves as being relatively happy. The definition of happiness used in such studies, unlike the concerns of Level 3 happiness, is "simply whatever people mean when describing their lives as happy" (Myers, 2000, p. 57). While not dismissing the importance of these conclusions, or of the strong correlations between reported happiness and a range of positive behaviors – less self-absorption, less hostility, more loving, more creative and healthy activity (see Myers, 2000 , pp. 57–58) – Nettle (2005) concluded that "the finding that most people are pretty happy is in part a reflection of an endearingly unrealistic psychology with which we address the world" (p. 54). Studies of Level 2 happiness, he asserted, generally rely on instruments that lack a frame of reference and depend predominantly on recent events and feelings, especially when those events are judged positive or strongly negative. For educators, having studies of subjective well-being without a frame of reference goes straight to the heart of our deepest concerns, as Noddings (2003) noted:

> Education, of all enterprises, cannot neglect [...] the normative aspect of happiness [...]. We hope that children will learn to derive some happiness from doing the right thing, from satisfying the demands of their souls. We shrink from people who are happily untroubled by the misery of those around them. There is a kind of happiness that creeps through, even in the presence of pain and misery, when we know that we have done what we can do to improve things. Thus education for happiness must include education for unhappiness. (p. 36)

Nettle raised additional important questions about the nature of Level 2 happiness, suggesting that "no organism should ever be completely satisfied for anything more than a short time" (pp. 57–58). In his and in Noddings' views, dissatisfaction and unhappiness influence human motivation, not so much in terms of what is felt when facing significant blocks to meeting life's goals, but rather in the sense of being helped to recognize that a situation might be better for others besides ourselves. Furthermore, Nettle observed that while most persons are reportedly happy in general, this often changes when specific contextual questions are posed. When internalized as an imaginative and positive ideal, a vision of another way of being and of being more deeply satisfied and happier inspires and invites human striving. Happiness is not merely meeting goals, but meeting worthy goals of ever-increasing significance. Otherwise, why seek happiness? Why not be satisfied with physical pleasure?

Ultimately, Nettle argued, humans are hardwired to seek happiness; a drive toward happiness is built into the species – into the operating systems of the brain that form a "happiness system" which keeps us moving, searching for ever larger and more enduring satisfactions and enjoyments. Nevertheless, Nettle (2005) concluded, "People will never be completely happy, whatever their external conditions" (p. 63). Striving, he argued, is what is most important for the future of humanity, not achieving of happiness, and striving is sustained by hope and stands as proof of its existence.

Support for Nettle's conclusion comes from Kegan's (1982) conception of human development and self-formation. For educators, Kegan's argument deepens the linkage between happiness Level 2 and Level 3 by broadening what counts as motivating and underscoring the centrality of growth to being happy and flourishing. Essential to his argument is how hope and happiness are bound together in identity, the kind of person we take ourselves to be and others take us to be (as hopeful and happy or not). Seeking to make sense of how humans develop over time, Kegan identified and described an inherent tension between two drives both essential to the survival of the species and essential to the individual's well-being: a drive toward self-preservation and another toward transcendence – contentment and satisfaction (Level 2 happiness) and growth and learning, and transcendence (Level 3 happiness). This view recognizes patterns of adaptation in every life, such that what is found to produce contentment at some point comes to be experienced as flatness or staleness at another; after adapting and feeling flat, a healthy person seeks a higher state of happiness (see Bullough & Baughman, 1997).

> While this evolutionary process may be described in purely biological terms, it is as true that the same ongoing tension between self-preservation and self-transformation is descriptive of the very activity of hope itself [...] "a dialectic of limit and possibility." Were we "all limit"

(all "assimilation"), there would be no hope; "all possibility" (all "accommodation"), no need of it. That "energy field" which to the evolutionary biologist may be about "adaptation," is as much as anything about the very exercise of hope. Might we better understand others in their predicament if we could somehow know how their way of living reflects the state of their hoping at this depth?—not the hopes they have or the hoping they do, but the hoping they are? (Kegan, 1982, p. 45)

For the individual lacking hope the tension fails, self-preservation dominates self-transformation, and striving ceases. Development stops. Children suffer. Speaking of happiness under such a condition is misleading, as other emotions come to fill life and characterize the self: the person becomes disinterested or perhaps sad, fearful, and anxious. At some point, emotions may become habitual, and the person is no longer who he was before. Certainly, such a person may still experience episodes of laughter and moments of pleasure – moments of feeling good, signs of Level 1 happiness – but it is unlikely that contentment can be sustained and unlikely that the happiness of eudaimonia will follow (Bullough, 2009). This is true in part because lower-hope individuals tend to avoid complex and especially challenging goals and situations if they can, while higher-hope individuals pursue "stretch" goals (Snyder et al., 1997, p. 110). Stretching involves choosing enjoyment over pleasure: the "good feelings people experience [...] when they do something that stretches them beyond what they were" (Seligman & Csikszentmihalyi, 2000, p. 12). Stretching implies a frame of reference and points toward avenues for experiencing self-transcendence and thereby the happiness of *eudaimonia*.

ON CULTURES

That measures of hope and happiness tend toward stability over time may seem to suggest that external contextual differences have comparatively little influence over forming and strengthening these critical emotional beliefs and habits: that internal rather than external factors seem more likely to determine outcomes. In part an artifact of measurement, arising because of the tendency to focus on adults (whose life habits and personalities appear rather fixed), such conclusions might lead to a kind of determinism, an acceptance that outside of gene splicing and therapy focused on recreating childhood memories, there is little that can strengthen hope or increase happiness. Common sense suggests otherwise, even as recognition of the power of early rearing practices and biology sets much of the difficulty of the challenge. Erikson (1968) has been helpful here: "The ontological source of faith and hope [is] a sense of basic trust: it is the first basic wholeness, for it seems to imply that the inside and the outside can be experienced as an interrelated goodness" (p. 82). Such trust forms very early in life and tends to persist. Yet, as Peterson (2006) wrote, contextual differences do matter, in part because basic trust comes in degrees and fortunately is not usually wholly lacking; there is almost always something to build upon: most children are hopeful, at least about some things and some relationships

CULTURES OF UNHAPPINESS

It is much easier to recognize ways in which hope and happiness are undermined than to understand how they may be built institutionally. But clearly within and outside families, the enduring strength of hope and happiness depends largely on the depth, quality, character, variety, and consistency of human relationships. While the relationships formed within schools are generally rather unstable (although less so in the lower grades) and to a degree intentionally guarded, attentiveness to relationships — how students and teachers are to live together in school and care for one another — stands as perhaps the most promising point of action when seeking to build hope and happiness. The challenge, observed long ago by Goodlad (1984), is daunting: In schools one finds "rather well-intentioned teachers going about their business somewhat detached from and not quite connecting with the 'other lives' of their students" (p. 80). Neoliberalism, with its emphasis on "disciplining the teachers" (Valli & Buese, 2007, p. 545) and testing the children, certainly encourages disconnection, caution, and elevates the value of self-protection among teachers. Instead, what is needed are the relationships of an "affectionate climate" (Martin, 1992, p. 38) — schools that are the "moral equivalent of home in which love transforms mundane activities [...] and joy is a daily accompaniment of learning" (p. 40).

CULTURES OF HOPE AND HAPPINESS

Consistent with the argument of this chapter, all schools should be, must be, hopeful and happy places, even as they are places engaged in serious work for both teachers and students. Most schools are not places of hopelessness or despair, despite occasional difficulties. Probably, no teacher wants to be a prophet of doom and gloom. When doom and gloom persist, one of the more prominent coping mechanisms for teachers facing exhaustion, depersonalization, and reduced personal accomplishment, the three signs of burnout (Maslach, 1999), is to leave teaching, and, as Kelchtermans (1999) observed, leaving often is not especially difficult even in harsh economic times. At some point, hope must be realized in happiness and longer-term well-being to convince a teacher to persist in teaching — there must be a positive point to teaching and continuing to teach. For students, there is a parallel reality: there must be a positive point to staying engaged in schooling.

As means for building hope and encouraging happiness among educators, the increasing interest in professional learning communities (PLCs) appears promising even though during the years of NCLB the percentage of teachers engaged in collaborative efforts reportedly dropped by more than half, to 16% (Darling-Hammond et al., 2018, p. 348). Generally linked to reform efforts and often driven by student test scores, the concept gains in power when bound to a different and competing language tradition: the language of *reform* dilates attention on organizational and institutional features and blocks recognition of educational improvement as fundamentally a matter of learning and of development. As Kelly (2013) argued, well-conceived PLCs build interdependence and sustain trusting relationships that enable the risk-taking demanded of learning. Compared to reform, *renewal* offers a much more hopeful alternative: a way of thinking that not only recognizes but also respects the historicity and humanity of those who work within schools — children and adults — and their need to learn and to grow together (Goodlad, Mantle-Bromley, & Goodlad, 2004).

Definitions of PLCs vary (see Cox & Richlin, 2004), but the concept is generally taken to mean a group of educators who "continuously seek and share learning, and act on their learning" (Hord, 1997, p. 6). Decisions are data-driven (DuFour, 2005), and efforts are consistently directed toward creating conditions that support continuous inquiry. Stoll et al. (2006) described the essential features of a PLC as including "shared beliefs and understandings; interaction and participation; interdependence; concern for individual and minority views [...] and meaningful relationships" (p. 225). Such conditions, it is believed, benefit children and educators. Shade (2006), whose concern was for developing school cultures that build hope, would add an additional and generally overlooked feature: that the most powerful and morally centered learning communities are likely those that explicitly develop what he described as "habits of hope" (p. 196). Raising test scores without attending carefully to the kind and quality of life lived within schools, to the relationships shared by teachers and students, and to whether or not that life encourages hope and enables happiness is an empty accomplishment (see Nichols & Berliner, 2007). Data of a different kind are called for: evidence that teachers and students are invested in learning and in the relationships that support hope and happiness and strengthen the sense of community belonging.

Persistence in the pursuit of worthy goals, resourcefulness and courage are among the habits of hope (Shade, 2006). Of these three habits, Shade argued:

> Each of hope's habits is itself a complex of other habits. Persistence requires habits of patience and self-control to maintain focus without losing commitment to a hoped-for end. Trust also proves important as an acknowledgment that other forces contribute to our ends; humility is similarly relevant in that we typically do not know all possible routes to our end [...]. Resourcefulness, which enables us to expand our abilities, is similarly constituted by a variety of abilities. These include habits that enable us to identify real conditions, to explore new means and abilities in a knowledgeable, skilled, and imaginative manner, and to intelligently formulate and adapt means and ends [...]. Realizing hope's ends involves transcending antecedent limitations [...]. Finally, courage also displays complexity. Hoping illuminates our limits and vulnerability and so calls for us to face weaknesses, dangers, and risks. Intelligence functions in courage as it does in other contexts to assess means and ends in the light of one another, though courage involves more than intelligent appraisal. It also indicates the willingness and ability *to act* on that appraisal. Those who are courageous must summon the energies to overcome risks and play an active role in bringing about conditions necessary to realize desired ends. (2006, pp. 196–197)

Noting that habits are developed by interacting with the environment, including with those sharing that environment and community, Shade called for the creation of a curriculum and a school culture characterized by experiences and human relationships that, by inspiring emulation, sustain hope and happiness, not as afterthoughts but as a central aim of education.

Shade's "habits" are related to Snyder's goal of encouraging agency and pathways as means for strengthening hope. McDermott and Hastings (2000) offered a broader view, suggesting means for encouraging the development of hope. Their position was framed by an important insight: "Hopeful thinking [...] is more than a set of shared behaviors or cognitive skills. Rather, it flows from core self-beliefs that the individual is capable of generating pathways and of sustaining the energy necessary to pursue goals" (p. 196). Hope is encouraged when children and adults work closely together toward valued and clearly articulated goals.

The process, as McDermott and Hastings, like Lasch (1991), observed, is slow and demanding, especially for those lacking hope, a point of importance for both teachers and children. Teachers are called upon to model hope for the young, even as they may need help holding to hope for themselves. Teachers need to guide children in setting, parsing, prioritizing, and then working toward worthy goals (see Duckworth, 2016). Children also need help learning how to identify and pursue alternative solutions to problems and how to get around them when intractable. Hence, building competence also builds hope, as Erickson suggested. When seeking to teach hope, teachers must demonstrate patience and learn to be realistically encouraging, helping children learn to pool their resources and work together to realize their goals. From a content perspective, building a curriculum of hope includes using stories about "high-hope protagonists" (McDermott & Hastings, 2000, p. 196), inviting children to identify with them and their struggles and to recognize in them the importance of hard work to hopefulness. Children's own stories and teachers' stories can make important contributions to building hopeful cultures. Shade (2006) added that teachers can "cultivate hope by explicitly focusing on it as a regular resource in student learning and classroom behavior" (p. 207).

Shade underscored the importance of the ways students are helped when facing difficult learning challenges, such as learning to read and write or to use statistics where persistence pays off. Failure, as I have written elsewhere (Bullough, 2006), must become "smart": failure can be an opportunity to celebrate honest effort (Duckworth, 2016) and clever though perhaps not wholly satisfying solutions to nagging problems. Rather than scorn, those who try and fail need opportunities to learn about and develop some of the most significant qualities of hopefulness. True stories of failure and triumph, such as biographies of Churchill, Lincoln, Gandhi, Mother Teresa, and Barack Obama, are particularly dramatic and compelling. The happiness of eudaimonia is the promise of activities of these and many other kinds where skilled and strongly invested and hopeful teachers build an interesting and stretching curriculum that supports children in confronting their limitations and helps them in their effort to move beyond present capabilities and limiting emotional habits. Building *teacher* hopefulness follows a similar pattern of engagement. This said, classrooms and schools ought also to evidence Level 1 happiness and Level 2 happiness, which most likely do – lots of laughter, feelings of well-being produced by living within a comparatively safe and interesting environment and of being known, valued, and trusted in that environment. But challenge is as important as is support if transcendence and greater competence are to follow.

Fullan's (1997) argument, noted previously, that hope is crucial to educational renewal, raises a difficult question: under current social, economic, and work conditions, how can teachers be helped to avoid disenchantment and remain or become more hopeful themselves? As suggested, in most respects, hope can be built among teachers as it is with the young. To build hope and to maximize teachers' happiness requires work conditions that enhance teachers' autonomy and agency, and competence and meaningful relationships (Ryan & Deci, 2001). Such conditions encourage engagement and invite and inspire self-transcendence. Teachers need to be encouraged and supported to do what they believe is best for children and to build to their strengths.

Respecting agency, Nettle (2005) made a particularly telling point: "Personal control is a much better predictor of happiness than income is (in statistical terms, it accounts for twenty times more of the variation)" (p. 74). Moreover, he observed that autonomy − which is closely related to agency − is related to health and well-being. Looking at the available data, he concluded, "People really don't like being told what to do, whatever the material inducements" (p. 75). For teachers facing ever-increasing accountability pressures, the point is perhaps obvious: happiness depends on having a relatively high degree of control over their own work life; rich and loving relationships with those they teach and those with whom they work; and receiving support in pursuing highly valued ethical goals. Moreover, happiness, most especially Level 3 happiness, like hope, is related to increasing competence and to teachers' as well as students' learning. Surely, such aims are within the reach of most if not all schools.

When hope is weak or lacking, both children and teachers need help developing explanatory styles that strengthen agency and blunt the threat of helplessness (see Peterson, 2000). Teachers, like students, may need help to recognize the place of prior beliefs in the judgments they make about experience and that guide their actions. As Gillham and Reivich (2004) suggested, hopefulness is promoted by understanding that there are multiple ways of perceiving and interpreting reality and that our sense of the world might be distorted, even wrong. Such insight is a first step toward recognizing that shifting perspectives can and often do change how we recognize and frame problems and, in turn, shape the outcome of our efforts to improve our situations and those of others we care about. Greater hope and happiness likely follow, and resilience may grow. The goal is not to exchange our positive for negative attributions, but to learn to think more deeply, accurately, and realistically about situations and resources, thereby to locate genuine points of action where agency holds the most promise. Where hope is concerned, the goals set and plans made are most promising when they can be widely shared, are morally inspiring, and require and support stretching beyond one's own capability and inevitable shortcomings. This point is supported by studies of distributed cognition (Moore, 2007): in effect, in a classroom or within a faculty, the thinking that takes place is greater than the total of the individuals' cognition, and thereby, hope becomes more realistic and powerful and less quaint or fanciful.

Temperaments differ. Some teachers and some children are less easily infected by hope or despair; some seem to always have an inner strength, the confidence noted by Erikson, that lightens even the darkest disappointments. In varying degrees, temperament, which is highly heritable (Kahneman, 2011, p. 401), forms the boundaries of emotionality, yet which emotions are activated and expressed and how they are expressed is influenced by learning and by the institutional, social, and economic contexts within which we live.

Institutions are characterized by different ways of living, thinking, and acting, and they support certain preferred ways of feeling, as Zembylas (2002) has suggested. As institutional cultures form and evolve, intentionally or unintentionally they come to embody "structures of feeling" (p. 187) that shape emotion and normalize experience. Some schools embody cultures of hope and happiness, and from such schools, a great deal can be learned. Such schools do not just happen; they are crafted and carefully tended. As noted, hope and happiness, like hopelessness and despair, are infectious. If the work of school renewal is to produce higher achievement among the young and increase the quality of teaching available to them, there is probably no better long-term strategy than to work to create conditions that invite and inspire teachers' hope and happiness, particularly the happiness associated with flourishing. Noddings (2003) underscored what is at stake in such efforts: "Children (and adults, too) learn best when they are happy" (p. 2). But there is no lasting happiness without hope.

POSTSCRIPT

A postscript is an addendum or sequel, and a follow-up or an upshot. In this instance, the upshot is a short set of eight propositions. Embedded in the arguments made within the essays that comprise this book, each proposition is deceptively simple but far-reaching in its consequences. When taken together and taken seriously, the propositions would disrupt the dominant discourses of teaching and teacher education. Instead of buttressing the propositions by piling up additional supporting sentences, I have sought to be clear, direct, and brief.

> *P1.* The work of education and of schools has little in common with the work of business enterprise. Expressed differently, business is no model for education.

I find it surprising that this proposition so often proves controversial. Young people, after all, are only in a very peculiar sense raw material. Their worth is much greater than their potential value as human capital. Lest we forget, the young are citizens with rights and, as Phillip Hallie (1997) suggested of children, they also are the "springtime" (p. 274). Despite the power of neoliberalism, its promotion of competition and its values centered in the market economy have failed and will continue to fail as strategies for improving education (as well as work done in a wide range of other human endeavors outside of business — and some inside of business as well) and most certainly for enriching the educational experience of the young. The reduction in education to a consumer good has fueled a vast and well-funded — and for public education, most devastating —

marketing campaign, which has fundamentally distorted educational aims and means and has seriously misrepresented the value of both public and higher education to democratic citizenship (Berliner & Glass, 2014; Lubienski & Lubienski, 2014; Ravitch, 2013; Schneider, 2016).

P2. While quality teaching is often invisible to the innocent eye, teaching is among the most complex and demanding of all human excellences.

Behind the performance of teaching resides a complex inner drama of confronting and transcending various limitations and of forming and transforming a sense of self, an identity. Teaching skills are subtle and proficiency is fluid, with so many consequential variables that impinge on practice and defy predictability. Great teachers are not born, although having potential matters a great deal, they are made, and achieving something that approaches teaching proficiency takes persistent, consistent, thoughtful, and well-supported hard and self-critical work. To say "well-supported" echoes a more general insight: it takes a village to raise a child *and* it takes a dedicated and invested professional community to develop a knowledgeable, competent, and committed educator. Given the complexity of the work of teaching, increasingly common forms of drive-by teacher education enabled by federal and state governments, which open wide the back door to just about anyone who might, for whatever reason, wish to teach while tightly regulating access to the front door, is foolish and unethical.

P3. To be energizing and positively productive, educational policies and supporting practices must get motivation right.

Economists did us a terrible disservice when they reduced humankind to homo economicus: beings who are primarily driven by pleasure seeking, motivated by external rewards, and who respond positively to threats and tight surveillance. Transferred to education, such assumptions have supported a psychology obsessed with identifying deficits and then remediating or fixing them. In the process, everything educational has been turned upside down: first and foremost teaching is a complex and peculiar kind of human relationship upon which everything else depends (Korthagen, Attem-Noordewier, & Zwart, 2014). As with other humans, the primary motivation for those who teach is to do well the work they find meaningful and worthwhile; have some input over both the aims and means that define that work; be supported in achieving greater competence; and enjoy, value, and be respected by those with whom they work. Thus, to achieve improved education requires less fixing than building to strength.

P4. For the young to flourish, those who seek to educate them must also flourish.

To broaden the statement, the well-being of the young is inextricably linked to the well-being of their teachers. To strengthen students' well-being requires investing in educators' well-being. A life is a testimony. The formal curriculum of teaching and learning rests on a hidden human curriculum, apparent though too seldom examined. Unhappy, angry, fearful, frustrated, discouraged, or disinterested educators always teach what and who they are. Conversely, happy, intellectually engaged, hard-working, affectively present, committed, courageous, and competent teachers also teach themselves (Kelchtermans, 2009).

P5. High-quality education and teacher education are expensive in time and resources as well as demanding of talent.

Because humans develop as we do and because we are intensely social creatures, there is never a quick fix or fast-forward device to becoming good, educated, or wise. Along the way, there is inevitably stumbling and starting over. Though missteps and repeated steps are costly in time and resources, talent cannot be developed in any other way, nor can the equally significant character traits required for democratic citizenship be developed.

P6. The early twentieth-century conception of teaching as primarily content transferal or transmission is deeply embedded in the consciousness of Americans and even many teachers, though it dramatically misrepresents what educators do and enjoy and what young people and their parents most value.

It is increasingly understood that the test fetish that has come to dominate public education hurts children. It also hurts teachers. Teaching is only partially about content delivery. Though the fetish is weakening, conceptual change of this sort requires time, determination, and genuinely compelling alternatives. Certainly, providing access to theories, concepts, and facts that have proven themselves useful is part of the charge of education and that for some teachers, and most certainly for a good many professors, these theories, concepts, and facts are beloved; however, teaching involves ever so much more than such content, as has been suggested.

P7. Preservice teacher education is about beginning and becoming, not being and completing teacher education.

Given how little time is dedicated to preservice teacher education, too much is expected and too much is packed into the curriculum. A long list of best practices stated in the form of academic and behavioral standards, complete with rubrics (statements of the conditions for the demonstration of mastery) defining what makes a teacher competent, not only sets a problem but is often thought to represent a guarantee. For someone new to teaching, the so-called best practice offers a place to begin problem framing, little more.

The promise of preservice teacher education cannot ever be mastery of teaching. What can be promised is sufficient knowledge about teaching and a level of essential teaching competence that assures students will not be harmed and the teacher has a high likelihood of a good beginning leading to a lifetime of professional learning. Skills develop with coaching and practice within specific contexts and find their value in what they enable: in their potentiality, in the artistry of their expression, and in the consequences of their use. This takes time, persistent work, and lots of focused support. Beginning teachers must never be left on their own to sink or swim.

> *P8.* Times may be tough, but we educators know what to do to build renewing and powerful institutional cultures, the sort of places where teaching can be life-affirming and learning is at times joyous.

The attack on public education, on teacher education, and (to a degree) on higher education in all likelihood will continue. Given the political climate of our times, we can easily get discouraged, so we need to be careful about who we listen to and believe. We ought not listen too carefully to our critics. We must listen carefully to one another, to be sure to those we serve, and particularly to those who share with us the responsibility to care for those we serve.

There are wise and experienced voices among us, and many educational practices have proven and are proving themselves as promising. For example, states and nations that offer competitive salaries to teachers, support high-quality teacher education, and invest significantly in professional development in-service as part of teaching and of the teachers' workday enjoy considerable success holding teachers and enabling high student achievement. Remarkably, as Darling-Hammond and her colleagues (2018) observed, many of the "innovative practices [of] various countries exist and were often launched in the United States, from which they spread elsewhere in the world" (p. 344). Yet, good ideas often receive only spotty support across the various states. In the US, for example, there is comparatively little investment in providing teacher mentoring or supporting teacher-led research; teachers spend almost all of their time with students and are rarely allotted workday time for learning and studying with colleagues to improve their own and their school's practices, and salaries generally remain noncompetitive. Formal partnerships between teacher education programs and public education remain a powerful idea (Bullough & Rosenberg, 2018), but rarely are they adequately supported within higher education institutions or by schools. Within higher education, despite the potential for high validity, local research remains a poor sister to other kinds of studies. Similarly, pedagogical studies are often not considered to represent serious scholarship at all.

The danger of listening too closely to critics is that with careful listening belief may develop. Belief may lead to the temptation to define our work and assess its value in terms set by those critics, many of whom recognize that in criticism comes the possibility of power and sometimes of gain (Ball, 2018). The problem is reminiscent of the story of Apelles' shoe. Seeing Apelles' painting, a shoemaker recognized that the renowned ancient Greek painter had painted one sandal loop too few. Respecting the shoemaker's knowledge, Apelles corrected his error. But when the shoemaker later criticized the figure's leg, Apelles rightly rebuked him (see Bullough & Rosenberg, 2018, pp. 57–58). Some criticism is simply wrong.

Often criticism is offered without expectation or even desire for improvement. Under such conditions, good news about teachers and teaching is really bad news. By way of example, on December 5, 2017, the *New York Times* reported with puzzlement that there were signs the much-maligned Chicago public schools were doing remarkably well, even when standardized test scores were used as the measure. Critics were puzzled because this success seemed to have little if anything to do with the legacy of federal education policy but a lot to do with the determined hard work and creative innovation of educators. Now, there is a surprise! We need to remember, despite frequent criticism, there has been and is a tremendous amount of good work being done at every level of education by smart, dedicated, committed, motivated — but also inevitably flawed — yet still hopeful human beings. Much of this work has been and is heroic, even when it has at times necessarily been subtly subversive. That said, except in the short term, counting on heroism to keep any system running probably is foolish.

A good deal of relatively recent research supports the proposition that we know what to do to build renewing cultures. Consider, for example, the body of relevant research on professional development (PD; see Whitworth & Chou, 2015). Over the past couple of decades, this research has given overwhelming support to the following principles. Influential PD has a clear content focus (something of importance is to be explored and learned), involves active learning among participants, offers program coherence, is extended in duration, includes collective participation within sites (context responsive) and, a point often neglected, engages school and district leadership. In such work, data can prove valuable, but the data must be valued by those who teach, which suggests they should be involved in data-gathering decisions as well as data analysis. You will notice that these findings support the view of motivation identified earlier with self-determination theory and its relationship to commitment. Distrust of those charged with a work always undermines commitment or generates commitment to the wrong things. Quality programs do not grow out of distrust.

I firmly believe that every school and teacher education faculty has within itself the goodwill, knowledge, and expertise needed for renewal, once identified and sometimes better focused and organized. Having long been an educator and having served on numerous merit and retention, promotion and tenure committees at every level from department to university, I know something about talent pools as well as about how little is generally known about the work our colleagues are doing. There is talent enough to accomplish the work that needs to be done, and there is much to be learned from our colleagues if we take seriously the challenge to build and renew our work cultures. This, of course, is why partnering is imperative. As I have said, most everything having to do with education is about relationships and relationship building. John Goodlad once remarked that there probably is no better indication of a school's quality than that the students are happy when they are there. So it is also with educators.

REFERENCES

Abrahamson, C. E. (1998). Storytelling as a pedagogical tool in higher education. *Education, 118*(3), 440–451.

Akkerman, S. F., & Meijer, P. C. (2011). A dialogical approach to conceptualizing teacher identity. *Teaching and Teacher Education, 27*(2), 308–319.

Alfi, O., Assor, A., & Katz, I. (2004). Learning to allow temporary failure: Potential benefits, supportive practices and teacher concerns. *Journal of Education for Teaching, 30*(1), 27–41.

Allen, D. W., & Ryan, K. (1969). *Microteaching.* Reading, MA: Addison-Wesley.

Apter, M. J. (1991). A structural-phenomenology of play. In J. H. Kerr & M. J. Apers (Eds.), *Adult play: A reversal theory approach* (pp. 13–29). Amsterdam: Swets & Zeitlinger.

Arendt, H. (1958). *The human condition.* Chicago, IL: University of Chicago Press.

Attardo, S. (2010). Preface: Working class humor. *Humor, 23*(2), 121–126.

Averill, J. R., & More, T. A. (2004). Happiness. In M. Lewis & J. M. Haviland-Jones (Eds.). *Handbook of emotions* (pp. 663–676). New York, NY: Guilford Press.

Baez, B., & Boyles, D. Y. (2009). *The politics of inquiry: Education research and the "culture of science."* Albany, NY: State University of New York Press.

Ball, D. L., & Forzani, F. M. (2009). The work of teaching and the challenge of teacher education. *Journal of Teacher Education, 60*(5), 497–511.

Ball, S. J. (2003). The teachers' soul and the terrors of performativity. *Journal of Education Policy, 18*(2), 215–228.

Ball, S. J. (2016). Subjectivity as a site of struggle: Refusing neoliberalism? *British Journal of Sociology of Education, 37*(8), 1129–1146.

Ball, S. J. (2018). Commercializing education: Profiting from reform. *Journal of Education Policy, 33*(5), 587–589.

Ballou, D., Sanders, W., & Wright, P. (2004). Controlling for student background in value added assessment of teachers. *Journal of Educational and Behavioral Statistics, 29*(1), 37–65.

Baron-Cohen, S. (2011). *The science of evil: On empathy and the origins of cruelty.* New York, NY: Basic Books.

Baskin, K. (2005). Complexity, stories, and knowing. *Emergence: Complexity & Organization, 7*(2), 32–40.

Baskin, K. (2008). Storied spaces: The human equivalent of complex adaptive systems. *Emergence: Complexity & Organization, 10*(2), 1–12.

Bates, J. E. (2000). Temperament as an emotional construct: Theoretical and practical issues. In M. Lewis & J. M. Haviland-Jones (Eds.), *Handbook of emotions* (pp. 382–396). New York, NY: The Guilford Press.

Bauer, J. J., McAdams, D. P., & Pals, J. L. (2008). Narrative identity and eudaimonic well-being. *Journal of Happiness Studies, 9*(1), 81–104.

Bauerlein, M., Gad-el-Hak, M., Grody, W., McKelvey, B., & Trimble, S. W. (2010). We must stop the avalanche of low-quality research. *The Chronicle of Higher Education, 56*(38), A80.

Bauman, Z. (2008). *Does ethics have a chance in a world of consumers?* Cambridge, MA: Harvard University Press.

Bauman, Z. (2011a). *Collateral damage: Social inequalities in a global age.* Cambridge: Polity Press.

Bauman, Z. (2011b). *Culture in a liquid modern world.* Cambridge: Polity Press.

Bauman, Z. (2012). *This is not a diary.* Cambridge: Polity Press.

Bauman, Z., & Donskis, L. (2013). *Moral blindness: The loss of sensitivity in liquid modernity.* Cambridge: Polity Press.

Bauman, Z., & Donskis, L. (2016). *Liquid evil.* Cambridge: Polity Press.

Bauman, Z., & Mazzeo, R. (2012). *On education: Conversations with Riccardo Mazzeo.* Cambridge: Polity Press.

Baxter, L. A. (2011). *Voicing relationships: A dialogic perspective.* Los Angeles, CA: Sage.

Beauchamp, C., & Thomas, L. (2009). Understanding teacher identity: An overview of issues in the literature and implications for teacher education. *Cambridge Journal of Education, 39*(2), 175–189.

Beck, C., & Kosnik, C. (2002). Components of a good practicum placement: Student teacher perceptions. *Teacher Education Quarterly, 29*(2), 81–98.

Beijaard, D., Meijer, P. C., & Verloop, N. (2004). Reconsidering research on teachers' professional identity. *Teaching & Teacher Education, 20*(2), 107–128.

Bell, T. H. (1988). *The thirteenth man: A Reagan cabinet memoir.* New York, NY: Free Press.

Bellah, R. N., Madsen, R., Sullivan, W. M., Swidler, A., & Tipton, S. M. (1985). *Habits of the heart: Individualism and commitment in American life.* Berkeley, CA: University of California Press.

Bereiter, C., & Scardamalia, M. (1993). *Surpassing ourselves: An inquiry into the nature and implications of expertise.* Chicago, IL: Open Court.

Berliner, D. C. (1986). In pursuit of the expert pedagogue. *Educational Researcher, 15*(7), 5–13.

Berliner, D. C. (2009). MCLB (Much curriculum left behind): A U.S. calamity in the making. *The Educational Forum, 73*(4), 284–296.

Berliner, D. C. (2011). Rational responses to high stakes testing: The case of curriculum narrowing and the harm that follows. *Cambridge Journal of Education, 41*(3), 287–302.

Berliner, D. C. (2014). Exogenous variables and value-added assessments: A fatal flaw. *Teachers College Record, 116*(1), 1–31.

Berliner, D. C. (2018). Between Scylla and Charybdis: Reflections on and problems associated with the evaluation of teachers in an era of metrification. *Education Policy Analysis Archives, 26*(54). doi:10.14507/eppa.26.3820

Berliner, D. C., & Glass, G. V. (2014). *50 myths & lies that threaten America's public schools: The real crisis in education.* New York, NY: Teachers College Press.

Biesta, G., Field, J., Hodkinson, P., Macleod, F. J., & Goodson, I. F. (2011). *Improving learning through the lifecourse.* New York, NY: Routledge.

Biesta, G., Hodkinson, P., & Goodson, I. F. (2004). *Combining life history and life-course approaches in researching lifelong learning: Some methodological observations from the 'Learning Lives' project.* Paper presented at Teaching and Learning Research Programme Annual Conference, Cardiff, Wales.

Blömeke, S., Houang, R., Hsieh, F.-J., & Wang, T.-Y. (2018). Comparative research on teachers and their work contexts. In M. Akiba & G. LeTendre (Eds.), *International handbook of teacher quality and policy* (pp. 319–335). New York, NY: Routledge.

Bloom, B. S., Engelhart, M. D., Furst, E. J., Hill, W. H., & Krathwohl, D. R. A. (1956). *Taxonomy of educational objectives: The classification of educational goals. Handbook 1: Cognitive domain.* New York, NY: David McKay.

Bloom, P. (2016). *Against empathy: The case for rational compassion.* New York, NY: HarperColling Publishers.

Bolkan, S., Griffin, D. J., & Goodboy, A. K. (2018). Humor in the classroom: The effects of integrated humor on student learning. *Communication Education, 67*(2), 144–164.

Bottery, M. (2003). The leadership of learning communities in a culture of unhappiness. *School Leadership & Management, 23*(2), 187–207.

Boyd, D., Grossman, P., Hammerness, K., Lankford, H., Loeb, S., Ronfeldt, M., & Wyckoff, J. (2012). Recruiting effective math teachers: Evidence from New York City. *American Educational Research Journal, 49*(6), 1008–1047.

Boyer, E. (1990). *Scholarship reconsidered: Priorities of the professoriate.* Princeton, NJ: The Carnegie Foundation for the Advancement of Teaching.

Boyer, E. L. (1983). *High school: A report on secondary education in America.* New York, NY: Harper & Row.

Bracey, G. (2009). Some thoughts as "research" turns 25. *Phi Delta Kappan, 90*(7), 530–531.

Braverman, H. (1974). *Labor and monopoly capitalism.* New York, NY: Monthly Review Press.

Brill, S. (2011). *Class warfare: Inside the fight to fix America's schools.* New York, NY: Simon & Schuster.

Brooks, D. (2018a). The strange failure of the educated elite. *New York Times,* May 29, A23.

Brooks, D. (2018b). The blindness of social wealth. *New York Times,* April 17, A23.

Broudy, H. S. (1988). *The uses of schooling.* New York, NY: Routledge.

Brouwers, A., & Tomic, W. (2000). A longitudinal study of teacher burnout and perceived self-efficacy in classroom management. *Teaching & Teacher Education, 16*(2), 239–253.

Brown, J. S., & Duguid., P. (2000). *The social life of information.* Boston, MA: Harvard Business School Press.

Brown, P., & Tanneck, T. (2009). Education, meritocracy and the global war for talent. *Journal of Education Policy, 24*(4), 377–392.

Buddhist parables: Tales to illuminate. (2002). Kent, UK: Grange Books PLC.

Bullough, R. V. Jr. (1979/1989). Curriculum history: Flight to the sidelines. In C. Kridel (Ed.), *Curriculum history: Conference presentations from the society for the Study of Curriculum History* (pp. 32–39). Lanham, MD: University Press of America.

Bullough, R. V., Jr. (1988). *The forgotten dream of American public education.* Ames, IA: Iowa State University Press.

Bullough, R. V., Jr. (1989). *First year teacher: A case study.* New York, NY: Teachers College Press.

Bullough, R. V. Jr. (1991). Exploring personal teaching metaphors in preservice teacher education. *Journal of Teacher Education, 42*(1) 43–51.

Bullough, R. V., Jr. (1992). Beginning teacher curriculum decisions making, personal teaching metaphors, and teacher education. *Teaching & Teacher Education, 8*(3), 239–252.

Bullough, R. V., Jr. (1993). Case records as personal teaching texts for study in preservice teacher education. *Teaching & Teacher Education, 9*(4), 385–396.

Bullough, R. V., Jr. (1997). Practicing theory and theorizing practice in teacher education. In J. Loughran & T. Russell (Eds.), *Purposes, passion and pedagogy in teacher education* (pp. 13–21). London: Falmer Press.

Bullough, R. V., Jr. (2001a). Pedagogical content knowledge circa 1907 and 1987: A study in the history of an idea. *Teaching and Teacher Education, 17*(6), 655–666.

Bullough, R. V. Jr. (2001b). *Uncertain lives: Children of promise, teachers of hope.* New York, NY: Teachers College.

Bullough, R. V. Jr. (2006). Developing scientifically-based researchers: Inter-disciplinarity and whatever happened to the humanities and education? *Educational Researcher, 35*(8), 3–10.

Bullough, R. V. Jr. (2008a). *Counternarratives: Studies of teacher education and becoming and being a teacher.* Albany, NY: State University of New York Press.

Bullough, R. V. Jr. (2008b). The writing of teachers' lives—Where personal troubles and social issue meet. *Teacher Education Quarterly, 35*(4), 7–26.

Bullough, R. V. Jr. (2009). Seeking eudaimonia: The emotions in learning to teach and to mentor. In P. Schutz & M. Zembylas (Eds.), *Teacher emotion research: The impact on teachers' lives* (pp. 33–53). New York, NY: Springer.

Bullough, R. V. Jr. (2010). Proceed with caution: Interactive rules and work sample scoring strategies, an ethnomethodological study. *Teachers College Record, 112*(3), 775–810.

Bullough, R. V. Jr. (2011a). *Adam's fall.* Santa Fe, NM: Sunstone Press.

Bullough, R. V. Jr. (2011b). Hope, happiness, teaching and learning. In C. Day & J. Lee (Eds.), *New understandings of teacher's work: Emotions and educational change* (pp. 17–32). New York, NY: Springer.

Bullough, R. V. Jr., & Baughman, K. (1997). *"First-year teacher" eight years later: An inquiry into teacher development.* New York, NY: Teachers College Press.

Bullough, R. V. Jr., Burbank, M., Gess-Newsome, J., Kauchak, D., & Kennedy, C. (1998). "What matters most: Teaching for America's future?" A faculty response to the report of the national commission on teaching and America's future. *Journal of Education for Teaching, 24,* 7–32.

Bullough, R. V. Jr., Clark, D. C., & Patterson, R. S. (2003). Getting in step: Accountability, accreditation and the standardization of teacher education in the United States. *Journal of Education for Teaching, 29*(1), 35–51.

Bullough, R. V. Jr., & Draper, R. J. (2004). Mentoring and the emotions. *Journal of Education for Teaching*, *30*(3), 271–288.

Bullough, R. V. Jr., & Gitlin, A. D. (1994). Challenging teacher education as training: Four propositions. *Journal of Education for Teaching*, *20*(1), 67–81.

Bullough, R. V. Jr., & Gitlin, A. D. (1995). *Becoming a student of teaching: Methodologies for exploring self and school context*. New York, NY: Garland.

Bullough, R. V. Jr., & Hall-Kenyon, K. M. (2011). The call to teach and teacher hopefulness. *Teacher Development*, *15*(2), 127–140.

Bullough, R. V. Jr., & Hall-Kenyon, K. M. (2018). *Preschool teachers' lives and work: Stories and studies from the field*. New York, NY: Routledge Publishers.

Bullough, R. V., Jr., Hobbs, S. F., Kauchak, D., Crow, N. A., & Stokes, D. (1997). Long-Term PDS development in research universities and the clinicalization of teacher education. *Journal of Teacher Education*, *48*, 85–95.

Bullough, R. V., Jr., & Knowles, J. G. (1990). Becoming a teacher: Struggles of a second-career beginning teacher. *Qualitative Studies in Education*, *3*(2), 101–112.

Bullough, R. V., Jr., & Knowles, J. G. (1991). Teaching and nurturing: Changing conceptions of self as teacher in a case study of becoming a teacher. *International Journal of Qualitative Studies in Education*, *4*(2), 121–140.

Bullough, R. V. Jr., Knowles, J. G., & Crow, N. A. (1991). *Emerging as a teacher*. London: Routledge.

Bullough, R. V. Jr., & Kridel, C. (2003). Workshops, in-service education, and the Eight Year Study. *Teaching & Teacher Education*, *19*(7), 665–679.

Bullough, R. V., Jr., & Kridel, C. (2007). *Stories of the eight-year study: Reexamining secondary education in America*. Albany, NY: State University of New York Press.

Bullough, R. V. Jr., & Rosenberg, J. R. (2018). *Schooling, democracy, and the quest for wisdom: Partnerships and the moral dimensions of teaching*. New Brunswick, NJ: Rutgers University Press.

Bullough, R. V. Jr., & Stokes, D. K. (1994). Analyzing personal teaching metaphors in preservice teacher education as a means for encouraging professional development. *American Educational Research Journal*, *31*(1), 197–224.

Bullough, R. V. Jr., Young, J., & Draper, R. J. (2004). One-year teaching internships and the dimensions of beginning teacher development. *Teachers and Teaching: Theory and Practice*, *10*(4), 365–394.

Burke, K. (1955). Linguistic approach to problems of education. In N. Henry (Ed.), *Modern philosophies and education: The fifty-fourth yearbook of the National Society for the Study of Education* (pp. 259–303). Chicago, IL: University of Chicago Press.

Burke, K. (1957). *The philosophy of literary form* (2nd ed.). New York, NY: Vintage Books.

Burke, K. (1989). *On symbols and society*. J. R. Gusfield (Ed.), Chicago, IL: The University of Chicago Press.

Buskist, W., Benson, T., & Sikorski, J. F. (2005). The call to teach. *Journal of Social and Clinical Psychology*, *24*(l), 111–122.

Carr, W., & Kemmis, S. (1986). *Becoming critical: Education, knowledge and action research*. London: Routledge/Falmer.

Carter, K. (1993). The place of story in the study of teaching and teacher education. *Educational Researcher*, *22*(1), 5–12, 18.

Carter, R. (1999). *Mapping the brain*. Berkeley, CA: University of California Press.

Castle, S., Fox, R. K., & Souder, K. O. H. (2006). Do professional development schools (PDSs) make a difference? A comparative study of PDS and non-PDS teacher candidates. *Journal of Teacher Education*, *57*(1), 65–80.

Charters, W. W., & Waples, D. (1929). *The commonwealth teacher training study*. Chicago, IL: The University of Chicago Press.

Christensen, C. M., & Eyring, H. J. (2011). *The innovative university: Changing the DNA of higher education from the inside out*. San Francisco, CA: Jossey-Bass.

Cilliers, P. (2006). Complexity and philosophy: On the importance of a certain slowness. *ECO*, *8*(3), 105–112.

Cilliers, P. (2010). Difference, identity and complexity. In P. Cilliers & R. Preiser (Eds.), *Complexity, difference and identity* (pp. 3–18). Dordrecht: Springer.

Clandinin, D. J. (Ed.). (2007). *Handbook of narrative inquiry: Mapping a methodology*. Thousand Oaks, CA: Sage.

Clandinin, D. J., & Connelly, F. M. (2000). *Narrative inquiry: Experience and story in qualitative research*. San Francisco, CA: Jossey-Bass.

Clark, C. M. (1983). Research on teacher planning: An inventory of the knowledge base. In D. C. Smith (Ed.), *Essential knowledge for beginning educators* (pp. 5–15). East Lansing, MI: Institute for Research on Teaching, Michigan State University.

Clifford, G. J. (1973). A history of the impact of research on teaching. In R. M. W. Travers (Ed.), *Second handbook of research on teaching* (pp. 1–46). Chicago, IL: Rand McNally College.

Clifford, G. J., & Guthrie, J. W. (1988). *Ed school: A brief for professional education*. Chicago, IL: University of Chicago Press.

Cochran-Smith, M., Feiman-Nemser, S., McIntyre, D. J., & Demers, K. E. (2008). *Handbook of research on teacher education* (3rd ed.). New York, NY: Routledge.

Cochran-Smith, M., Piazza, P., & Power, C. (2013). The politics of accountability: Assessing teacher education in the United States. *Educational Forum, 77*, 6–27.

Cochran-Smith, M., & Zeichner, K. M. (2005). *Studying teacher education: The report of the AERA panel on research and teacher education*. Mahwah, NJ: Lawrence Erlbaum Associates.

Cohler, B. J., & Hostetler, A. (2004). Linking life course and life story: Social change and the narrative study of lives over time. In J. R. Mortimer & M. J. Shanahan (Eds.), *Handbook of the life course* (pp. 555–576). New York, NY: Springer.

Cohn, M. A., Fredrickson, B. L., Brown, S. L., Mikels, J. A., & Conway, A. M. (2009). Happiness unpacked: Positive emotions increase life satisfaction by building resilience. *Emotion, 9*(3), 361–368.

Coles, R. (1989). *The call of stories: Teaching and the moral imagination*. Boston, MA: Houghton Mifflin.

Collinson, D. L. (2002). Managing humour. *Journal of Management Studies, 39*(3), 269–288.

Common, D. L. (1991). In search of expertise in teaching. *Canadian Journal of Education, 16*(2), 184–197.

Connelly, F. M., & Clandinin, D. J. (1988). *Teachers as curriculum planners: Narratives of experience*. New York, NY: Teachers College Press.

Connelly, F. M., & Clandinin, D. J. (1990). Stories of experience and narrative inquiry. *Education Researcher, 19*(5), 2–14.

Convery, A. (1999). Listening to teachers' stories: Are we sitting too comfortably? *Qualitative Studies in Education, 12*(2), 131–146.

Conway, M. A., & Pleydell-Pearce, C. W. (2000). The construction of autobiographical memories in the self-memory system. *Psychological Review, 107*(2), 261–288.

Coplan, A. (2011). Understanding empathy: Its features and effects. In A. Coplan & P. Goldie (Eds.), *Empathy: Philosophical and psychological perspectives* (pp. 3–18). Oxford: Oxford University Press.

Coplan, A., & Goldie, P. (Eds.). (2014). *Empathy: Philosophical and psychological perspectives*. Oxford, UK: Oxford University Press.

Coplan, A., & Goldie, P. (2011). *Empathy: Philosophical and psychological perspectives*. Oxford: Oxford University Press.

Council for the Accreditation of Educator Preparation Commission on Standards and Performance Report. (2013). *Draft recommendations for the CAEP Board*. Washington, DC: Council for the Accreditation of Educator Preparation.

Council of Chief State Officers. (2011). *InTASC model core teaching standards: A resource for state dialogue*. Washington, DC: Council of Chief State Officers.

Cox, M. D., & Richlin, L. (Eds.). (2004). *Building faculty teaming communities: New directions for teaching and learning*. San Francisco, CA: Jossey-Bass.

Csikszentmihalyi, M. (1990). *Flow: The psychology of optimal experience*. New York, NY: Harper & Row.

Csikszentmihalyi, M. (1993). *The evolving self: A psychology for the third millennium.* New York, NY: HarperCollins.

CSTPP. (2010). *Preparing teachers: Building evidence for sound policy.* Washington, DC: National Academies Press.

Cummings, W. K., & Shin, J. C. (2013). Teaching and research in contemporary higher education: An overview. In J. C. Shin, A. W. Arimoto, W. K. Cummings, & U. Teichler (Eds.), *Teaching and research in contemporary higher education* (pp. 1–12). Dordrecht: Springer.

Cunningham, L. L. (1973). Effecting reform in a college of education. In D. J. McCarthy & associates (Eds.), *New perspectives on teacher education* (pp. 139–159). San Francisco, CA: Jossey-Bass.

Dale, M., & Frye, E. M. (2009). Vulnerability and love of learning as necessities for wise teacher education. *Journal of Teacher Education, 60*(2), 123–130.

Daly, M. (2011). Cathie Black, in the truest and worst sense of the word, is a chancellor. *New York Daily News.* Retrieved from http://www.NYDailyNews.com

Darling-Hammond, L., & Bransford, J. (2005). *Preparing teachers for a changing world: What teachers should learn and be able to do.* San Francisco, CA: Jossey-Bass.

Darling-Hammond, L., Burns, D., Campbell, C., Goodwin, A. L., & Low, E. L. (2018). International lessons in teacher education. In M. Akiba & G. LeTendre (Eds.), *International handbook of teacher quality and policy* (p. 349). New York, NY: Routledge.

Davis, B., & Harre, R. (1999). Positioning and personhood. In R. Harre & L. van Langehove (Eds.), *Positioning theory* (pp. 32–52). Oxford: Blackwell.

Davis, M. H. (1983). Measuring individual differences in empathy: Evidence for a multidimensional approach. *Journal of Personality and Social Psychology, 44*(1), 113–126.

Day, C., & Gu, Q. (2007). Variations in the conditions for teachers' professional learning and development: Sustaining commitment and effectiveness over a career. *Oxford Review of Education, 33*(4), 423–443.

Day, C., & Gu, Q. (2010). *The new lives of teachers.* London: Routledge.

Day, C., Kington, A., Stobart, G., & Sammons, P. (2006). The personal and professional selves of teachers: Stable and unstable identities. *British Educational Research Journal, 32*(4), 601–616.

Decety, J., & Jackson, P. L. (2004). The functional architecture of human empathy. *Behavioral and Cognitive Neuroscience Reviews, 3*(2), 71–100.

Decety, J., & Lamm, C. (2009). Empathy versus personal distress: Recent evidence from social neuroscience. In J. Decety & W. Ickes (Eds.), *The social neuroscience of empathy* (pp. 119–213). Cambridge, MA: The MIT Press.

Decker, L. E., & Rimm-Kaufman, S. E. (2008). Personality characteristics and teacher beliefs among pre-service teachers. *Teacher Education Quarterly, 35*(2), 45–64.

Dedousis-Wallace, A., Shut, R., Varlow, M., Murrihy, R., & Kidman, T. (2014). Predictors of teacher intervention in indirect bullying at school and outcome of a professional development presentation for teachers. *Educational Psychology, 34*(7), 862–875.

De Jong, D., Grundmeyer, T., & Yankey, J. (2017). Identifying and addressing themes of job dissatisfaction for secondary principals. *School Leadership & Management, 37*(4), 354–371.

de Waal, F. (2009). *The age of empathy: Nature's lessons for a kinder society.* New York, NY: Harmony Books.

Dewey, J. (1904). The relation of theory to practice in the education of teachers. In C. A. McMurry (Ed.), *The third yearbook of the National Society for the Scientific Study of Education. Part I* (pp. 9–30). Chicago, IL: University of Chicago Press.

Dewey, J. (1910). *The influence of Darwin on philosophy and other essays in contemporary thought.* New York, NY: Henry Holt.

Dewey, J. (1916). *Democracy and education: An introduction to the philosophy of education.* New York, NY: Macmillan.

Dewey, J. (1922). *Human nature and conduct.* New York, NY: Henry Holt and Company.

Dewey, J. (1929a). *The quest for certainty: A study of the relation of knowledge and action.* New York, NY: Minton, Balch & Company.

Dewey, J. (1929b). *The sources of a science of education.* New York, NY: Horace Liveright.

Dewey, J. (1933). *How we think.* Boston, MA: D.C. Heath & Company.

Dewey, J. (1938). *Experience and education.* New York, NY: Macmillan.

Diener, E., & Lucas, R. E. (2000). Subjective emotional well-being. In M. Lewis & J. M. Haviland-Jones (Eds.), *Handbook of emotions* (pp. 325–337). New York, NY: Guilford Press.

Dobson, A. (2014). *Listening for democracy: Recognition, representation, reconciliation.* New York, NY: Oxford University Press.

Doyle, W. (1990). Themes in teacher education research. In W. R. Houston (Ed.), *Handbook of research on teacher education* (pp. 3–25). New York, NY: Macmillan.

Duckworth, A. (2016). *Grit: The power of passion and perserverance.* New York, NY: Scribner.

Dufour, R. (2005). What is a professional learning community? In R. Dufour, R. Eaker, & R. Dufour (Eds.), *On common ground* (pp. 31–43). Bloomington, IN: Solution Tree.

Education Policy Initiative at Carolina. (2015). *Measuring up: The National Council on Teacher Quality's ratings of teacher preparation programs and measures of teacher performance.* Retrieved from Publicpolicy,unc.edu/files/2015/07/measuring-up-the-national-council-on-teacher-qualitys-ratings-of-teacher-preparation-pgorams-and-measures-of-teacher-performance.pdf

Egan, K. (1988). *Teaching as story-telling: An alternative approach to teaching and the curriculum.* London: Routledge.

Eisenberg, N., Smith, C. L., & Spinrad. (2004). Effortful control: Relations with emotion regulation, adjustment, and socialization in childhood. In K. D. Vohs & R. F. Baumeister (Eds.), *Handbook of self-regulation* (pp. 263–283). New York, NY: Guildford Press.

Ekman, P. (1992). An argument for basic emotions. *Cognition and Emotion, 6*(314), 169–200.

Elbaz, F. (1983). *Teacher thinking: A study of practical knowledge.* London: Croom Helm.

Elbaz, F. (1992). Hope, attentiveness, and caring for difference: The moral voice in teaching. *Teaching & Teacher Education, 8*(5/6), 412–432.

Elbow, P. (1986). *Embracing contraries: Explorations in learning and teaching.* Oxford: Oxford University Press.

Elder, G. H., Jr., Johnson, M. K., & Crosnoe, R. (2004). The emergence and development of life course theory. In J. T. Mortimer & M. J. Shanahan (Eds.), *Handbook of the life course* (pp. 3–19). New York, NY: Springer.

Elliot, J. (1991). *Action research for educational change.* Philadelphia, PA: Open University Press.

Ellis, V., Glackin, M., Heighes, D., Norman, M., Nicol, S., Norris, K., & McNicoll, J. (2013). A difficult realization: The proletarianization of higher education-based teacher educators. *Journal of Education for Teaching, 39*(3), 266–280.

Emonson, A. C., & Roloff, K. S. (2009). Overcoming barriers to collaboration: Psychological safety and learning in diverse teams. In E. Salas, G. Goodwin, & S. Burke (Eds.), *Team effectiveness in complex organizations: Cross-disciplinary perspectives* (pp. 183–208). New York, NY: Psychology Press.

Epstein, J. (1997). The personal essay: A form of discovery. In J. Epstein (Ed.), *The Norton book of personal essays* (pp. 11–24). New York, NY: W. W. Norton.

Erasmus, D. (1549/1942). *The praise of folly.* Roslyn, NY: Walter J. Black.

Eriksen, T. H. (2007). *The key concepts of globalization.* Oxford: Berg.

Erikson, E. H. (1958). *Young man Luther: A study in psychoanalysis and history.* New York, NY: W. W. Norton.

Erikson, E. H. (1964). *Insight and responsibility.* New York, NY: W. W. Norton.

Erikson, E. H. (1968). *Identity, youth and crisis.* New York, NY: W. W. Norton.

Erikson, E. H. (1975). *Life history and the historical moment.* New York, NY: W. W. Norton and Company.

Feiman-Nemser, S. (2001). From preparation to practice: Designing a continuum to strengthen and sustain teaching. *Teachers College Record, 103*(6), 1013–1055.

Feistritzer, C. E. (2011). *Profile of teachers in the U.S., 2011.* Washington, DC: National Center for Education Information.

Feyerabend, P. (1975). *Against method.* London: NLB.

Feyerabend, P. (1994). *Against method* (3rd ed.). New York, NY: Verso.

Figley, C. R. (2002). Compassion fatigue: Psychotherapists' chronic lack of self care. *JCLP/In Session: Psychotherapy in Practice, 58*(11), 1433–1441.

Filion, K. B., & Pless, I. B. (2008). Factors related to the frequency of citation of epidemiologic publications. *Epidemiologic Perspective & Innovations, 5*(3). doi:10.1186/1742–5573-5-3

Fine, G. A., & De Sucey, M. (2005). Joking cultures: Humor themes as social regulation in group life. *Humor, 8*(1), 1–22.

Fisher, P. (2002). *The vehement passions.* Princeton, NJ: Princeton University Press.

Ford, T. G., Van Sickle, M. E., Clark, L. V., Fazio-Brunson, M., & Schween, D. C. (2017). Teacher self-efficacy, professional commitment, and high-stakes teacher evaluation policy in Louisiana. *Educational Policy, 31*(2), 202–248.

Frankl, V. (1970). *Man's search for meaning.* New York, NY: Touchstone Books.

Fraser, J. W. (2007). *Preparing America's teachers: A history.* New York, NY: Teachers College Press.

Fredman, N., & Doughney, J. (2012). Academic dissatisfaction, managerial change and neoliberalism. *Higher Education, 64*(1), 41–58.

Fredrickson, B. L., & Branigan, C. (2005). Positive emotions broaden the scope of attention and thought-action repertoires. *Cognition and Emotion, 19*(3), 313–332.

Fredrickson, B. L., Cohn, M. A., Coffey, K. A., Pek, J., & Finkel, S. M. (2008). Open hearts build lives: Positive emotions, induced through loving-kindness meditation, build consequential personal resources. *Journal of Personality and Social Psychology, 95*(5), 1045–1062.

Freedman, D. H. (2010). Lies, damned lies, and medical science. *The Atlantic, 306*(4), 76–86.

Freire, P. (1970). *Pedagogy of the oppressed.* New York, NY: Herder and Herder.

Freud, S. (1920). *A general introduction to psychoanalysis.* New York, NY: Liveright Publishing Corporation.

Fuller, F. E., & Bown, O. (1975). Becoming a teacher. In K. Ryan (Ed.), *Teacher education: The seventy-fourth yearbook of the National Society for the Study of Education, Part II* (pp. 25–52). Chicago, IL: University of Chicago Press.

Furlong, J., Whitty, G., Whiting, C., Miles, S., Baron, L., & Barrett, E. (1996). Redefining partnership: Revolution or reform in initial teacher education? *Journal of Education for Teaching, 22*(1), 39–55.

Furnham, A., Richards, S. C., & Paulhus, D. L. (2013). The dark triad of personality: A 10 year review. *Social and Personality Psychology Compass, 7*(3), 199–216.

Gage, N. L. (1972). *Teacher effectiveness and teacher education: The search for a scientific basis.* Palo Alto, CA: Pacific Books.

Gale, R. M. (2010). *John Dewey's quest for unity: The journey of a Promethean mystic.* Amherst, NY: Prometheus Books.

Gallagher, S., & LaBrie, J. (2012). Online learning 2.0: Strategies for a mature market. *Continuing Higher Education Review, 76,* 65–73.

Gallimore, R., Ermeling, B. A., Saunders, W. M., & Goldenberg, C. (2009). Moving the learning of teaching closer to practice: Teacher education implications of school-based inquiry teams. *Elementary School Journal, 109*(5), 537–553.

Garand, D. (2009). Misunderstanding: A typology of performance (K. B. Shelton, Trans.). *Common Knowledge, 15*(3), 472–500.

Garner, J. T., Chandler, R. C., & Wallace, J. D. (2015). Nothing to laugh about: Student interns' use of humor in response to workplace dissatisfaction. *Southern Communication Journal, 80*(2), 102–118.

Garrison, J. (1997). *Dewey and eros: Wisdom and desire in the art of teaching.* New York, NY: Teachers College Press.

Gergen, K. J. (1999). *An invitation to social construction.* Thousand Oaks, CA: Sage.

Giles, H. H., McCutchen, S. P., & Zechiel, A. N. (1942). *Exploring the curriculum: The work of the thirty schools from the viewpoint of curriculum consultants.* New York, NY: Harper & Brothers.

Gillham, J., & Reivich, K. (2004). Cultivating optimism in childhood and adolescence. *Annals of the American Academy of Political and Social Science, 591,* 146–163.

Girod, G. R., (2002). *Connecting teaching and learning: A handbook for teacher educators on teacher work sample methodology.* Washington, DC: AACTE.

Glazer, J. (2018). Learning from those who no longer teach: Viewing teacher attrition through a resistance lens. *Teaching & Teacher Education, 74,* 62–71.

Glenn, D. (2010). Doctoral-program rankings, delayed years, may be merely a historical record. *Chronicle of Higher Education, 56*(38), A1–A9.

Goddard, J. T., & Foster, R. Y. (2001). The experiences of neophyte teachers: A critical constructivist assessment. *Teaching & Teacher Education, 17*(3), 349–365.

Goldstein, D., & Casselman, B. (2018). Teachers find support as campaign for higher salaries goes to voters. *New York Times*, June 1, A13.

Good, T. L. (1980). Recent classroom research: Implications for teacher education. In D. C. Smith (Ed.), *Essential knowledge for beginning educators* (pp. 55–64). Washington, DC: American Association of Colleges for Teacher Education.

Good, T. L. (1990). Building the knowledge base of teaching. In D. D. Dill & associates, *What teachers need to know: The knowledge, skills, and values essential to good teaching* (pp. 17–75). San Francisco, CA: Jossey-Bass.

Good, T. L., & Brophy, J. E. (1973). *Looking in classrooms.* New York, NY: Harper & Row.

Goodlad, J. I. (1984). *A place called school: Prospects for the future.* New York, NY: McGraw-Hill.

Goodlad, J. I. (1994). *Educational renewal: Better teachers, better schools.* San Francisco, CA: Jossey-Bass.

Goodlad, J. I. (1999). Rediscovering teacher education: School renewal and educating educators. *Change, 31*(5), 28–33.

Goodlad, J. I., Mantle-Bromley, C., & Goodlad, S. J. (2004). *Education for everyone.* San Francisco, CA: Jossey-Bass.

Goodson, I. F., & Sikes, P. J. (2001). *Life history research in educational settings: Learning from lives.* Buckingham: Open University Press.

Gould, S. J. (1983). *Hen's teeth and horse's toes.* New York, NY: Norton.

Greeley, A. M. (1972). *Unsecular man.* New York, NY: Schocken Books.

Green, T. F. (1999). *Voices: The educational formation of conscience.* Notre Dame, IN: University of Notre Dame Press.

Greene, M. (1967). The professional significance of history of education. *History of Education Quarterly, 7*(2), 182–190.

Greene, M. (1977). Toward wide-awakeness: An argument for the arts and humanities. *Teachers College Record, 79*(1), 119–125.

Greene, M. (1995). *Releasing the imagination: Essays on education, the arts, and social change.* San Francisco, CA: Jossey-Bass.

Grimes, D. R., Bauch, C. T., & Ioannidis, J. P. A. (2018). Modelling science trustworthiness under publish or perish pressure. *Royal Society Open Science, 5*(1), 171511. doi:10.1098/rsos.171511

Gu, Q., & Day, C. (2007). Teacher resilience: A necessary condition for effectiveness. *Teaching & Teacher Education, 23*(8), 1302–1316.

Guerlac, S. (2001). Humanities 2.0: E-learning in the digital world. *Representations, 116*, 102–127.

Habermas, T., & Bluck, S. (2000). Getting a life: The emergence of the life story in adolescence. *Psychological Bulletin, 126*(5), 748–769.

Hacking, I. (1990). *The taming of chance.* Cambridge: Cambridge University Press.

Haggis, T. (2008). Knowledge must be contextual: Some possible implications of complexity and dynamic systems theories for educational research. In M. Mason (Ed.), *Complexity theory and the philosophy of education* (pp. 150–168). Chichester: John Wiley.

Hall, D., & McGinity, R. (2015). Conceptualizing teacher professional identity in neoliberal times: Resistance, compliance and reform. *Education Policy Analysis Archives, 23*(88), 1–15.

Hall, S. S. (2010). *Wisdom: From philosophy to neuroscience.* New York, NY: Alfred A. Knopf.

Hallie, P. (1997). *Lest innocent blood be shed.* New York, NY: Harper & Row.

Hamilton, R. F. (1997). *The social misconstruction of reality.* New Haven, CT: Yale University Press.

Hamman, D., Gosselin, K., Romano, J., & Bunuan, R. (2010). Using possible-selves theory to understand the identity development of new teachers. *Teaching & Teacher Education, 26*(7), 1349–1361.

Hammerness, K., Darling-Hammond, L., & Bransford, J. (2005). How teachers learn and develop. In L. Darling-Hammond & J. Bransford (Eds.), *Preparing teachers for a changing world: What teachers should learn and be able to do* (pp. 358–389). San Francisco, CA: Jossey-Bass.

Hansen, D. T. (1995). *The call to teach.* New York, NY: Teachers College Press.

Harari, Y. N. (2017). *Home Deus: A brief history of tomorrow.* New York, NY: Harper.

Hargreaves, A. (2000). Four ages of professionalism and professional learning. *Teachers and Teaching: Theory and Practice, 6,* 151–182.

Harre, R., & van Langenhove, L. (Eds.). (1999). *Positioning theory.* Oxford: Blackwell.

Hartley, D. (2003). The instrumentalisation of the expressive in education. *British Journal of Educational Studies, 51*(1), 6–19.

Hartwick, J. M. M., & Kang, S. J. (2013). Spiritual practices as a means of coping with and ameliorating stress to reduce teacher attrition. *Journal of Research on Christian Education, 22,* 165–188.

Harvey, J. (1995). Humor as social act: Ethical issues. *The Journal of Value Inquiry, 29*(1), 19–30.

Hawkey, K. (1997). Roles, responsibilities, and relationships in mentoring: A literature review and agenda for research. *Journal of Teacher Education, 48*(5), 325–335.

Hedges, C. (2009). *Empire of illusion.* New York, NY: Nation Books.

Helsing, D. (2007). Regarding uncertainty in teachers and teaching. *Teaching & Teacher education, 23*(8), 1317–1333.

Hickok, G. (2014). *The myth of mirror neurons: The real neuroscience of communication and cognition.* New York, NY: W.W. Norton & Company.

Ho, S. K. (2016). Relationships among humor, self-esteem, and social support to burnout in school teachers. *Social Psychology of Education, 19*(1), 41–59.

Hochschild, A. R. (2016). *Strangers in their own land: Anger and mourning on the American right.* New York, NY: The New Press.

Hodges, S. D., Lewis, K. L., & Ickes, W. (2015). The matter of other minds: Empathic accuracy and the factors that influence it. In M. Mikulincer & P. R. Shaver (Eds.), *APA handbook of personality and social psychology: Vol. 3. Interpersonal relations* (pp. 319–348). Washington, DC: The American Psychological Association.

Hoffman, M. L. (2000). *Empathy and moral development: Implications for caring and justice.* Cambridge: Cambridge University Press.

Hoffman, M. L. (2014). Empathy, justice, and social change. In H. L. Maibom (Ed.), *Empathy and morality* (pp. 69–96). New York, NY: Oxford University Press.

Holmes Group. (1986). *Tomorrow's teachers: A report of the Holmes Group.* East Lansing, MI: Holmes Group.

Holmes Group. (1990). *Tomorrow's schools of education: A report of the Holmes group.* East Lansing, MI: Holmes Group.

Holmes, J., & Marra, M. (2002). Having a laugh at work: How humour contributes to workplace culture. *Journal of Pragmatics, 34*(12), 1683–1710.

Hord, S. M. (1997). *Professional learning communities: Communities of continuous inquiry and improvement.* Austin, TX: Southwest Educational Development Laboratory.

Hord, S. M. (2003). *Learning together, leading together: Changing schools through professional learning communities.* New York, NY: Teachers College Press.

Hord, S. M. (2009). *Guiding professional learning communities: Inspiration, surprise, and meaning.* Thousand Oaks, CA: Corwin Press.

Hord, S. M., & Sommers, W. A. (2008). *Leading professional learning communities: Voices from research and practice.* Thousand Oaks, CA: Corwin Press.

Horne, H. H. (1916). *Story-telling, questioning and studying.* New York, NY: Macmillan.

Howe, H. (1973). Improving teacher education through exposures to reality. In D. J. McCarthy & Associates (Eds.), *New perspectives on teacher education* (pp. 53–65). San Francisco, CA: Jossey-Bass.

Hoy, A. W., Hoy, W. K., & Kurz, N. M. (2008). Teachers' academic optimism: The development and testing of a new construct. *Teaching & Teacher Education, 24*(4), 821–835.

Hoy, A. W., Hoy, W. K., & Tarter, C. J. (2006). Academic optimism of schools: A force for student achievement. *American Educational Research Journal, 43*(3), 425–446.

Huberman, M. (1989). The professional life cycle of teachers. *Teachers College Record, 91,* 31–57.

Huberman, M. (1992). Teacher development and instructional mastery. In A. Hargreaves & M. G. Fullan (Eds.), *Understanding teacher development* (pp. 122–142). New York, NY: Teachers College Press.

Hunt, D. E. (1987). *Beginning with ourselves: In practice, theory, and human affairs.* Cambridge, MA: Brookline Books.

Hunt, M. (1993). *The story of psychology.* New York, NY: Doubleday.

Iacoboni, M. (2008). *The new science of how we connect with others: Mirroring people.* New York, NY: Farrar, Straus and Giroux.

Ickes, W. (2003). *Everyday mind reading: Understanding what other people think and feel.* Amherst, NY: Prometheus Books.

Ickes, W. (2009). Empathic accuracy: Its links to clinical, cognitive, developmental, social, and physiological psychology. In J. Decety & W. Ickes (Eds.), *The social neuroscience of empathy* (pp. 57–70). Cambridge, MA: The MIT Press.

Ingersoll, R. (2003). *Who controls teaching?* Cambridge, MA: Harvard University Press.

Ingersoll, R. (2007). Misdiagnosing the teacher quality problem. *CPRE Policy Briefs.* Retrieved from http://repository.upenn.cpre_policybriefs/35.

Ingersoll, R., Merrill, L., & May, H. (2014). What are the effects of teacher education preparation on beginning teacher attrition? *CRPE Research Reports.* doi:10.12698/cpre.2014.rr82

Interstate New Teacher Assessment and Support Consortium. (1992). *Model standards for beginning teacher licensing, assessment and development: A resource for state dialogue.* Washington, DC: Council of Chief State School Officers.

Ioannidis, J. P. A. (2017). The reproducibility wars: Successful, unsuccessful, uninterpretable, exact, conceptual, triangulated, contested replication. *Clinical Chemistry, 63*(5), 1–3.

James, W. (1922/1899). *Talks to teachers on psychology: And to students on some of life's ideals.* New York, NY: Henry Holt.

Jamison, L. (2014). *The empathy exams: Essays.* Minneapolis, MN: Graywolf Press.

Jensen, B., Whiting, E. F., & Chapman, S. (2018). Measuring the multicultural dispositions of preservice teachers. *Journal of Psychoeducational Assessment, 36*(2), 120–135.

Jensen, K. (2007). The desire to learn: An analysis of knowledge-seeking practices among professionals. *Oxford Review of Education, 33*(4), 489–502.

Jiang, J., Vauras, M., Volet, S., & Wang, Y. (2016). Teachers' emotions and emotion regulation strategies: Self- and students' perceptions. *Teaching and Teacher Education, 54,* 22–31.

Johnson, D. D., Johnson, B., Farenga, S. J., & Ness, D. (2005). *Trivializing teacher education: The accreditation squeeze.* Lanham, MD: Rowman & Littlefield Education.

Johnson, M. (1993). *Moral imagination: Implications of cognitive science for ethics.* Chicago, IL: University of Chicago Press.

Johnston, P. (1989). Constructing evaluation and the improvement of teaching and learning. *Teachers College Record, 90*(4), 509–528.

Judson, K. M., & Taylor, S. A. (2014). Moving from marketization to marketing of higher education: The co-creation of value in higher education. *Higher Education Studies, 4*(1), 51–67.

Kahneman, D. (2011). *Thinking, fast and slow.* New York, NY: Farrar, Straus and Giroux.

Kane, R. (2010). *Ethics and the quest for wisdom.* Cambridge, MA: Cambridge University Press.

Kantor, H., & Lowe, R. (2013). Educationalizing the welfare state and privatizing education: The evolution of social policy since the New Deal. In P. L. Carter (Ed.), *Closing the opportunity gap* (pp. 25–39). New York, NY: Oxford University Press.

Kauppinen, A. (2014). Empathy, emotion regulation and moral judgment. In H. L. Maibom (Ed.), *Empathy and morality* (pp. 97–121). New York, NY: Oxford University Press.

Kegan, R. (1982). *The evolving self: Problem and process in human development.* Cambridge, MA: Harvard University Press.

Kelchtermans, G. (1996). Teacher vulnerability: Understanding its moral and political roots. *Cambridge Journal of Education, 26*(3), 307–324.

Kelchtermans, G. (1999). Teaching career: Between burnout and fading away? In R. Vandenberghe & A. M. Huberman (Eds.), *Understanding and preventing teacher burnout: A sourcebook of international research and practice* (pp. 176–191). Cambridge: Cambridge University Press.

Kelchtermans, G. (2005). Teachers' emotions in educational reforms: Self-understanding, vulnerable commitment and micropolitical literacy. *Teaching & Teacher Education, 21*(8), 995–1006.

Kelchtermans, G. (2009). Who I am in how I teach is the message: Self-understanding, vulnerability, and reflection. *Teachers and Teaching: Theory and Practice, 15*(2), 257–272.

Kelchtermans, G. (2011). Vulnerability in teaching: The moral and political roots of a structural condition. In C. Day & J. Lee (Eds.), *New understandings of teacher's work: Emotions and educational change* (pp. 65–82). New York, NY: Springer.

Kelchtermans, G., & Ballet, K. (2002). The micropolitics of teacher induction: A narrative biographical study of teacher socialization. *Teaching & Teacher Education, 18*(1), 105–120.

Kelly, J. (2013). Professional learning communities: The emergence of vulnerability. *Professional Development in Education, 39*(5), 862–864.

Kent, P. (2008). How statistics and league tables are failing schools. *Secondary Headship, 68*(Oct), 1–2.

Kolata, G. (2016, August). Food and exercise studies one big problem. *New York Times*, A3.

Korthagen, F. A. J., Attem-Noordewier, S., & Zwart, R. C. (2014). Teacher-student contact: Exploring a basic but complicated concept. *Teaching and Teacher Education, 40*, 22–32.

Kounin, J. S. (1970). *Discipline and group management in classrooms*. New York, NY: Holt, Rinehart and Winston.

Kuhn, T. (1970). *The structure of scientific revolutions*. Chicago, IL: University of Chicago Press.

Kuiper, N. A., Grimshaw, M., Leite, C., & Kirsh, G. (2004). Humor is not always the best medicine: Specific components of sense of humor and psychological well-being. *Humor, 17*(1–2), 135–168.

Kuntz, M. A., Petrovic, J. E., & Ginocchio, L. (2012). A changing sense of place: A case study of academic culture and the built environment. *Higher Education Policy, 25*, 433–451.

Kuttner, R. (2018). *Can democracy survive global capitalism*. New York, NY: W. W. Norton.

Lakoff, G., & Johnson, M. (1980/2003). *Metaphors we live by*. Chicago, IL: University of Chicago Press.

Lasch, C. (1991). *The true and only heaven: Progress and its critics*. New York, NY: W. W. Norton.

Lawrence Sheriff School Inspection Report. (2007). Retrieved from http://www.ofsted.gov.uk/oxedu-reports/download(id)/90176(as)125753–315304.pdf

Lazarus, R. S. (1999). Hope: An emotion and a vital coping resource against despair. *Social Research, 66*(2), 653–678.

Leisering, L. (2004). Government and the life course. In, J. T. Mortimer & M. J. Shanahan (Eds.), *Handbook of the life course* (pp. 205–225). New York, NY: Springer.

Lemke, J. L., & Sabelli, N. H. (2008). Complex systems and educational change: Towards a new research agenda. In M. Mason (Ed.), *Complexity theory and the philosophy of education* (pp. 112–123). Oxford: Wiley-Blackwell.

Levinas, E. (1969). *Totality and infinity: An essay on exteriority*. Pittsburgh, PA: Duquesne University Press.

Lewis, P. (2006). *Cracking up: American humor in a time of conflict*. Chicago, IL: University of Chicago Press.

Lipari, L. (2014). *Listening, thinking, being: Toward an ethics of attunement*. University Park, PA: Pennsylvania State University Press.

Loftus, E. (2003). Our changeable memories: Legal and practical implications. *Nature Reviews: Neuroscience, 4*(3), 231–234.

Lottie, D. C. (1975). *Schoolteacher: A sociological study*. Chicago, IL: University of Chicago Press.

Loughran, J. J., Hamilton, M. L., LaBoskey, V. K., & Russell, T. L. (Eds.). (2004). *International handbook of self-study of teaching and teacher education practices*. Dordrecht: Kluwer Academic Publishers.

Lozano, G. A., Laiviere, V., & Gingras, Y. (2012). The weakening relationship between Impact Factor and papers' citations in the digital age. *The Journal of the Association for Information Science and Technology. 63*(11), 2140–2145.

Lubienski, C. A., & Lubienski, S. T. (2014). *The public school advantage: Why public schools outperform private ones*. Chicago, IL: University of Chicago Press.

Lucas, C. J. (1999). *Teacher education in America: Reform agendas for the twenty-first century*. New York, NY: St. Martin's Press.

Maddern, K. (2009). Not enough talent to go round: How schools struggle to fill headships. *TES Connect*. Retrieved from https://www.tes.com/news/not-enough-talent-go-round-how-schools-struggle-fill-headships

Maguire, M. (2001). Bullying and the postgraduate secondary trainee teacher: An English case study. *Journal of Education for Teaching, 27*(1), 95–110.

Maibom, H. L. (Ed.). (2014a). *Empathy and morality*. New York, NY: Oxford University Press.

Maibom, H. L. (2014b). Introduction. In H. L. Maibom (Ed.), *Empathy and morality* (pp. 1–40). New York, NY: Oxford University Press.

Majcher, A. (2008). The battle over professorship: Reform of human resource management and academic careers in a comparative perspective. *Higher Education Policy, 21*, 345–358.

Manuel, J., & Brindley, S. (2005). The call to teach: Identifying pre-service teachers' motivations, expectations and key experiences during initial teacher education in Australia and the United Kingdom. *English in Australia, 144*, 38–49.

Manzi, J. (2012). *Uncontrolled: The surprising payoff of trial and error for business, politics, and society*. New York, NY: Basic Books.

Margolis, J. (2008). What will keep today's teachers teaching? Looking for a hook as a new career cycle emerges. *Teachers College Record, 110*(1), 160–194.

Martin, J. R. (1992). *The schoolhome: Rethinking schools for changing families*. Cambridge, MA: Harvard University Press.

Martin, R. A. (2007). *The psychology of humor: An integrative approach*. San Diego, CA: Elsevier Academic Press.

Martineau, J. A. (2006). Distorting value added: The use of longitudinal, vertically scaled student achievement data for growth-based, value-added accountability. *Journal of Educational and Behavioral Statistics, 31*(1), 35–62.

Maslach, C. (1999). Progress in understanding teacher burnout. In R. Vandenberghe & A. M. Huberman (Eds.), *Understanding and preventing teacher burnout: A sourcebook of international research and practice* (pp. 211–222). New York, NY: Cambridge University Press.

Mason, M. (Ed.). (2008). *Complexity theory and the philosophy of education*. Oxford: Wiley-Blackwell.

Mattingly, P. H. (1975). *The classless profession*. New York, NY: New York University Press.

Mayes, C. T. (2005a). Teaching and time: Foundations of a temporal pedagogy. *Teacher Education Quarterly, 32*(2), 143–160.

Mayes, C. T. (2005b). *Teaching mysteries: Foundations of a spiritual pedagogy*. Lanham, MD: University Press of America.

Mayes, C. T. (2005c). *Jung and education: Elements of an archetypal pedagogy*. Lanham, MD: Rowman & Littlefield Education.

Mayes, C. T. (2007). *Inside education: Depth psychology in teaching and learning*. Madison, WI: Atwood.

Mayes, C. T., Mayes, P. B., & Sagmiller, K. (2005). The sense of spiritual calling among teacher education program students. *Religion and Education, 30*(2), 84–103.

Mayo, C. (2010). Incongruity and provisional safety: Thinking through humor. *Studies in the Philosophy of Education, 29*(6), 509–521.

McAdams, D. P. (1990). Unity and purpose in human lives: The emergence of identity as a life story. In A. I. Rabin (Ed.), *Studying persons and lives* (pp. 148–200). New York, NY: Springer.

McAdams, D. P. (2001). The psychology of life stories. *Review of General Psychology, 5*(2), 100–122.

McAdams, D. P. (2004). The redemptive self: Narrative identity in America today. In D. R. Beike, J. M. Lampinen, & D. A. Behrend (Eds.), *The self and memory* (pp. 95–115). New York, NY: Psychology Press.

McAdams, D. P. (2005). *Redemptive self: Stories Americans live by*. Oxford: Oxford University Press.

McAdams, D. P. (2006). The problem of narrative coherence. *The Journal of Constructivist Psychology, 19*(2), 109–125.

McAdams, D. P., Bauer, J. J., Sakaeda, A. R., Anyidoho, N. A., Machado, M. A., Magrino-Failla, K., Whie, K. W., & Pals, J. L. (2006). Continuity and change in the life story: A longitudinal study of autobiographical memories in emerging adulthood. *Journal of Personality, 74*(5), 1371–1400.

McAdams, D. P., Diamon, A., de St Aubin, E., & Mansfield, E. (1997). Stories of commitment: The psychosocial construction of generative lives. *Journal of Personality and Social Psychology, 72*(3), 678–694.

McCabe, C., Sprute, K., & Underdown, K. (2017). Laughter to learning: How humor can build relationships and increase learning in the online classroom. *Journal of Instructional Research, 6,* 4–7.

McCaw, N. (2011). Close reading, writing and culture. *International Journal for the Practice and Theory of Creative Writing, 8*(1), 25–34.

McCollough, C. (2008). *The art of parables.* Kelowna: Copper-House.

McCraw, T. K. (1992). The trouble with Adam Smith. *American Scholar, 61*(3), 353–373.

McDermott, D., & Hastings, S. (2000). Children: Raising future hopes. In C. R. Snyder (Ed.), *Handbook of hope: Theory, measures and applications* (pp. 185–199). San Diego, CA: Academic Press.

McDiarmid, G. W. (1990). Challenging perspective teachers' beliefs during field experience: A quixotic understanding. *Journal of Teacher Education, 41*(3), 12–30.

Meidl, T., & Baumann, B. (2015). Extreme make over: Disposition development of pre-service teachers. *Journal of Community Engagement and Scholarship, 8*(1), 90–97.

Menzies, H. &, Newson, J. (2007). No time to think: Academics' life in the globally wired university. *Time & Society, 16*(1), 83–98.

Metlife. (2013). *The MetLife survey of the American teacher: Challenges for school leadership.* Retrieved from https://www.metlife.com/assets/cao/foundation/MetLifeTeacher-Survey-2012.pdf

Meyer, F., Le Fevre, D. M., & Robinson, V. M. J. (2017). How leaders communicate their vulnerability: Implications for trust building. *International Journal of Educational Management, 31*(2), 221–235.

Mikics, D. (2007). *A new handbook of literary terms.* New Haven, CT: Yale University Press.

Miles, M. B., & Huberman, A. M. (1984). *Qualitative data analysis.* Newbury Park, CA: Sage.

Mills, C. W. (1959). *The sociological imagination.* New York, NY: Oxford University Press.

Mitchell, M. (2009). *Complexity: A guided tour.* New York, NY: Oxford University Press.

Mohrman, K., Wanhua, M., & Baker, D. (2008). The research university in transition: The emerging global model. *Higher Education Policy, 21,* 5–27.

Monroe, W. S. (1952). *Teaching-learning theory and teacher education: 1890–1950.* Urbana, IL: The University of Illinois Press.

Moore, D. T. (2007). Analyzing learning at work: An interdisciplinary framework. *Learning Inquiry, 1,* 175–188.

Moran, C. (2015). Time as a social practice. *Time & Society. 24*(3), 283–303.

Morreall, J. (1983). *Taking humor seriously.* Albany, NY: State University of New York Press.

Morreall, J. (1997). *Humor works.* Amherst, MA: HRD Press.

Morreall, J. (2009). *Comic relief: A comprehensive philosophy of humor.* Malden, MA: Wiley-Blackwell.

Morrison, K. (2008). Educational philosophy and the challenge of complexity theory. In M. Mason (Ed.), *Complexity theory and the philosophy of education* (pp. 16–31). Chichester: John Wiley.

Mullan, C. A., Samier, E., Brindley, S., English, F. W., & Carr, N. K. (2013). An epistemic frame analysis of neoliberal culture and politics in the U.S., U.K., and the UAE. *Interchange, 43,* 187–228.

Mullen, C. A. (Ed.). (2009). *Leadership and building learning communities.* New York, NY: Palgrave Macmillan.

Myers, D. G. (2000). The funds, friends, and faith of happy people. *American Psychologist, 55*(1), 56–67.

National Commission on Excellence in Education. (1983). *A nation at risk: The imperative for educational reform.* Washington, DC: U.S. Government Printing Office.

National Commission on Teaching and America's Future. (1996a). *Summary report.* New York, NY: National Commission on Teaching and America's Future.

National Commission on Teaching and America's Future. (1996b). *What matters most: Teaching for America's future.* New York, NY: National Commission on Teaching and America's Future.

National Education Goals Panel. (1995). *The national education goals report: Building a nation of learners.* Washington, DC: U.S. Government Printing Office.

National Research Council. (2002). *Scientific research in education.* Committee on scientific principles for education research (R. J. Savelson & L. Towne (Eds.). Washington, DC: The National Academies Press.

National Research Council. (2010). *Preparing teachers: Building evidence for sound policy.* Committee on the Study of Teacher Preparation Programs in the United States. Washington, DC: The National Academies Press.

Natriello, G. (2007). Imagining, seeking, inventing: The future of learning and the emerging discovery networks. *Learning Inquiry, 1*(1), 7–18.

Nettle, D. (2005). *Happiness: The science behind your smile.* New York, NY: Oxford University Press.

Newfield, C. (2003). *Ivy and industry: Business and the making of the American university, 1880–1980.* Durham, NC: Duke University Press.

Newfield, C. (2008). *The unmaking of the public university: The forty-year assault on the middle class.* Cambridge, MA: Harvard University Press.

Nezleck, J. B., & Derks, P. (2001). Use of humor as a coping mechanism, psychological adjustment, and social interaction. *Humor, 14*(4), 395–413.

Nias, J. (1989). *Primary teachers talking: A study of teaching as work.* New York, NY: Routledge.

Nichel, P. M. (Ed.). (2012). *North American critical theory after postmodernism: Contemporary dialogues.* New York, NY: Palgrave Macmillan.

Nichols, S. L., & Berliner, D. C. (2007). *Collateral damage: How high stakes testing corrupts America's schools.* Cambridge, MA: Harvard Education Press.

Niebuhr, R. (1945). *The children of light and the children of darkness.* New York, NY: Charles Scribner's Sons.

Nigg, J. T. (2017). Annual research review: On the relations among self-regulation, self-control, executive functioning, effortful control, cognitive control, impulsivity, risk-taking, and inhibition for developmental psychopathology. *Journal of Child Psychology and Psychiatry, 58*(4), 361–383.

Noddings, N. (2003). *Happiness and education.* New York, NY: Cambridge University Press.

Nuttall, J., Brennan, M., Zipin, L., Tuinamuana, K., & Cameron, L. (2013). Lost in production: The erasure of the teacher educators in Australian university job advertisements. *Journal of Education for Teaching, 39*(3), 329–343.

Nutting, W. C. (1981). Professional development centers: The Utah experiment. *Phi Delta Kappan, 63,* 394–395.

Oden, T. C. (Ed.). (1978). *Parables of Kierkegaard.* Princeton, NJ: Princeton University Press.

Ofsted. (2018). *School inspection handbook.* Reference no: 150066, www.gov.uk/government/publications/school-inspection-handbook-from-september-2015

Olsen, B., & Sexton, D. (2009). Threat rigidity, school reform, and how teachers view their work inside current education policy contexts. *American Educational Research Journal, 46*(1), 9–44.

Orlando, L. (2006). *School superintendent's inappropriate video could get him fired.* Retrieved from http://www.buzzle.com/articles. Accessed on February 18, 2011.

Oxenham, M. (2013). *Higher education in liquid modernity.* New York, NY: Routledge.

Page, M. L., Rudney, G. L., & Marxen, C. E. (2004). Leading preservice teachers to water…and helping them drink. *Teacher Education Quarterly, 31*(2), 25–41.

Palmer, P. (1998). *The courage to teach.* San Francisco, CA: Jossey-Bass.

Palmer, P. (2009). *A hidden wholeness: The journey toward an undivided life.* San Francisco, CA: Jossey-Bass.

Papay, J. P. (2011). Different tests, different answers: The stability of teacher value-added estimates across outcome measures. *American Educational Research Journal, 48*(1), 163–193.

Park, I. (2005). Teacher commitment and its effects on student achievement in American high schools. *Educational Research and Evaluation, 11*(5), 461–485.

Pearson, C. (2009). Teacher perceptions of high-stakes testing. *Policy and Practice in Education, 15,* 21–42.

Penprase, B., Oakley, B., Ternes, R., & Driscoll, D. (2015). Do higher dispositions for empathy predispose males toward careers in nursing? A descriptive correlational design. *Nursing Forum*, *50*(1), 1–8.

Peters, J. S. (2005). Law, literature, and the vanishing real: On the future of an interdisciplinary illusion. *PMLA*, *120*(2), 442–453.

Peterson, C. (2000). The future of optimism. *American Psychologist*, *55*(1), 44–55.

Peterson, C. (2006). *A primer in positive psychology*. New York, NY: Oxford University Press.

Pinnegar, S. (1996). Sharing stories: A teacher educator accounts for narrative in her teaching. *Action in Teacher Education*, *18*(3), 13–22.

Pinnegar, S., & Hamilton, M. L. (2009). *Self study of practice as a genre of qualitative research: Theory, methodology and practice*. New York, NY: Springer.

Pinnegar, S., Mangelson, J., Reed, M., & Groves, S. (2011). Exploring preservice teachers' metaphor plotlines. *Teaching & Teacher Education*, *27*(3), 639–647.

Platsidou, M., & Agaliotis, I. (2017). Does empathy predict instructional assignment-related stress? A study in special and general education teachers. *International Journal of Disability, Development and Education*, *64*(1), 57–75.

Popham, W. J. (1973). *Evaluating instruction*. Englewood Cliffs, NJ: Prentice-Hall.

Popham, W. J., & Baker, E. L. (1973a). *Classroom instructional tactics*. Englewood Cliffs, NJ: Prentice-Hall.

Popham, W. J., & Baker, E. L. (1973b). *Expanding dimensions of instructional objectives*. Englewood Cliffs, NJ: Prentice-Hall.

Porter, T. M. (1986). *The rise of statistical thinking: 1820–1900*. Princeton, NJ: Princeton University Press.

Praag, L. V., Stevens, P. A. J., & Houtte, M. V. (2017). How humor makes or breaks student-teacher relationships: A classroom ethnography in Belgium. *Teaching & Teacher Education*, *66*, 393–401.

Rabinow, P. (2008). *Marking time*. Princeton, NJ: Princeton University Press.

Radford, M. (2008). Complexity and truth in educational research. In M. Mason (Ed.), *Complexity theory and the philosophy of education* (pp. 137–149). Chichester: John Wiley.

Ravitch, D. (2013). *Reign of error: The hoax of the privatization movement and the danger to America's public schools*. New York, NY: Alfred A. Knopf.

Redding, C., & Smith, T. M. (2016). Easy in, easy out: Are alternatively certified teachers turning over at increased rates? *American Educational Research Journal*, *53*(4), 1086–1125.

Rentner, D. S., Kober, N., Ferguson, M., Frizzell, M., & Center on Education Policy. (2016). *Listen to us: Teacher views and voices*. Retrieved from http://www.cep-dc.org

Reynolds, M. C. (1989). *Knowledge base for the beginning teacher*. New York, NY: Pergamon Press.

Rhoades, G. (2006). The higher education we choose: A question of balance. *Review of Higher Education*, *39*(3), 381–404.

Rhoads, R., Berdan, J., & Toven-Lindsey, B. (2013). The open courseware movement in higher education: Unmasking power and raising questions about the movement's democratic potential. *Educational Theory*, *63*(1), 87–109.

Rice, J. (2013). What I learned in MOOC. *College Composition and Communication*, *64*(4), 695.

Rich, M. (2013, September 10). Loud voice fighting tide of new trend in education. *New York Times*, A12.

Richards, J. (2004). *From the inside out: Learning from the positive deviance in our organization*. Washington, DC: National Staff Development Council.

Richardson, P. W., & Watt, H. M. G. (2006). Who chooses teaching and why? Profiling characteristics and motivations across three Australian universities. *Asia-Pacific Journal of Teacher Education*, *34*(1), 27–56.

Rodgers, C. R., & Scott, K. H. (2008). The development of the personal self and professional identity in learning to teach. In M. Cochran-Smith, S. Nemser-Feiman, D. J. McIntyre, & K. E. Demers (Eds.), *Handbook of Research on Teacher Education* (pp. 732–755). New York, NY: Routledge.

Rodrigues, S. B., & Collinson, D. L. (1995). "Having fun"?: Humor as resistance in Brazil. *Organizational Studies*, *16*(5), 739–768.

Rodriguez, S. Monreal, T., & Howard, J. (2018). "It's about hearing and understanding their stories": Teacher empathy and socio-political awareness toward newcomer undocumented students in the New Latino Sough. *Journal of Latinos and Education*. doi.org/1080.15348431.2018.

Rosenshine, B., & Furst, N. (1971). Research in teacher performance criteria. In B. O. Smith (Ed.), *Teacher expectation and pupil's intellectual development* (pp. 37−72). Englewood Cliffs, NJ: Prentice-Hall.

Ryan, R. M., & Deci, E. L. (2000). Self-determination theory and the facilitation of intrinsic motivation, social development, and well-being. *American Psychologist, 55*(1), 68−78.

Ryan, R. M., & Deci, E. L. (2001). On happiness and human potentials: A review of research on hedonic and eudaimonic well-being. *Annual Review of Psychology, 52*, 141−166.

Santoro, D. A. (2011). Good teaching in difficult times: Demoralization in the pursuit of good work. *American Journal of Education, 118*(1), 1−23.

Schmidt, W. H., Houang, R. T., & McKnight, C. C. (2005). Value-addedresearch: Right idea but wrong solution. In R. W. Lissitz (Ed.), *Value-added models in education: Theory and application* (pp. 145−165). Grove, MN: JAM Press.

Schneider, M. K. (2016). *School choice: The end of public education?* New York, NY: Teachers College Press.

Schön, D. A. (1983). *The reflective practitioner*. New York, NY: Basic Books.

Schön, D. A. (1987). *Educating the reflective practitioner: Toward a new design for teaching and learning in the professions*. San Francisco, CA: Jossey-Bass.

Schonfeld, I. S. (1992). A longitudinal study of occupational stressors and depressive symptoms in first-year female teachers. *Teaching & Teacher education, 8*(2), 151−158.

Schroyer, T. (1975). *The critique of domination*. Boston, MA: Beacon Press.

Schubert, W., & Ayers, W. (1992). *Teacher lore: Learning from our own experience*. New York, NY: Longman.

Scott, C., & Dinham, S. (2008). Born not made: The nativist myth and teachers' thinking. *Teacher Development, 12*(2), 115−124.

Seelye, K. Q., Schmidt, M. S., & Rashbaum, W. K. (2013). Surviving suspect is charged by U.S. in Boston attack. *New York Times*, A1.

Seligman, A. B. (1997). *The problem of trust*. Princeton, NJ: Princeton University Press.

Seligman, M. E. P., & Csikszentmihalyi, M. (2000). Positive psychology. *American Psychologist, 55*(1), 5−14.

Serow, R. C. (1994). Called to teach: A study of highly motivated preservice teachers. *The Journal of Research and Development in Education, 27*(2), 65−72.

Serow, R. C., Eaker, D. J., & Forrest, K. D. (1994). "I want to see some kind of growth out of them": What the service ethic means to teacher-education students. *American Educational Research Journal, 31*(1), 27−48.

Shade, P. (2006). Educating hopes. *Studies in Philosophy and Education, 25*, 191−225.

Shanahan, M. J., & Macmillan, R. (2008). *Biography and the sociological imagination*. New York, NY: W.W. Norton.

Shell, E. R. (2018, May 16). College may not be worth it anymore. *New York Times*, A23.

Shrum, E. (2012). A bibliographic essay on the university, the market, and professors. *The Hedgehog Review, 14*(1), 43−51.

Shulman, L. S. (1986a). Paradigms and research programs in the study of teaching: A contemporary perspective. In M. C. Wittrock (Ed.), *Handbook of research on teaching* (pp. 3−36). New York, NY: Macmillan.

Shulman, L. S. (1986b). Those who understand: Knowledge growth in teaching. *Educational Researcher, 15*, 4−14.

Sirotnik, K. A. (2001). *Renewing schools & teacher education: An odyssey in educational change*. New York, NY: AACTE.

Slick, S. K. (1997). Assessing versus assisting: The supervisor's role in the complex dynamics of the student teaching triad. *Teaching & Teacher Education, 13*(7), 713−726.

Smith, A. (1759/1937). *An inquiry into the nature and causes of the wealth of nations*. New York, NY: The Modern Library.

Smith, D. C. (1983). *Essential knowledge for beginning educators*. Washington, DC: American Association of Colleges for Teacher Education.

Smith, T. W., & Colby, S. A. (2010). Perspectives on decisions of researchers who examine the efficacy of the advanced certification system of the National Board for Professional Teacher Standards. *Studies in Educational Evaluation, 36*, 143–152.

Snyder, C. R., Cheavens, J., & Sympson, S. C. (1997). Hope: An individual motive for social commerce. *Group Dynamics: Theory, Research, and Practice, 1*(2), 107–118.

Snyder, C. R., Harris, C., Anderson, J. R., Holleran, S. A., Irving, L. M., Sigmon, S. T., … Harney, P. (1991). The will and the ways: Development and validation of an individual-differences measure of hope. *Journal of Personality and Social Psychology, 60*(4), 570–585.

Snyder, C. R., Rand, K. L., & Sigmon, D. R. (2005). Hope theory: A member of the positive psychology family. In C. R. Snyder & S. J. Lopez (Eds.), *Handbook of positive psychology* (pp. 257–312). New York, NY: Oxford University Press.

Snyder, C. R., Sympson, S. C., Ybasco, F. C., Borders, T. F., Babyak, M. A., & Higgins, R. L. (1996). Development and validation of the state Hope Scale. *Journal of Social Psychology, 70*(2), 321–335.

Solomon, R. C. (1993). *The passions: Emotions and the meaning of life*. Indianapolis, IN: Hackett.

Spencer, I. (2013). Doing the "second shift": Gendered labour and the symbolic annihilation of teacher educators' work. *Journal of Education for Teaching, 39*(2), 301–313.

Spinrad, T. L., & Eisenberg, N. (2014). Empathy and morality: A developmental psychology perspective. In H. L. Maibom (Ed.), *Empathy and morality* (pp. 59–70). New York, NY: Oxford University Press.

Spinrad, T. L., & Eisenberg, N. (2015). Effortful control. In R. Scott & S. Kosslyn (Eds.), *Emerging trends in the social and behavioral Sciences* (pp. 2–11). New York, NY: John Wiley & Sons.

Sprat, T. (1958). *History of the Royal Society of London*. St. Louis, MO: Washington UniversityStudies.

Sprinthall, N. A., Reiman, A. J., & Thies-Sprinthall, L. (1996). Teacher professional development. In J. Sikula (Ed.), *Handbook of research on teacher education* (pp. 666–703). New York, NY: Macmillan.

Stein, K. (2012). Time off: The social experience of time on vacation. *Qualitative Sociology, 35*, 335–353.

Stewart, M. (2018). The birth of a new American aristocracy. *The Atlantic, 321*(5), 48–63.

Stigler, S. M. (1999). *Statistics on the table: The history of statistical concepts and methods*. Cambridge, MA: Harvard University Press.

Stoll, L., Bolam, R., McMahon, A., Wallace, M., & Thomas, S. (2006). Professional learning communities: A review of the literature. *Journal of Educational Change, 7*, 221–258.

Strong, M., & Baron, W. (2004). An analysis of mentoring conversations with beginning teachers: Suggestions and responses. *Teaching & Teacher Education, 20*(1), 47–57.

Sutherland, T. (2013). Getting nowhere fast: A teleological conception of sociotechnical acceleration. *Time & Society. 23*(1), 49–68

Sutton, R. E., Mudrey-Camino, R., & Knight, C. C. (2009). Teachers' emotion regulation and classroom management. *Theory into Practice, 48*(2), 130–137.

Swann, W. B. Jr. (1996). *Self-traps*. New York, NY: W. H. Freeman and Company.

Swarns, R. L. (2014, January 19). Crowded out of the ivory tower, adjuncts see a life less lofty. *New York Times*, A11.

Sykes, G., & Bird, T. (1992). Teacher education and the case idea. In G. Grant (Ed.), *Review of research in education* (pp. 457–521). Washington, DC: American Educational Research Association.

Terkel, S. (1970). *Hard times: An oral history of the great depression*. New York, NY: Pantheon Books.

Thomas, W. I., & Thomas, D. W. (1928). *The child in America*. New York, NY: Alfred A. Knopf.

Tirri, K., Husu, J., & Kansanen, P. (1999). The epistemological stance between the knower and the known. *Teaching & Teacher Education, 15*(8), 911–922.

Toulmin, S. (2001). *Return to reason*. Cambridge, MA: Harvard University Press.

Tumkaya, S. (2007). Burnout and humor relationships among university lectures. *Humor, 20*(1), 73–92.

US Department of Education. (2009). *Race to the top program: Executive summary*. Retrieved from https://ww2.ed.gov/programs/racetothetop/executive-summary.pdg

US Department of Education. (2012). *Early K-12 teaching experiences of 2007–2008, Bachelor's degree recipients*. Retrieved from http://nces.ed.gov/pubs2013/2013154.pdf

Valli, L., & Buese, D. (2007). The changing roles of teachers in an era of high-stakes accountability. *American Educational Research Journal, 44*(3), 519–558.

Van Eekelen, I. M., Vermunt, J. D., & Boshuizen, H. P. A. (2006). Exploring teachers' will to learn. *Teaching & Teacher education, 22*(4), 408–413.

van Langehove, L., & Harre, R. (1999). Introducing positioning theory. In R. Harre & L. van Langenhove (Eds.), *Positioning theory* (pp. 14–31). Oxford: Blackwell.

Veronneau, M. H., Fosco, K., & Dishion, T. J. (2014). The contribution of adolescent effortful control to early adult educational attainment. *Journal of Educational psychology, 106*(3), 730–743.

Vescio, V., Ross, D., & Adams, A. (2008). A review of research on the impact of professional learning communities on teaching practice and student learning. *Teaching & Teacher Education, 24*(1), 80–91.

Wallinger, L. M. (1997). Don't smile before Christmas: The role of humor in education. *NASSP Bulletin, 81*(589), 27–34.

Wang, J. (2001). Context of mentoring and opportunities for learning to each: A comparative study of mentoring practice. *Teaching & Teacher Education, 17*(1), 51–73.

Wanzer, M. B., Frymier, A. B., Wojtaszczyk, A. M., & Smith, T. (2006). Appropriate and inappropriate uses of humor by teachers. *Communication Education, 55*(2), 178–196.

Ward, I. (1993). The educative ambition of law and literature. *Legal Studies, 13*(3), 323–331.

Ward, I. (1994). From literature to ethics: The strategies and ambitions of law and literature. *Oxford Journal of Legal Studies, 14*(3), 389–400.

Warren, C. A. (2014). Towards a pedagogy for the application of empathy in culturally diverse classrooms. *Urban Review, 46*(3), 395–419.

Watson, C. (2009). 'Teachers are meant to be orthodox': Narrative and counter narrative in the discursive construction of 'identity' in teaching. *Qualitative Studies in Education, 22*(4), 469–483.

Weinberg, M. (2018). Paradox and trespass: Possibilities for ethical practice in times of austerity. *Ethics & Social Welfare, 12*(1), 5–19.

Weiner, L. (2007). A lethal threat to U.S. teacher education. *Journal of Teacher Education, 58*(4), 274–286.

Weinstein, C. S. (1989). Teacher education students' preconceptions of teaching. *Journal of Teacher Education, 40*(2), 53–60.

Wenger, E. (1998). *Communities of practice: Learning, meaning, and identity*. Cambridge: Cambridge University Press.

Whitworth, B., & Chou, J. (2015). Professional development and teacher change: The missing leadership link. *Journal of Science Teacher Education, 26*, 121–137.

Winitzky, N., O'Keefe, P., & Stoddart, T. (1992). Great expectations: Emergent professional development schools. *Journal of Teacher Education, 43*, 3–18.

Wood, P. B. (1980). Methodology and apologetics: Thomas Sprat's history of the Royal Society. *British Journal for the History of Science, 13*(1), 1–26.

Yee, S. M. (1990). *Careers in the classroom: When teaching is more than a job*. New York, NY: Teachers College Press.

Ylijoki, O.-H. (2013). Boundary-work between work and life in the high-speed university. *Studies in Higher Education, 38*(2), 242–255.

Ylijoki, O.-H., & Mantyla, H. (2003). Conflicting time perspectives in academic work. *Time & Society, 12*(1), 55–78.

Young, J. R., Bullough, R. V. Jr., Draper, R. J., Smith, L. K., & Erickson, L. B. (2005). Novice teacher growth and personal models of mentoring: Choosing compassion over inquiry. *Mentoring & Tutoring: Partnership in Learning, 13*(2), 169–188.

Zembylas, M. (2002). "Structures of feeling" in curriculum and teaching: Theorizing the emotional rules. *Educational Theory, 52*(2), 187–208.

INDEX